# TIBETAN ASTROLOGY

# A TIBETAN ASTROLOGY

PHILIPPE CORNU

*Translated from the French by*
*Hamish Gregor*

SHAMBHALA
*Boston & London*
2002

Shambhala Publications, Inc.
Horticultural Hall
300 Massachusetts Avenue
Boston, Massachusetts 02115
http://www.shambhala.com

© 1990 Les Djinns
Translation © 1997 by Hamish Gregor

Published by arrangement with Editions les Djinns, Paris.

Designed by Ruth Kolbert

9  8  7  6  5  4  3  2  1

First Paperback Edition

Printed in the United States of America

⊗ This edition is printed on acid-free paper that meets the
American National Standards Institute Z39.48 Standard.
Distributed in the United States by Random House, Inc.,
and in Canada by Random House of Canada Ltd

The Library of Congress catalogs the hardcover edition of this book as follows:

Cornu, Philippe.
[Astrologie tibétaine. English]
Tibetan astrology/Philippe Cornu; translated from the French by
Hamish Gregor.—1st ed.
p.  cm.
Includes bibliographical references.
ISBN 1-57062-217-5 (alk. paper)
ISBN 1-57062-963-3
1. Astrology, Tibetan.  I. Title.
BF1714.T53C6713  1997        96-39527
133.5'92515—dc21              CIP

*To my spiritual masters:*
*Sogyal Rinpoche, Namkhai Norbu, Dudjom Rinpoche,*
*Dingo Khyentse Rinpoche, and many others*

With a heart full of devotion,
I pay homage to you, Mañjuśrī,
You, the eternally youthful,
The Supreme Deity
And Spiritual doctor.
You change into ambrosia,
Bringing gifts and virtues
To all sentient beings.
You are the full moon
Of omniscient wisdom,
And you have abandoned all stains
Of saṃsāric defilement.

—GYALWA KELZANG GYATSO, Seventh Karmapa,
*Rosary of Precious Questions*

# TRANSLATOR'S NOTE

In translating this work, I have departed in certain minor respects from M. Cornu's presentation: I have supplied diacritics for all Sanskrit terms, and for the convenience of students of Tibetan, I have compiled a glossary of Tibetan terms in Wylie transcription (Appendix 3). I have also supplied a number of footnotes. Those details aside, I have attempted to adhere to the principle that a translator should be sympathetically invisible.

I would like to record my gratitude to my wife, Krisztina, for her invaluable assistance in preparing this translation.

—H.G.

# CONTENTS

# *Preface*

Even in the 1950s, Tibet and its civilization were hardly known to the public except through the accounts of certain travelers and a few translations of texts; and only Tibetologists had carried out any in-depth study of the country. For most Westerners, "Thibet" remained poorly known, a semi-legendary kingdom shrouded in mystery.

The political tragedy of 1959 suddenly and brutally changed that situation. In the face of Chinese occupation, many Tibetans chose to follow the Fourteenth Dalai Lama and most of the major religious figures into exile. They have been welcomed, often in difficult conditions, in India, Nepal, and neighboring Himalayan regions. Although threatening the survival of Tibetan culture, these historical events have contributed to the emergence of Tibetan Buddhism from its geographical setting and have encouraged its spread throughout the world.

For the last fifteen years or so, many lamas have been traveling the world, particularly in the West. In response to the requests of many Western students, certain of these lamas have founded centers of Tibetan studies, where they teach meditation and the techniques of the Vajrayāna, the form of Buddhism practiced in Tibet; and a growing number of Westerners have begun to take an internal and personalized approach to these teachings. There is now great interest not only in Buddhism but also in traditional Tibetan medicine. Nevertheless, certain arts considered as "minor," such as Tibetan astrology and divination, remain practically unknown to this day.

The purpose of this book is to open a crack in a door, that of the study of Tibetan astrology. Very little has appeared on this vast subject in the West. I have therefore been obliged to study and translate the Tibetan texts, a difficult task in view of the great number of technical terms often omitted from dictionaries. Only after much cross-checking, verification, and comparison with Chinese and Indian astrology did this book begin to take shape. Despite its lacunae and imperfections, I hope this work will be a modest contribution to the knowledge of the Tibetan universe. Even at the ethnological level, astrology is seldom studied and is often regarded with a degree of contempt. Nonetheless, it remains a source of knowledge regarding the civilization that produced it, and is the vehicle for numerous myths and ancient cultural influences.

Particularly for Tibetans, astrology can only be understood as part of a cosmology—a vision of humanity in the universe, in the planetary environment. I invite the reader to a discovery of this vision.

## ACKNOWLEDGMENTS

I wish to thank Madame Yvette Caroutch and Messrs. Lucien Biton and Patric Carré for their assistance, and Catherine for her great patience.

# PART ONE

# General Considerations

# I

## THE
## TIBETAN
## SETTING

Tibetan astrology is a tree with many branches. But before examining those branches, we shall consider its roots, which draw on a number of sources, some of them ancient—the "nameless religion," for example, and the ancient Bön religion of Tibet—and others more recent, such as ancient Chinese and Indian astrology. Its growth and development are intimately linked to the unique geographical location of Tibet and its religious history.

### THE TIBETAN AREA

Tibet, sometimes called the Roof of the World, is for the most part a vast plateau encircled by a barrier of high mountains: to the south the Himalayas, and to the west the Pamirs and the Karakorams; Tian Shan and Altyn Tagh to the north and the Chinese Kun-lun and Nan-shan ranges to the east. This enormous high plateau covers an area of more than two million square kilometers and comprises four main regions: the great steppes of Chang-thang to the north, a semidesert, high-altitude plateau; at a lower altitude, the "central" regions of U and

Tsang, where the main towns of Lhasa, the capital, and Shigatse are situated. To the west, Ngari is the region surrounding Mount Kailash. Finally, in the east, the Do-Kham area comprises two large regions bordering China: Kham to the south, a mountainous region with fertile wooded valleys; and Amdo to the north, a region of grasslands and salt lakes.

The mountainous belt that surrounds Tibet keeps out most of the rain, thus accounting for the country's arid and contrasting climate. Only the regions of the south and east are mild and fertile, and it is here that the majority of the population is concentrated—the steppes of the north are populated only by yak-breeding nomads. It is noteworthy, nevertheless, that most of the great rivers of Asia rise in Tibet, including the Huang Ho, the Yang-tze, the Salween and the Mekong in the east, and the Indus and the Brahmaputra in the west.

The Tibetan cultural area is not confined to the great Tibetan plateau, however, but extends to the south into certain areas of Nepal such as the Dolpo and the Sherpa lands, as well as into the enclaves of the small Himalayan kingdoms of Sikkim[1] and Bhutan. To the west, it includes the highlands of "Little Tibet," Ladakh, Spiti, Zangskar, and Lahul.

Although Tibet is seemingly isolated, the cultures of all the surrounding countries have influenced it: India and Nepal to the south; China to the east; Kashmir and Afghanistan to the west, the gateways to Central Asia; and Mongolia to the north. Tibet has always maintained cultural and commercial relations with its neighbors. Far from being a country closed to foreign influence, as it is often described, Tibet has always been an important meeting place of Indian and Chinese culture and a melting pot for their integration with the local character.

---

## A LITTLE HISTORY

The origins of a civilization are often lost in legend, and the interpretation of historical events varies according to different

---

1. Sikkim became a state of India in 1975.

sources, different authors, different political influences, and the currents of opinion. Tibetan history is no exception.

We have two major sources for Tibetan history: the ancient chronicles and religious histories of the Bön; and those of the Buddhists. The manuscripts discovered at Tun-huang represent a valuable source for ancient history. According to Bön sources, it appears certain that a very ancient kingdom known as Zhang-Zhung existed well before Tibet itself was born. The royal chronicles attest to the great antiquity of this kingdom, which occupied a sizable area around Mount Kailash, in the west of Tibet. It was probably in this region that the founder of the Bön religion, Shenrab Miwo, was born, approximately three to four hundred years before the appearance of the Buddha in India.[2] This, therefore, was the first source of Tibet's civilization, the origin of its first great religion.

Later, in the regions of Yarlung to the south, there arose what is known as Pö Yül, or Tibet. Both the Buddhist and Bön royal chronicles agree as to the succession of Tibetan kings, the first of whom are semilegendary, related to the sky, then to the atmosphere and later to the earth. The first king was Nyatri Tsenpo, and both he and his successors are said to have been connected to the sky by a magic thread, the *mu* cord, which reached from the crown of their heads to the world above. These kings left no corpse when they died but returned to the sky whence they had come.

The eighth king, Drigum, began the religious persecutions against the Bönpos of Zhang-Zhung, attesting to the influence

2. The various schools of Buddhism accept widely differing chronologies for the Buddha Śākyamuni. In Chinese and Tibetan tradition, for example, the Buddha's dates are set as impossibly early as 1027–947 B.C.E. See George Roerich (tr.), *The Blue Annals* (2nd ed., Delhi: Motilal Banarsidas, 1976), pp. 18–22. Such dates derive largely from efforts to prove that Śākyamuni predated Lao-tzu, in the face of Chinese claims to the contrary. See Kenneth Ch'en, *Buddhism in China* (Princeton, N.J.: Princeton University Press, 1964), pp. 184–185. Modern scholarship accepts much later dates, e.g., 466–383 B.C.E. See Hirakawa Akira, *A History of Indian Buddhism* (University of Hawaii Press, 1990), pp. 14 ff.; Etienne Lamotte, *Histoire du Bouddhisme Indien* (Louvain: Institute Orientaliste Louvain-LaNeuve, 1976), pp. 16 ff, 95 ff.

which that kingdom had upon Tibet at the time. Drigum accidentally cut the magic cord in the course of a magic contest, and thereafter the kings left a corpse behind when they died.

The twenty-eighth king, Lhalhathori, was, according to the Buddhist annals, the first to make contact with Buddhism, toward the year 333 of the common era. This contact was miraculous: he received from the sky a magic casket containing two sūtras, a stūpa, and the mantra of Chenrezi (Skt. Avalokiteśvara), but being unable to understand these relics, he piously stored them away.

Under the reign of Namri Songtsen, thirty-second in the line, Chinese medical and astrological texts reached Tibet. His successor, Songtsen Gampo (569–650), was the first Buddhist king, at a time when Tibet was becoming an important political and military power. With a view to fostering good relations with the kingdom of Zhang-Zhung, he gave his daughter in marriage to King Ligmikya, and himself took a princess of Zhang-Zhung as his first wife. Later, in order to establish firm relations with his other neighbors, King Songtsen Gampo married a Nepalese Buddhist princess, who brought certain precious statues to Tibet. He later asked the emperor T'ai Tsung for the hand of a Chinese Tsang princess, a difficult enterprise which, according to legend, required all the force and ability of his minister, Gar. When Princess Konjo arrived in Tibet, she brought with her not only precious statues but also Chinese scholars and astrologers. Also under Songtsen Gampo's reign, the minister Thön-mi Sambhota, assisted by Indian *paṇḍitas*, definitively fixed the Tibetan writing system and wrote a grammar in order to promote the study and translation of Buddhist Sanskrit texts.

Tibet soon became a powerful state, and after King Ligmikya had been assassinated by order of Songtsen Gampo, it finally annexed Zhang-Zhung. Nevertheless, the Bön religion remained powerful under the reigns of his successors, until the appearance of the great king Trisong Detsen (755–797), thirty-eighth in the dynasty. In order to establish Buddhism firmly in Tibet, this king invited Śāntarakṣita, a celebrated Indian scholar. After encountering numerous obstacles caused by the resistance of the

Bön priests and the local deities, Śāntarakṣita suggested to the king that he should invite the great tantric master Padmasambhava, more commonly known by the Tibetans as Guru Rinpoche or "Precious Master."

Padmasambhava overcame all obstacles, and with his help the king founded the first monastery at Samye. With the support of the king and Śāntarakṣita, Padmasambhava assembled a team of translators and scholars, such as Vairocana, and had a large number of sūtras and tantras translated. He had twenty-five main disciples, including the king himself, all of whom attained a high level of spiritual realization. At this time, he initiated the oral master-to-disciple transmission lineage known as *Kāma* and the direct hidden-treasure transmission, or *terma*. Foreseeing the almost complete destruction of the Dharma by an irreligious king, he hid numerous teachings as "hidden treasures," or *termas* in various secret places and predicted that only future incarnations of his disciples and of himself, known as *tertöns*, would be able to find these and reveal their content to humanity at the appropriate times. Having thus assured the first spread of Buddhism in Tibet, Padmasambhava miraculously left the country to continue his work in other places. The school of Buddhism founded at this time later came to be known as the *Nyingma*, or "Old School."

During the reign of Trisong Detsen, Tibet reached the height of its political power and enjoyed cultural relations with all of Asia. Thus the first medical congress was held under the aegis of the king, gathering together practitioners from China, India, Nepal, Kashmir, Persia, Mongolia, and Tibet. Astrology was enriched at this time by numerous contributions, both Indian and Chinese.

Under the reigns of Ralpachen and Senalek, the work of translation was continued; but as Padmasambhava had foreseen, the monastic establishments and the monks and lamas suffered systematic persecution at the instigation of King Langdarma, whose assassination marks the end of the royal period. For a hundred years or so thereafter, political chaos reigned. Little by little, however, Buddhism was reborn thanks to a second diffusion through the work of Tibetan translators, or *lotsawas*, who undertook numerous journeys to India in search of transmissions from Indian masters. Among the foremost of these we may note Rinchen Zangpo, Marpa, the master of the yogi-poet Milarepa, founder of the Kagyü school, and Virupa, founder of the Sakya school.[3] An important part was played by Atīśa toward 1025 in the introduction of the Kālacakra Tantra to Tibet, as well as all the principles of esoteric astrology.

In concluding this brief historical overview, we may note the foundation of the Geluk school by the master Je Tsongkapa during the fifteenth century. It was in this school, the most recent of the four main traditions of Tibetan Buddhism, that the institution of the Dalai Lamas was born, under Mongolian tutelage. Since that time, successive Dalai Lamas have been both temporal and spiritual sovereigns of Tibet as incarnations of Avalokiteśvara, the bodhisattva of compassion. The most notable of the Dalai Lamas have been the Fifth, a great mystic and politician, builder of the Potala at Lhasa; the Sixth, noted for his erotic verse; and the Seventh, author of numerous religious works. The Thirteenth (1876–1933) proclaimed Tibetan independence in 1912, Tibet having until then been more or less under Mongolian and then Chinese suzerainty.[4]

In 1951, Chinese troops entered Tibet; and despite the negotiations that the Fourteenth Dalai Lama carried on with the Chinese, he was obliged to flee his country in 1959, when widespread repression began in Tibet. During the Cultural Revolution, Tibet suffered virtual genocide: most religious buildings

---

3. The names of the founders of the Sakya school are generally given as Drok Mi (*'Brog mi*) and his disciple, Khön Könchog Gyalpo/Nyingpo (*'Khon dkon mchog rgyal po/snying po*), the latter of whom founded the first Sakya monastery in 1073. See David Snellgrove, *Indo-Tibetan Buddhism* (Boston: Shambhala, 1987), p. 488; George Roerich (tr.), op. cit., pp. 205–210.
4. The political status of Tibet before 1912 is a complex matter surrounded by some controversy. For discussion of that subject and the temporal authority of the Dalai Lamas, see David Snellgrove and Hugh Richardson, *A Cultural History of Tibet* (Boston: Shambhala, 1968); Hugh Richardson, *Tibet and Its History* (Boston and London: Shambhala, 1984); Geoffrey Samuel, *Civilized Shamans* (Washington, D.C.: Smithsonian Institution Press, 1993).

were destroyed or damaged, many lamas were executed and the practice of religion was forbidden. Since that time, many Tibetan refugees both in India and elsewhere have attempted, under the inspiration of the Dalai Lama, to preserve their threatened culture and to make it better known throughout the world. Today, the conditions of Tibetans living in Tibet have hardly changed. Although they are free to practice their religion once more and although some temples have been rebuilt, the loss of ancient knowledge, the arrival of tourists, and above all the influx of Chinese colonists in large numbers constitute new threats to this remarkable culture.[5]

## THE TIBETANS

There is a considerable diversity of physical characteristics in the various regions of Tibet, and the origins of the Tibetan people remain poorly understood. Ancient Chinese sources mention the presence of nomadic Tibeto-Mongol peoples in the northeast of Tibet, but many other peoples seem to have contributed to the formation of the Tibetan peoples. The Indo-European Dards from the west and the Hors, a Turko-Mongol people, began to be assimilated toward the seventh century. Although the majority of Tibetans have clearly Mongoloid features, these are more commonly found in the eastern regions than in central Tibet, and there are even fair-haired, blue-eyed people among the Amdo in the northeast. Ethnic groups show great diversity, such as the Golok of the extreme east, the Lo of the Kongpo region, and the Mön of the south. Spoken Tibetan has numerous dialects and there are significant differences between Ladakhi, spoken in the west, and the official language of Lhasa in the center; and also between these and the Tibetan spoken to the east by the Khampas, the Amdopas, and the Golok. On the other hand,

5. For an account of postoccupation Tibet and the reestablishment of Tibetan institutions in India, see John Avadon, *In Exile from the Land of Snows* (London: Wisdom Publications, 1985).

there is a cultural unity based on cultural traits and a common written language.

The Tibetans form two distinct groups according to their lifestyle: the sedentary agriculturalists known as the Zhingpa or Sonampa; and the nomadic yak-breeders, the Drokpa, who live in tents. These two peoples do not mix. The Drokpa are free men who avoid taxation and census, and they affect to despise the peasants and their attachment to the land. The latter, in their turn, consider the Drokpa as bumpkins; but this does not in any way prevent commercial relations across their borders.

Some peasants have not only land but also herds—these are the Samadrok, "neither too attached to the land nor nomads," and it is not uncommon for one part of a family to be concerned with agriculture while the other takes the herds to pasture during summer. The nomads are more numerous in the north and east, in the steppes and the high plateaus, while the sedentary agriculturalists occupy the valleys below the tree line and the snow line.

The main crop is barley, which grows well at high altitudes and from which *tsampa* (roasted barley) is made, the staple food of the Tibetans. In addition, radishes, turnips, and cabbages are grown. The yak and the *dri*, or female yak, provide meat, milk, butter, and cheese. Other domestic animals include the *dzo*, a cross between the yak and the cow. Tea, imported from China, serves as the basis for the famous Tibetan salted butter tea, a refreshing and invigorating drink. All these products, as well as salt, skins, and crafts, form the basis of commerce between regions, as well as with neighboring countries, carried on by the caravans of traders who until recent times traveled the roads.

Traditional Tibetan society was stratified according to criteria of property and religion, which were, moreover, frequently linked. The nobles or Gerpa were the descendants of the old fiefholding clans. In central Tibet, most had become high government officials, but in Kham they still held a number of petty kingdoms and fiefs, which were in effect independent before the Chinese occupation.

Often originating from the same ancestral clans, the Ngakpas were tantric practitioners, married laymen who passed on their office through the family line, either to a son or to a nephew. These Ngakpas married only the daughters of Ngakpas. They enjoyed the respect of the people, received offerings from them, and played an important ritual role. Certain Ngakpas became famous saints, such as Marpa, the teacher of the poet-yogi Milarepa, and Drukpa Kunley, the famous crazy yogi. Many astrologers and doctors came from Ngakpa families.

Agriculturalists, traders, and itinerant agricultural workers, collectively known as Mi ser, made up approximately 85 percent of the Tibetan population.

The monastic clergy occupied a very important place in Tibetan society. Monasteries were extremely numerous before the cultural revolution, some comprising no more than a few cells around a temple and others being enormous and virtually constituting townships. These large monasteries often held several thousand monks, the great majority of whom were concerned more with administrative and economic duties or estate management than with religious practice. A minority of monks, selected for their abilities and tested in often highly difficult examinations, carried on religious studies that they later pursued further in colleges specializing in philosophical and tantric studies. Graduation from a monastery could offer opportunities for social advancement, and it was from monastery graduates that government officials were selected. It may be estimated that more than 20 percent of the population lived in the monasteries.[6] At the head of the monastery was the *khenpo* or abbot, or alternatively a *tulku*, a lama whose successive incarnations directed the monastery.

Power and property were arranged as follows: in the villages, the peasants were the "hereditary tenants" of lands belonging either to the government or to the lord, to whom they paid taxes in various forms, whether part of the harvest, the use of beasts

---

6. Figures for the monastic population of traditional Tibet are by no means certain and have been the subject of much debate. See Geoffrey Samuel, op. cit., appendix 1.

of burden for caravans, or boonwork. The village was administered by a headman elected by a council of elders. A fief was composed of a given number of villages governed by a *dzong pön*, or lord, who might be a government official, the abbot of a monastery, or an independent king (as in Ladakh, Kham, and Amdo). The land "rented" to a peasant was inalienable and passed to his heirs.

The family was the base unit of Tibetan society, and all forms of marriage were known in Tibet. Monogamous marriage was practiced everywhere and was the most common form in Amdo; while polygamy existed to all intents and purposes only among the nobility and the rich, allowing as it did the formation of matrimonial alliances. The most famous form of marriage among the Tibetans was polyandry, where one woman married several men, usually brothers or at least considered as such after the marriage. The elder brother was the head of the family and ensured the cohesion of the group, which shared the duties of tillage and tending the herds. This form of marriage, which prevented the breakup of property, was found chiefly among agriculturalists and peasants. If the oldest brother died or had no children, a younger brother succeeded him. It was not uncommon in this system for one or more of the younger brothers to enter a monastery without prejudice to the family.

In all these forms of marriage, however, one rule was constant: exogamy, which forbids marriage to a member of the familial clan; that is, anyone sharing kin of any sort over seven generations.

Although marriage was not considered in Tibet as a religious or sacred act, it gave rise to many ritualized customs, which were important in the life cycle. The choice of a partner was free when there were no lands to be considered. However, it was the parents or the uncle and aunt of the boy who would ask a girl's hand from her parents, taking beer and gifts. Sometimes there was a real or mock abduction. If the contract was fulfilled, the bride had to come to the groom's house, bringing a dowry with her. A village priest (*bönpo*) performed a ritual to ensure that good luck (*yang*) should not desert the bride's family. He prepared a ritual cake (*torma*), which was thrown on the bride's path to ensure that she was not bringing any demons to her new home. On her arrival, her new family introduced her to the household gods. As we shall see, all these ceremonies were closely linked to astrology.

As long as there were no children, divorce was easy and each party reclaimed his or her possessions.

Many other rituals were celebrated in the life cycle: rituals for prosperity, exorcisms against demons in the case of inexplicable illness, rituals for the buying back of the soul, and funeral rituals. And in all cases, the astrologer played an important role.

## THE TIBETANS AND THE NATURAL ENVIRONMENT

Tibet consists of vast spaces bordered by imposing mountain ranges. The dry climate produces sharp, clear colors and vividly contrasting shapes. The Tibetans viewed their natural environment as a horizontal space divided into boxes whose sides were oriented to the four cardinal points. Under the influence of Indian civilization, the Tibetans regarded the east-west axis as particularly important, as can be seen in the representations of *mandalas*, where the eastern gate of the palace is shown at the foot of the diagram, the south gate at the left, the west gate at the top, and the north gate at the right. This is why the Tibetans call West Tibet the "high" country and Eastern Tibet the "low" country. This organization of horizontal space is also found in the architecture of houses and temples. However, the Tibetans are essentially a mountain people and they attach great importance to the vertical plane of the landscape. Ideally, in the center of the box of the earth, there is an axial mountain, which exemplifies the vertical. It was from such a mountain that the first legendary king of the country descended. This mountain forms the link between heaven and earth, between the world of the gods and that of men. The king descends from the sky by means of a rainbow-cord.

The vertical axis is divided into three levels: "Above, the white gods; below, the black underground gods (*nāga*); in the middle, the *tsen* gods and men, yellow." This tripartite division plays a vital role in Tibetan culture. Each of these three levels is characterized by a dominant color: the highest level is the color of the glaciers, and the mountain gods are shown in crystal armor. The middle level is the color of earth and stones—this is the realm of men and the local deities of the rocks. Finally, the lower level is the same color as rivers and lakes, turquoise blue—this is the blue or black world of the subterranean waters, inhabited by the *lu* or *nāgas*, beings with snakelike bodies.

The same organization is found in the Tibetan house: the first floor is reserved for animals, while the second floor is the human habitation properly so called, with a fireplace. The third floor is a terraced roof, and here a chapel is often built, a place of practice and offerings. This is therefore the ideal "high place," related to the upper world. Here is found the fire for smoke offerings and the banners showing the Wind Horse, intended to bring good luck to the hearth. A vertical axis passes through the center of these three levels: this opening to the sky, located at the level of the central hearth, is the "sky door," which is sometimes "closed" during certain astrological rituals in order to avoid problems related to the gods above. This may also be the "earth door," located at the bottom, which is closed in order to break communication with the subterranean deities.

The whole human dwelling and the nature of its environment are thus inhabited by all manner of beings, gods and demons with whom one tries to maintain harmonious relations. The Tibetan land itself is a demon, nailed to the soil by the temples built at the time of King Songtsen Gampo in the sixth century. The Tibetans, convinced of the magical character of their natural environment, have always taken care not to defile or destroy that environment. The local mountain peak is the dwelling of the mountain god who reigns over the area; the rocks are the dwelling of the red *tsen;* the trees are sometimes inhabited by the yellow *nyen;* and the lakes and rivers are the province of the *lu.* Various sudden or serious illnesses are attributed to defilement or violation of the natural environment: pollution injures the local deities, who in revenge cause illness to strike those responsible.

In order to ensure the aid or the benevolence of the local deities, the Tibetans go to the cult site or dwelling of the *yül lha*, the local god, which is decorated with a pile of stones, weapons, arrows, a lance, helmet and buckler, with colored ribbons and banners showing the wind horse. There they perform the *lha sang*, the offering of juniper smoke to the gods. They also perform dances, chant, and stage theatrical performances and sporting contests such as archery and horse racing, all in honor of the local deity, who is often a *dra lha* or warlike god. The people's prosperity, good harvests, and protection from bands of warriors—all depend on the presence and the benevolence of the local god. If the local god is a *lha ri* or mountain god, he is the support of the vital soul of the king or lord.

## THE ASTROLOGER IN TIBETAN SOCIETY

In Tibet, the astrologer (*tsipa*) is generally a lama, whether monk or layman. In the large monastic establishments, it was the duty of the astrologer monks to fix favorable dates for ceremonies and to compile calendars for religious events and holidays. The astrologers responsible for writing almanacs also provided monthly and annual forecasts for climate and harvests. The role of the astrologer was often associated with that of the *mopa*, or diviner. In smaller areas, this role was taken by the village lama, who was consulted on all sorts of occasions. When a child was born, the astrologer would cast his horoscope and determine which rituals were necessary in order to ward off negative planetary influences and safeguard the child's life. The astrologer also played an important part at weddings: he checked the astrological profiles of the couple and studied the compatibility of their horoscopes. If the judgment was positive, the representatives of the intending groom visited the bride's family with the "requesting beer." If this was accepted by the family, the arrangements for the marriage were then discussed. In the case of important marriages, the astrologer determined the most favorable date for the ceremonies in order to ensure the couple's future prosperity.

The astrologer also acted as meteorologist, forecasting drought or rain in accordance with the phases of the moon and the relationships between the moon and other astrological elements. Farmers would ask him to carry out divinations in connection with the harvest. If any threat was revealed, the *tsipa* would indicate which rites should be performed in order to appease the local deities; and he would in most cases perform those rites himself in his capacity as tantric practitioner.

At the moment of death, the astrologer would draw up a special horoscope in accordance with the "astrology of the dead" in order to determine the best way to proceed with the funeral arrangements. Taking account of the moment of death and the astrological characteristics of the deceased, he would determine the moment for taking the corpse out of the house, the direction in which it should be carried, and the way in which the ceremonies should be conducted. The funeral arrangements were connected with the elements: Air (dismemberment of the corpse and offering different parts of it to the vultures); Fire (funeral pyre); Earth (burial); or Water (immersion in a river). "Sky burial" was the most frequent form of funeral in areas poor in wood and light soil. It is possible that this custom derives from Persian influence, for the Parsees expose their dead to the vultures on top of towers. Certainly, Tibetan funeral customs have never failed to strike the Western imagination. Cremation was rare, and was reserved for religious dignitaries, while the other two types of funeral were exceptional. Certain great lamas were embalmed in salt and their bodies became relics.

When the correct funeral procedures were not observed, it was said that negative effects would be felt by the deceased's family, such as sickness, poverty, and so on. The astrologer-lama would indicate which practices should be performed for the benefit of the deceased: ritual readings, the offering of butter lamps, and so on, practices intended to purify the deceased and guide him or her to a better rebirth. These practices were normally conducted by monks at the nearest monastery. Divination was sometimes carried out in order to determine what sort of rebirth the deceased would take.

Astrology was also studied as part of the medical curriculum. A doctor was required to know the best time for making medicines and administering them to his patients. Diagnosis by inspection of urine and taking of pulses was closely linked to the astrology of the seasonal elements. The great medical colleges were required to produce doctors trained not only in the four medical tantras and their commentaries and applications, but also in the Dharma—the teachings and practices of Buddhism—and astrology.

Under the reign of the Thirteenth Dalai Lama (1876–1933), the Men Tsi Khang, or College of Medicine and Astrology, was founded at Lhasa; it continued to function until about 1960. After the Chinese invasion and the exile of the Tibetans, the Tibetan Medical Center was established at Dharamsala in India, including an astrological institute among whose duties is the compilation of the calendar and yearly almanacs (*lotho*).

Astrology has not been officially taught in Tibet since the 1960s, when the Chinese occupied the country, but it is still very much alive among the Tibetan people. Many almanacs are in circulation and astrological texts can easily be found in the markets. Astrology also retains its importance in those neighboring countries that have Tibetan populations, such as Ladakh, Bhutan, the Sherpa and Dolpo countries, and Nepal, as well as among the refugees in India. Tibetans, however, clearly show their attachment to the old lunar calendar. We may note finally the recent editions of astrological texts published by "Tibetan Popular Editions" under Chinese control.

# 2

# THE
# SOURCES
# OF TIBETAN
# ASTROLOGY

The Tibetan science of astrology has many sources, among which four in particular may be distinguished: the Bön religion, Chinese astrology, Indian astrology, and the Buddhist *Kālacakra Tantra*.

## THE BÖN RELIGION

The ancient Bön religion of Tibet comprises a number of branches, and it developed in various stages. In Bön sources, the original site of Bön merges with the birthplace of its founder, Shenrab Miwo, who was born miraculously at Olmo Lungring, which some sources locate in the land of Takzig or Persia; while others identify it with the kingdom of Zhang-Zhung. Whatever the truth of the matter, Bön spread thanks to the cultural influence of Zhang-Zhung and reached Tibet well before there was any contact with Buddhism. It appears that in Tibet, Bön merged with ancient magical and folk beliefs, the "nameless religion," and eventually came to form what is known as "organized Bön." There were two types of priest, the *shen* and the *bön*, and the teaching included royal rituals, methods of divination and astrology, rites for prosperity, longevity, healing, and exorcism, as well as very exalted spiritual teachings such as Dzogchen, which is also found in Buddhism.

When it eventually made contact with Buddhism, Bön had to integrate numerous Buddhist elements in order to survive the prohibitions that were placed upon it. This osmosis was so successful that nowadays the Bön is often regarded as a marginal school of lamaism, known as transformed Bön or Gyur Bön.

Modern Bön has its monastic orders and canonical texts, and its various practices are classified into nine vehicles, following the model used by the Nyingma Buddhists. Only some of these, however, correspond, namely those which deal with discipline, Tantrism, and Dzogchen. There is no doubt that certain interchanges occurred between Buddhism and Bön, some by force and others voluntarily. It would be absurd, however, to suggest that the highest spiritual elements of Bön are all late borrowings from Buddhism.

Astrology assumes considerable importance in the Bön tradition: in the first vehicle, the *Chag Shen gyi Thekpa*, the "Vehicle of the Shen of Prediction," astrology is associated with other methods of divination and enters into different rites intended to ward off the negative influences that sometimes threaten the lives of human beings. It also plays a part in medical diagnosis.

According to the *Ziji*, which has been translated in part by David Snellgrove,[1] this vehicle uses four methods: divination or *mo;* astrological calculations or *tsi*, ritual or *to*, and diagnostics or *che*. As far as astrology is concerned:

> There are four types of astrological calculation: The mirror of magical horoscopes; the circle of Parkhas (trigrams) and Mewas (magic squares in 9 colours); the Wheel of Time of the elements; and the calculation of interdependence by the *Jushak* method.

1. David Snellgrove, *The Nine Ways of Bon* (London: Oxford University Press, 1977).

Of these methods, Mewa and Parkha are of Chinese origin and as we shall see, they are highly developed in both Chinese and Tibetan Jungtsi astrology. The Mewas, combined in cycles of 60 years, form great cycles of 180 years, the *metreng*, which the Bönpos have long used in chronology—the first *metreng* cycle is regarded as beginning with the birth of Shenrab Miwo.

We may also note the importance of the astrology of the elements in certain rituals intended to strengthen vitality and improve good luck and prosperity, such as the Wind Horse, the *namkha*, colored threads wound together and used to rebalance elemental forces, the *dö* rituals, and so on, all of which constitute a cycle of ancient rites found in Bön and later adopted by Buddhism.

The cosmogonic myths of Bön assume numerous forms, but there are always two constants: creation from cosmic eggs; and the dualistic nature of creation, which begins with the formation of a divine world of light and a demonic world of darkness. The influence of the Persian Mazda religions is clear in these dualistic myths, and it can be assumed that Mesopotamian astrological knowledge also reached Tibet through Bön.

At the center of the world is the axial mountain, Mount Ti Se. This is the meeting point between heaven and earth, and at its peak there is a celestial ladder, *namtak*, analogous to the *mu* cord of the first kings. This is also where the 360 Gekö gods dwell, symbolizing the 360 days of the lunar year.

The divine palace is in the form of a square, with four doors representing the four cardinal points. These doors are guarded by a white tiger (East), a turtle (North), a red bird (West), and a turquoise dragon (South), the divinities of the four directions. Here we see a probable Chinese influence.

The 360 Gekö gods are also associated with a Bön divination method, *Juthik* which uses small pieces of string. These represent the retinue of a very important god, Balchen Gekö, who is described as follows: he has nine heads and eighteen arms, is yellow and very wrathful. The eagle Khyung flies above his head and he carries a sword marked with a swastika. He sits on eight snakes and he is adorned with the skins of men and demons. In his belt, five poisonous snakes are intertwined, and the Eight Mahādevas or great gods form his crown. His symbols are the eight planets, and the twenty-eight lunar mansions are his clothes. Since he is said to govern time and the three worlds of existence, he may be the supreme deity of Bön astrology, analogous in this respect to Kālacakra among the Buddhists or Śiva among the Hindus.

The Bön vehicle includes important cultural elements and has played a seminal role in the development of Tibetan astrology.

## CHINESE ORIGINS

Chinese astrology forms the basis of two great systems within Tibetan astrology: *Naktsi*, or "black astrology," which refers to the Tibetan name for China, *Gyanak*, meaning "black area";[2] and *Jungtsi*, the "astrology of the elements," which is concerned with the calendar and which we shall later examine in detail.

Here we find cycles of sixty and twelve years, the five elements of the Chinese tradition, the nine magic squares, or Mewas, and the eight Parkhas, identical to the *pa-kua* or trigrams of the *I Ching*. This system is connected with ancient Tibetan concepts deriving from the "nameless religion" as well as from Bön, and suggests very early Chinese influence upon Tibet.

Chinese astrology is one of the oldest systems in the world. Its mythical origins are merged with the origins of civilization; and the emperor Fu-Hsi is credited with inventing the trigrams of the *I Ching* over five thousand years ago. The founder of Chinese civilization first "raised his eyes to heaven and contemplated the stars, then lowered his gaze and saw what was happening on earth." This quotation summarizes Chinese astrology: the knowledge of heaven and earth, together with a desire to harmonize the terrestrial and the celestial orders.

Fu Hsi is also credited with the invention of *Ho Tu*, "the De-

---

2. *Gyanak* (*rgya nag*) is normally explained as "the vast country (*rgya*) where people dress in black (*nag*)."

sign of the River," based on certain signs he saw on a horse-dragon emerging from the Yellow River. This diagram is composed of rows of black and white figures representing the four directions, the four seasons, and the five elements, and symbolizes cosmic order.

Under the reign of Huang Ti, the Yellow Emperor, the writing system was fixed and arithmetic and astronomy were codified. The most ancient of the medical treatises, the *Nei Ching*, which contains a number of astrological concepts, is also attributed to the Yellow Emperor.

Emperor Yao (2357–2286 B.C.E.) created the calendar in order to connect human activities with the celestial order. He employed four astronomers to watch the four celestial regions, and they calculated the seasons, observing the cycles of beings' activities in the course of the seasons. Connecting seasons with directions, they divided the year into four periods: spring (East), summer (South), autumn (West), and winter (North). Yao invented the intercalary months in order to connect the solar and lunar calendars.

The Great Emperor Yu (2206–2197 B.C.E.), founder of the Hia dynasty, composed the "Great Rule" treatise, inspired by the designs he saw on the back of a tortoise emerging from the River Lo. This design, the *Lo Shu*, is the magic square from which the nine Mewas of the Tibetans originated.

The *I Ching* as we know it in its definitive form comes down to us from King Wen and dates from the time when he was imprisoned by order of the tyrant Chou Hsin (ca. 1132 B.C.E.). Later, his son, the Duke of Chou, wrote the commentary to it.

Systems of astrology and geomancy had thus been completely formulated in China by the first millennium before our era. It is not, then, surprising that these systems should have reached Tibet quite early.

We may now discuss the origin of the cycles of twelve and sixty years, used by the Chinese as well as the Mongols, the Tibetans, the Turko-Mongols, and the Vietnamese. Since remote antiquity, Chinese astronomers had conceived a chronology based on the combination of two sets of symbols: the twelve terrestrial branches and the ten celestial trunks, whose terms follow one another according to the alternations of Yin and Yang. From this was derived the sexagenary cycle of Chinese chronology, of which the first cycle begins in the year 2697 B.C.E., under the reign of Huang Ti. The ten celestial trunks were soon assimilated to the five elements, Yin alternating with Yang.

At the same time, there developed in China the system of twelve animals. Originally there were only four of these: the Spring Dragon of the East, the Summer Bird of the South, the Autumn Tiger of the West, and the Winter Turtle of the North. Later developments gave rise to six, eight, and finally twelve animals, as Lois de Saussure has conclusively demonstrated. These twelve animals were later assimilated to the twelve terrestrial branches, although they were of a different nature. This merging of the two systems took place at the beginning of our era, and it was the system of twelve animals and five elements that was introduced and popularized throughout Central Asia. According to late Tibetan sources, it was the princess Kongjo who introduced this system to Tibet in 642, although this is by no means certain. Be that as it may, the Tibetans have named their years according to this system of animals ever since, although they did not use the sixty-year cycles at this time.

The *Padma Thangyik*, the biography of Padmasambhava, gives an account of the introduction of Chinese astrology to Tibet. King Tridetsuk Tsen (705–755) adopted the rules of Chinese astrology and protected the Tibetans through astrology and medicine (cf. *Song LIV*). At the birth of his son, the future king Trisong Detsen, it was a Chinese astrologer, Birje the Famous, who cast his horoscope and predicted his coming greatness.

## INDIAN ASTROLOGY

Tibetan astrology owes as much to Indian as to Chinese astrology. The branch of astrology deriving from India is known in

Tibetan as *Kartsi* or "white astrology," from the Tibetan name for India, *Gyakar* (*rgya gar*), meaning white area.[3]

According to Hindu tradition, astrology is a branch of the Vedas, a *Vedānga*. These are the ancient teachings of the *mahārisis*, who, by virtue of their spiritual power, entered into communication with the Lord Brahmā, the Creator, and received from him initiation into this divine science. The *risis* then spread the teaching for the benefit of humanity.

From the historical point of view, we know that as early as the third millenium B.C.E., a very advanced civilization flourished at Mohenjo-Daro in the Indus valley. This non-Indo-European culture enjoyed regular trading contact with the Sumerians of Mesopotamia, as witness the numerous objects discovered at archaeological sites. From this era onwards, ideas circulated between these two centers of civilization.

Indian astrology shows evidence of this cultural interchange in its adoption of a zodiac identical to that of the Mesopotamians: thus Indian astrology uses a system of twelve signs and twelve houses; while the decans are common to Egypt, Mesopotamia, Greece, and India. Indian and Western astrology thus share common origins, but in contrast to the Western system, Indian astrology remains faithful to the early sidereal zodiac, based on fixed stars.

India also had early contact with China, and there are certainly connections linking the twenty-eight Chinese lunar constellations or *Siu* and the twenty-seven or twenty-eight Indian *Naksatras*, mentioned in the Vedas. The Chinese *Siu* were known at the time of the emperor Yao (second millennium B.C.E.). These two systems probably had a common origin before they diverged in accordance with differing astronomical conceptions. (A system of twenty-eight lunar constellations, the twenty-eight *Menazils*, later penetrated the Moslem world.) Indian astrology also shares with China the importance attached to the lunar nodes, *Rāhu* and *Ketu*, the head and tail of the dragon in the Chinese system.

3. *Gyakar*, "The vast country (*rgya*) where people dress in white (*dkar*)."

Indian astrology has developed numerous original techniques of exceptional precision, such as the many subdivisions of the zodiac and the sophisticated mathematical system used to calculate rulers and planetary strengths.

Indian astrology undoubtedly reached Tibet in a number of different forms at different times; and the proximity of Shaivite Kashmir, frequent trading expeditions and the travels of the Indian masters all served to ease its passage. As we have seen, Bön was familiar with the principles of Indian astrology. Among the sūtras and tantras translated during the reign of Trisong Detsen, many contained elements of astrology.

Be that as it may, however, it was principally with the introduction of the *Kālacakra Tantra* that Indian astrology was fully established in Tibet in Buddhist form.

---

## THE KĀLACAKRA

*Kālacakra* (Tib. *Dükyi khorlo*) means "Wheel of Time." This text is not simply an astrological treatise, but a complete system of Tantric teaching and practice belonging to the class of nondual *Anuttara Yoga Tantra*, the highest of the Tantras.

The Kālacakra teachings operate at three levels. "External Kalacakra" deals with the world and external phenomena. It is concerned with the study of the elements of the universe in their dynamic relations; that is, with the interactions of cosmic phenomena and their transformation in time. The Tantra deals with cosmology, chronology and all astrological calculations, and describes the formation and constitution of the universe and the planets, constellations, and solar systems. The entire science of Indian astrology is described, along with its principles and its applications.

"Internal Kālacakra" deals with internal phenomena, namely, the subtle composition of the body of the yogi. It deals with the nature and functions of the subtle channels (*nādis*), the wheels or energy centers (*cakras*) and the internal winds that circulate in them (*prāṇa*), and the essential drops of energy (*bindu*). The circulation of the winds in the channels and the energy centers is linked to the cosmic energy of the stars and the planets.

The body is the basis for these subtle structures and is therefore considered as a perfect universe, a *maṇḍala*, in which our limbs, our organs and our centers (*cakras*) are sacred sites or the dwellings of gods. These deities are none other than our internal elements, our passions, our sensory awareness, and so on—in other words, the combination of our mental and physical constituents in their original purity. This combination is known as the Diamond Body (Vajrakāya).

These first two levels of Kālacakra are concerned with the external universe or macrocosm and the internal universe or microcosm, which are linked by a set of astrological correspondences. In order to reach enlightenment, the state of buddhahood, the yogi must purify his gross perceptions regarding both external and internal.

"Alternative Kālacakra" describes the methods for purifying our impure perceptions. Before putting these methods into practice, the yogi must receive the "transmission of power" or "initiation" from a fully qualified master. He is thus placed in contact with the energy of enlightenment, which is incarnate in the deity Kālacakra. He then devotes himself to practice according to two complementary systems:

1. In the development or creation stage (*kyerim*), the practitioner creates a visualisation in which the whole environment becomes the maṇḍala, the pure realm of Kālacakra. He himself becomes Kālacakra, the central deity of the maṇḍala, adorned with all Kālacakra's divine attributes. He thus purifies his gross perceptions and gradually develops a sacred perception in which all beings, all phenomena, and the world are luminous manifestations of emptiness. At the heart of the practice, the yogi recites the deity's mantra and thus activates the energy of the deity's word, from which he is not different.

2. In the perfection stage (*dzogrim*), continuing to visualize himself as the deity, he practices the yoga of the channels, winds, and essential drops. By means of this practice, he transforms his internal elements and comes to realize the state in

which bliss and emptiness are united, the Mahāmudrā or "Great Symbol."

The history of Kālacakra and its arrival in Tibet is by no means simple. According to tradition, the root tantra of Kālacakra was taught by the Buddha Śākyamuni himself at the request of Sucandra, king of Shambhala; and it was at the stūpa of Dhānyakaṭaka, in South India, at the full moon of the third lunar month that the Buddha, then eighty years old, taught this tantra.

King Sucandra, an incarnation of Vajrapāṇi, Bodhisattva of Enlightened Energy, then returned to his kingdom and wrote the first commentary (*Kālacakra Tantra*). Later, the first Kulika king of Shambhala, Mañjuśrīkīrti, wrote a condensed commentary (*Laghu Kālacakra*), and his son Kulika Puṇḍarīka wrote an expanded commentary, "The Immaculate Light" (*Vimalaprabhā*). Thus the Kālacakra teachings were spread among the inhabitants of Shambhala.

What is this mysterious land of Shambhala that has caused so much wandering among travelers and esotericists? We shall quote in this connection two eminent masters of the Kālacakra tradition. According to the present Dalai Lama, His Holiness Tenzin Gyatso: "Although Shambhala is a spot situated in some part of this planet, it is a place that cannot be seen except by those whose mind and karmic propensities are pure." In other words, although one might locate Shambhala somewhere in the north of Asia, it is a sort of Pure Land and reaching it depends on the yogi's purity of perception. Thus the Third Panchen Lama's *Shambhale Lamyik* (Guide to the Road to Shambhala) describes the path as simultaneously physical and spiritual. We read in this work:

> He who wishes to go to this land in this corporeal form must be a man possessing the strength of virtue and a knowledge of the Tantras. If this is not the case, he must fear lest the yakśas, nāgas, and other wrathful beings of the same sort should kill him on the road.

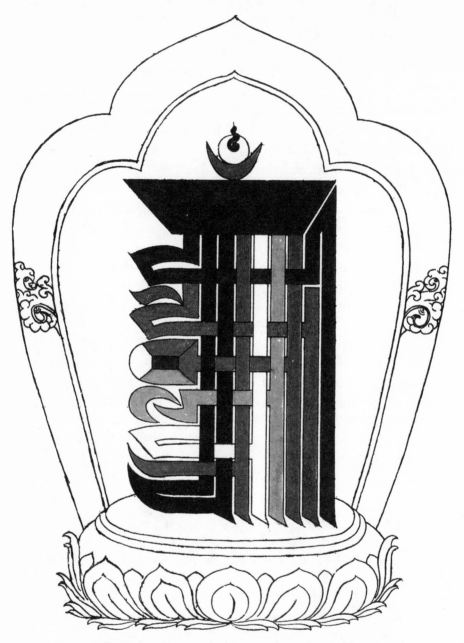

*The Kalacakra symbol* (rnams bcu dbang ldan)

These demons on the road symbolize the emotional defilements and gross passions that present obstacles to our progress.

For a description of the kingdom of Shambhala, we may turn to Khenpo Kalu Rinpoche:

> The country of this deity (Kālacakra) is located in the north of this world. A great city is located there, the capital, to which are connected 9,600,000 secondary towns. The whole is called Shambhala and is surrounded by snowcapped mountains. In this realm, divinity exists in human form in an uninterrupted line of kings . . . who turn the wheel of many teachings of the Dharma, principally Kālacakra. Thanks to this, innumerable disciples are established on the path to Liberation.

After seven great kings, including Sucandra, the lineage of the Kulika kings was founded. At present, the Twenty-first Kulika king reigns in Shambhala, Magakpa, who ascended the throne in 1927. He will be succeeded by Miyi Senge in the year of the Fire Sheep of the seventeenth cycle (2027). It is predicted that under the Twenty-fifth king, Rūdra the Bearer of the Wheel, Drakpo Khorlo Chang, a great war will break out in the year 2425 of our era between all the negative forces of the planet and the kingdom of Shambhala. The victory of the Kulika king will usher in a new era of prosperity on earth and the teachings of the Buddha will flourish again for eighteen hundred years. At the end of this period, 5,014 years after the Buddha's *parinirvāṇa*,[4] the teachings will fade. This is the story told of the kingdom of Shambhala and its relations with our world.

An Indian master, Chilupa, set out for the kingdom of Shambhala during the tenth century. On the way, he met an emanation of Mañjuśrī, who gave him the complete transmission of the Kālacakra and its commentaries. On his return, toward 966, Kālacakra was spread in India, Nepal, and Kashmir by certain of his disciples, including Nādapāda. It was these Indian masters, such as Somanātha the Kashmiri and Atīśa, who introduced the

---

4. The Buddha's death.

Tantra to Tibet in 1024. At present there exist in Tibet three great lineages of Kālacakra masters. The first, that of Dro, comes from Dro Lotsawa, who translated the Tantra into Tibetan. This lineage has been handed down in the Jonang school, and later in the Kagyü school, until the present day. The second, known as the Tsami tradition, was passed on by the Third Karmapa and the Kagyü school. The third, the Ra tradition, derives from Ra Lotsawa, a Tibetan translator who received the transmission from Samantaśrībhadra in Nepal. This lineage was transmitted by Butön Rinchen Drup (1290–1364) and flourishes in the Sakya, Geluk, and Kagyü schools.

We may add that in our own time, the Kālacakra initiation has been given numerous times all over the world, by both the Dalai Lama and the Venerable Kalu Rinpoche, in order to promote world peace. However, very few people are able to practice the internal and alternative levels of Kālacakra, which are undertaken in long retreats.

The influence of Kālacakra on Tibetan astrology has been considerable. It is noteworthy that it contains not only all the elements of Indian astrology but also a synthesis of the principles of Chinese astrology. Thus the sixty-year cycle, adopted by the Tibetans in 1027, is based on the merging of the Indian sexagenary cycle of the Kālacakra with that of Chinese astrology.

## THE BIRTH OF ASTROLOGY
### ACCORDING TO THE *PADMA THANGYIK*

In concluding this account of the history of Tibetan astrology, we present that history as told in the *Padma Thangyik*, the biography of Padmasambhava. This voluminous work is a treasure text, or *terma*, discovered by Orgyen Lingpa in the fourteenth century. It contains 108 chapters telling the story not only of Guru Rinpoche but also of eighth-century Tibet and the great masters of the time. The section dealing with astrology portrays Mañjuśrī, Bodhisattva of Wisdom and all divine sciences, in which capacity he presides over all the arts of writing, the sacred word, grammar, astrology, and divination. His divine consort, Sarasvatī, inspires music and the arts.

Mañjuśrī is portrayed as a young prince sixteen years of age, smiling and graceful. His perfect body is a beautiful saffron yellow, adorned with silks and jewels. He sits cross-legged on a snow lion or on a lotus in a moon-disk. In his right hand, he wields the flaming sword of supreme knowledge (*prajñā*), which dispels the darkness of ignorance. In his left hand, he holds a lotus stalk at his heart, the flower on his left shoulder bearing a book, symbol of knowledge. His thunderlike voice arouses beings from the sleep of ignorance. Mañjuśrī is invoked at the commencement of any astrological undertaking. Every morning, monks and lamas recite his prayer in order to dispel ignorance and develop intelligence, memory, eloquence, and understanding.

There is an astrological legend according to which Mañjuśrī plays the role virtually of a demiurge: at the beginning of the present age or *kalpa*, while the future universe was still immense chaos, Mañjuśrī caused a giant golden turtle to arise from his own mind, and this turtle emerged from the waters of the primordial ocean. Seeing in a dream that the universe in formation required a stable base, Mañjuśrī pierced the flank of the turtle with a golden arrow. The injured animal turned on its back and sank into the ocean, giving forth blood and excrement, from which there arose the constituent elements of the universe. The created world thenceforth rested on the flat belly of the turtle, upon which Mañjuśrī wrote all the secrets of the times to come in the form of sacred hieroglyphic signs.

# 3

## THE FOUNDATIONS OF TIBETAN ASTROLOGY

Tibetan astrology is known as *tsi rik*, the "science of calculation." It is not only a divinatory art but is also used in the study of the rhythms and cycles of time, whence the working out of Tibetan chronology and the compilation of the calendar also fall within the domain of the Tibetan astrologer.

Astrology is one of the five secondary sciences, along with the literary arts. It is also a valuable adjunct to traditional medicine, assisting in the confirmation of certain diagnoses and in determining the most auspicious times for the preparation and administration of medicines. The preparation and performance of many Buddhist and Bön rituals, moreover, require a good knowledge of the astrological conditions of the moment. Astrology is also crucial at the most important moments in the life cycle, such as birth, marriage, and death.

Astrology is thus ubiquitous in the daily life of the Tibetans and is always combined with religious life. It is therefore important to understand its relationship with Buddhism and the place that it occupies within that context.

## THE TWO REALITIES

If there is a single essential concept in Mahāyāna Buddhism, it is that of the coexistence of two aspects of reality: ultimate reality and apparent or conventional reality. Candrakīrti (sixth century), the great commentator on Nāgārjuna,[1] describes these as follows:

> All phenomena possess two natures:
> That which is revealed by correct perception
> And that which is induced by deceptive perception.
> The object of correct perception is ultimate reality,
> The object of deceptive perception is conventional reality.
> —MADHYAMAKĀVATĀRA, VI, 23

The same phenomenon, therefore, may be perceived according to its ultimate nature or its apparent nature.

Ultimate reality is also called "emptiness." "Emptiness" does not mean that all phenomena are nothing, but rather that they do not exist in themselves. Although phenomena, the universe, thoughts, beings, time, and so on, seem to be very real in themselves, ultimately they are not.

Each of us can perceive the changing and unpredictable nature of existence. There is not a single being or a single object that is not subject to birth and death, creation and destruction, from our own lives and our constuctions, the earth and the planets, down to atoms and subatomic particles, as scientists have discovered.

This transitory nature of phenomena, impermanence, is the first sign of emptiness.

Let us consider a rainbow. At first sight, when it appears in the sky, it seems real, but this appearance is very ephemeral. In order for such a phenomenon to appear, there must be a primary

---

1. Nāgārjuna is a key figure in the development of Mahāyāna Buddhist thought. His dates are unknown, but most authorities agree in placing him in the second century C.E.

cause—the rays of the sun—and a contributory cause—rain in the opposite direction to the sun. When these two causes come together at the same time, the sun's light is reflected and refracted in the droplets of rain and a rainbow appears. If the sun is hidden or if the shower stops, the rainbow disappears. What can be concluded from this? That the rainbow has no existence in itself. It is a phenomenon composed of light, and depends on precise causes and conditions in order to appear. When these change, the rainbow phenomenon cannot subsist.

What we have just described is the interdependence of phenomena, or their dependent production. The "rainbow" phenomenon, in fact, depends on the phenomena "sun rays," "rain," and "time": it therefore does not exist of itself. The emptiness of a phenomenon means that it exists neither in itself nor of itself.

What we have said regarding the rainbow can equally be applied to other phenomena. Ask yourself, what is "I"? Although we identify with it, this "I" is also a transitory compound, an assemblage of feelings, perceptions, sensations, ideas, and so on, whose nature is always open to question. Its ultimate nature is none other than emptiness. There is thus the emptiness of phenomena and the emptiness of self, the emptiness of subject and object.

What about time? The idea of time is closely linked to that of the succession of events, that is, to actions, to causes and effects. When you act, your action feeds on your past. The result proceeding from that action becomes the cause of a future event. An action connects the present to the future and the past. But neither the past nor the future has any existence. So what are the bases for your action?

We could also say that the ideas of past, present, and future exist only in our thoughts. A present thought is connected with past thoughts and gives rise to future thoughts. When a past thought vanishes and before a future thought arises, what can one say in the present about a present thought that is not linked to the other two times? It also has no existence. If a thought does not exist in itself, time does not exist either.

"Apparent" or "relative" truth is the aspect of things that we all perceive at first sight. It is our conventional interpretation of the world in which we live. Known in Tibetan as *kün dzop*, "the reality that encloses all things,"[2] this is none other than the appearance of phenomena as we perceive them through our senses.

Since the perception of each being is different, there will be as many perceptions of phenomenal appearances as there are beings in the universe. One day, according to a legend, the astrologer of a small Indian kingdom warned the king that there would soon fall on the land a rain "that would send people mad." This news quickly spread, and everyone, from the humblest to the most powerful, hurried to stock as much drinking water as possible. The rain began to fall, as predicted. The less consequential people, who had few reserves, were soon obliged to drink the rainwater and became mad. Then it was the turn of the merchants, the rich people, and finally the ministers themselves—all were forced to drink the contaminated water. Only the king, with his vast reserves, remained sane. And everyone throughout the kingdom was convinced that it was the king who was mad. This story illustrates the relative nature of conventional reality.

Our mode of perceiving the world depends on our mental disposition and our karma. By the word *karma*, I mean here all the conditioning created by our past actions. Every action is in effect a cause. A positive action will have positive effects, while a negative action will produce a bitter fruit. It is the performer of an action who will experience its consequences. By the same token, all our actions leave a trace in the current of our consciousness; and when conditions allow, this imprint will show the mental proclivities that are firmly rooted in us. These proclivities permeate our psyche and condition our view of things.

The overall result of the tendencies connected with our past karma is very complex and differs from individual to individual. However, we humans have a "common karmic vision" of the world, thanks to which we are able to communicate through concepts and words. Thus all human beings share a certain type

2. *Kün dzop* (*kun dzob*) translates literally as "entirely spurious."

of karmic tendency. We all agree about concepts such as "table," and "color"; but this does not apply to value judgments: here each individual has his or her own vision, his or her own opinion. If I say, "This is a table," everyone will agree, but if I add, "This is a fine table," opinions may differ.

Buddhism recognizes six classes of being that inhabit the universe, and we are told that the perception of the world is different in each class. Where a human being sees a river, a being of the hot hells sees a stream of burning molten bronze, a being of the cold hells sees a glacier, a hungry ghost sees defilement and pus, a god sees a stream of nectar, and a titan sees a violent river bearing weapons.

Since sensory perception is conditioned by our karmic tendencies, it is at the same time "relative" and "misleading." Karma, indeed, is always connected with ignorance. This fundamental ignorance that obscures our being is a sort of unawareness that prevents us from seeing the true nature of things. Rooted in ignorance, our actions are blind and are the origin of all illusion and all evil.

What, then, are the relations between these two levels of reality? The absolute and apparent reality of the same phenomenon are opposed to each other—indeed, since perception varies from one individual to another, the apparent nature of an object varies also, and for this reason its apparent nature cannot be its ultimate nature, which is unique.

The two realities are inseparable—according to the *Prajñāpāramitā Hṛdaya Sūtra.*

> Form is emptiness, emptiness is form. There is no emptiness
> other than form, no form other than emptiness.

Thus all phenomena are empty, but we see them as appearances. Conversely, all apparent phenomena have no existence in themselves. These two aspects are inseparable, and there is no third reality outside these two.

The two realities have the same essence. Indeed, existing things do not "become empty"—they are empty from the beginning. That is their essence. Apparent reality can be compared to a building whose component parts are brought together in order to support each other but in which no component part rests on the earth. The building is in a state of constant collapse: it is a sketch of existence, completely relative, in which phenomena only exist in relation to others and whose essence is empty since the beginning.

Thus phenomena are not "destroyed" by emptiness: they continue to appear in dependence upon each other, all empty. The two realities are like the two sides of the same coin.

## SAṂSĀRA AND NIRVĀṆA

Why does Buddhism emphasize emptiness? Not knowing the ultimate nature of things means believing that their appearance is the only reality. This belief leads one to cling to appearances as something real, and can only lead to illusion, disappointment, and suffering. Ignorance of ultimate reality is therefore the cause of suffering.

What is called "mind" is also essentially empty. But this empty mind has a luminous nature, and its clarity is none other than its capacity to perceive, to know, to think, to conceptualize, to analyze, and to create. The creativity of the mind is endless and has infinite possibilities; because of this the mind is sometimes referred to as "the king that creates everything." Within the mind, emptiness and clarity are inseparable, and their union gives rise to the unfolding of the infinite variety of appearances.

The person who recognizes the nature of the mind is enlightened, a buddha. For him, all phenomena are empty and luminous and are no more than the constant and spontaneous play of the mind. In this nonduality, he is free from any limited beliefs. Beyond nonexistence and beyond the eternal, beyond interior and exterior, hope and fear, he is beyond suffering. This is the sense of the word *nirvāṇa* in Tibetan.[3] Since a buddha is estab-

3. *Nirvāṇa* is, of course, Sanskrit. The corresponding Tibetan term is *nyang de* (*myang 'das*), "beyond suffering."

lished in the primordial purity of the mind, the origin of all things, he is omniscient, he knows all phenomena both in their essence (emptiness) and in detail (distinct appearances).

When, on the other hand, we do not have this awareness, we are deceived as to the true nature of things. Under the power of ignorance, we perceive the luminous creativity of the mind as "external" and "foreign" to ourselves. Doubt is set up and soon becomes duality, "I" and "others." "Others" includes all external phenomena, to which we attribute real and independent existence. We form three sorts of relationship with these others: attraction or desire for those phenomena that are judged as pleasant; revulsion or anger for unpleasant phenomena; and indifference or neutrality toward phenomena regarded as being of no interest. From these three reactions are born the five passions: ignorance, anger, desire/attachment, pride, and jealousy. When these passions dominate the mind, they are translated into thoughts, concepts, and finally concrete actions. These are known as karma. In accordance with their tone, whether negative or positive, our actions provide the causes for the later experience of effects of the same nature. We ceaselessly experience the fruits of past karma, and at the same time we continue to create new karma.

In this way, we chain ourselves to the vicious circle of existence, or *saṃsāra*. Our feeling of "I" is confirmed, and with it our mental habits. Karma is accumulated and it becomes more and more difficult to recognize the deep illusion in which we are sunk.

When one particular passion predominates and our perceptions take on a particular hue, this is known as "karmic vision." There are six types of karmic vision, corresponding to six realms of existence: the hell realms, the realms of the hungry ghosts or *pretas*, the animal realm, the human realm, the realm of the titans or *āsuras*, and the realm of the gods or *devas*. These realms are dominated respectively by anger, greed, ignorance, desire, jealousy, and pride. We wander from one to another of these realms under the influence of karma; and this transmigration from life to life does not cease until the nature of the mind is understood.

This entire process resembles the crystallization or solidification of phenomena created spontaneously by the mind. Thus, the five elements are the origin of the mind's pure and spontaneous manifestation of wisdom, appearing as a five-colored light. This luminosity has never been different from our mind, but as a result of ignorance we mistake it for the multitude of external objects. Thus externally the five colors of this light become the five gross elements, Ether, Air, Water, Fire, and Earth, and internally they become the gross constituents of the body: "hollows," wind, blood, heat, and flesh.

The mind is indeed "the king that creates everything," the basis of all things or *kün zhi*. Recognizing it as such is to realize its functioning and to unite with its radiant luminosity. This is the path of the buddhas. Not recognizing it leads to attachment to one's own perceptions and one thus falls into illusion. This is the path of saṃsāra and suffering.

In the original mind, neither saṃsāra nor nirvāṇa exists. Ignorance creates the conditions of saṃsāra, and as its antithesis there arises the search for nirvāṇa or the "extinction" of saṃsāra.

The practice taught by the buddhas consists of ridding ourselves of illusion, developing strong compassion for all suffering beings, liberating ourselves from the grip of karma, dissolving our crystallizations, and reintegrating them into our void and luminous nature.

## THE PLACE AND ROLE OF ASTROLOGY

In the light of the foregoing discussion, it will be clear that astrology is concerned with the realm of apparent reality; and this, moreover, is the meaning of the legend of the *Padma Thangyik* quoted in the previous chapter. Having been unable to teach the ultimate truth in China,[4] the Buddha instructed Mañjuśrī to awaken peoples' minds by means of astrology, the science of relative truth. Unfortunately, people were ensnared by their calculations and predictions, and thus they were closed to spirituality. This clearly shows the limitations of astrology: although it opens the door to many higher teachings, it can become a trap if one stays with it too long, and can prevent access to the ultimate.

Because of this danger, Mañjuśrī decided to take astrology away from humans and hide its texts. Unable to foresee anything, blind and powerless in the face of the circumstances of life, beings then suffered innumerable ills. Since only astrology can help to relieve these disasters, it will finally be returned to humans so that they may make good use of it.

Astrology is a means, not an end. It is used to calculate the cycles of time, to reveal their meaning, and to foresee certain events. Armed with this knowledge, human beings have the capacity to avoid or reduce suffering. This applies at both the collective and the individual level. Astrology is a practical discipline intended to reduce suffering and uncertainty, which are the lot of beings wandering in saṃsāra. The correct motivation for an astrologer is none other than compassion—without that, astrology falls to the level of the ordinary disciplines.

As a science of time, the fundamental doctrinal basis of astrology is a perfect understanding of the laws of causality: in other words, karma and the links of interdependence, the two chief mechanisms of relative existence.

## THE WHEEL OF LIFE
## AND THE LAWS OF CAUSALITY

In Tibet, there is a well-known graphic description of the laws of causality: the Wheel of Life or *Sipe Khorlo*, which illustrates the mechanisms binding us to saṃsāra. The wheel indicates the turbulent nature of existence and the vicious circle of saṃsāra: karma acts as the centrifugal force that prevents us from tearing ourselves away from the cycle. The more we struggle to satisfy our ambitions and desires, the more we revolve in the wheel of existence.

The entire wheel is held in the claws of a terrifying monster, Yama, death, the inevitable price of ignorance and dualism. At the center of the wheel there are three animals, each biting the tail of the one in front: a cock, a snake, and a pig, symbolizing respectively desire, anger, and ignorance, the three "poisons" that lie at the root of all our conditioned behavior.

The next circle, moving from the hub of the wheel toward the outside, shows human beings, some rising toward higher states of existence and others falling into the lower worlds—this symbolizes the power of karma, which, according to whether it is positive or negative, leads to an endless alternation of favorable and unfavorable conditions.

The next circle shows the six realms of saṃsāric existence, which are beings' different karmic visions. The force of the passions is so strong that it completely conditions our perception of the world. The three upper areas show the realms of humans, gods, and titans, while the three lower areas show those of the animals, the hungry ghosts, and the hot and cold hells. The outermost circle, which is divided into twelve sections, describes the twelve elements of causation or *nidānas*, the links of the chain of cause and effect, the motor that drives conditioned existence and every set of circumstances we meet.

Outside the wheel is the Buddha, the Awakened One, pointing to a text or a wheel with eight spokes, symbolizing the Dharma, his liberating teachings, which lead to the destruction of the chains and limitations of conditioned existence.

## THE TWELVE LINKS OF CAUSATION

The nidānas (Tib. *tendrel*) are the twelve links of the causal chain. As we have seen, phenomena exist only in dependence upon other phenomena, as is illustrated by this teaching, which comes from the sūtras. It shows that our existence is a succession of causes and effects, invariably linked to each other. The chain thus formed equally describes our conditioning as it arises from the past, our present circumstances, and the causes of our future existence. This teaching is of great importance in astrology for two reasons:

1. Only the teachings of interdependent origination can jus-

tify astrology from a doctrinal point of view. How is it possible to explain the interrelation between the state of the heavens at the moment of birth and a being's future existence? The idea that external stars guide or influence an individual's destiny is hardly adequate as a firm foundation for astrology. It is also necessary to establish a precise link between those external objects, the stars, and the internal "I" of beings; and without such a link, no interaction is possible.

The *Kālacakra Tantra* explains that the cosmos is a vast external maṇḍala, that the body of the yogi is the internal maṇḍala, and that these two are in complete correlation. This theory of the correspondence between macrocosm and microcosm is also found in the West, most notably in Paracelsus (1493–1541), the doctor and hermetic astrologer. This theory is borne out by the teaching of the tantras. As we have discussed, all phenomena arise from the luminous creativity of the mind, but under the influence of ignorance, we conceive the existence of a dualistic world in which we distinguish "I" and others, subject and object, internal and external. Thus the gross external elements and the gross internal constituents of the body are one and the same in their origin, as explained above. It follows that at an absolute level, such dualistic distinctions as internal and external disappear, while at the relative dualistic level, a real relationship of interdependence still obtains between the internal and the external.

Again, we are living in the temporal realm where everything is transitory and subject to change. This dynamic of phenomena is none other than the play of interdependence. If, as a result of observing the course of the stars in the sky, astrologers have been able to calculate their movement in advance, to determine the laws that govern their behavior, and above all to establish a clear and replicable correlation with individuals' destiny, astrology is vindicated.

2. From the practical point of view, the twelve nidānas are used in Tibetan astrology to designate the months of the year, as well as in daily prediction. There is also a correlation between the twelve nidānas and the twelve signs of the Indian zodiac.

The chain of interdependence, known as *pratītyasamutpāda*, is described as follows in the sūtras:

> Upon ignorance depend the karmic formations,
> Upon the karmic formations depends consciousness,
> Upon consciousness depend name and form,
> Upon name and form depend the sense organs,
> Upon the sense organs depends contact,
> Upon contact depends sensation,
> Upon sensation depends desire,
> Upon desire depends attachment,
> Upon attachment depends becoming,
> Upon becoming depends birth,
> Upon birth depend old age and death,
> In this way, the aggregates of suffering arise one from
> the other.

As they relate to the past, the first two nidānas are the causes that have brought us to our present situation:

*Ignorance (avidyā)* is represented in the Wheel of Life by an old blind woman feeling her way with a stick, ignorance lies at the root of saṃsāric confusion. There are two kinds of ignorance: the first, innate ignorance, is an unawareness of the true nature of the mind and phenomena, a state of distraction and confusion. When, as a result of this ignorance, one does not recognize appearances for what they are, one "imagines" that the world is dual. This is the second kind or imaginary ignorance.

*The karmic formations (saṃskhārāḥ karmāḥ)* are represented by a potter throwing pots on a wheel. Ignorance leads to the accumulation of impulses known as "conditioned actions." These karma-bearing actions are manifested in the body, speech, and mind as forces that structure our existence. Depending on whether our acts are virtuous, neutral, or negative, we are led by these actions to a more or less favorable rebirth.

The following seven nidānas are the "chains of the present." The first five describe the process of birth:

*Consciousness (vijñāna)* is represented by a monkey climbing a tree, leaping from branch to branch in search of fruit to pick. This rebirthing consciousness, formed at the time of conception in the womb, is the kernel of the "I" created by past karma. The new personality arranges itself around this kernel, fed by karmic proclivities.

*Name and form* (*nāmarūpa*) are represented by a boat with four passengers and a helmsman. As it explores its environment, consciousness "names" and labels things. When form is attributed to appearances, they crystallize. It is at this level that there occurs the formation of the five gross elements that shape the body and the physical world.

*The six sense fields* (*ṣaḍāyatana*) are represented by an empty house with six windows. The six senses are sight, hearing, smell, taste, touch, and the mental sense. Each sensory field comprises a sensory consciousness (for example, the consciousness of vision), an organ (for example, the eye) that establishes communication with the outside, and a sensory object (for example, shapes and colors).

*Contact* (*sparśa*) is represented by a couple embracing. The meeting of the senses and their objects creates contact—thus sight makes contact with forms, hearing makes contact with sounds, and so on.

*Sensation* (*vedanā*) is represented by a man with an arrow piercing his eye. Contact is a precondition for sensation, which may be pleasant, painful, or neutral.

The two following nidānas describe how we continue to create karma which will condition our future existence.

*Desire or thirst* (*tṛṣṇa*) is represented by a man slaking his thirst. Desire is conditioned by the sensation experienced when we come into contact with an object. There are three sorts of desire: desire for pleasure; desire for eternity, or thirst for existence; and desire for annihilation or nonexistence, which is regarded as pathological.

*Attachment or grasping* (*upādāna*) is represented by a monkey grasping a fruit. Desire demands satisfaction, otherwise it is frustrated and becomes a cause of suffering. Attachment to the desired object is therefore the result of desire. Four types of attachment giving rise to rebirth are distinguished: attachment to sense pleasures, erroneous views, rules and rituals, and the notion of a self.

The three last nidānas deal with the next life:

*Becoming (bhava)* is represented by a pregnant woman. Becoming is a consequence of attachment to existence and to the "I," and thus it is nothing less than the pursuit of existence, constantly fed by new karmic tendencies, which will ripen in the future. This is therefore also a process of conception.

*Birth or rebirth (jāti)* is represented by a woman in childbirth. Attachment to life and the constant creation of new karma give rise to our rebirth. The "newborn" being is in fact "old-born"—it carries its karma with it, and according to the nature of that karma, it is born in one of the six realms of existence.

*Old age and death (jarāmarana)* are represented by a man carrying a corpse to the charnel ground. Everything that is born grows, declines, and finally dies. It is in the nature of all existence that it is transitory. When the cohesion of a being's elements ceases, there is dissolution, and this results when life-karma is exhausted. Death is therefore a process of dissolution in which a being is gradually stripped first of the gross and then of the subtle elements of the "I," as the skins of an onion are peeled away one by one. When this process is complete, the mind appears for an instant in its nakedness, void and luminous. The trained yogi can then recognize the nature of his mind and liberate himself. But most beings are incapable of this and are soon submerged again by their karmic tendencies. Impelled by these tendencies as if by a strong wind, they seek refuge in a new womb and take birth. The chain of the twelve nidānas is closed.

Another brief observation is appropriate regarding the application of astrology in prediction. There is no element of fate in this law of causality. Every event is simply the result of a combination of causes and conditions converging at the same time in the same place. When an event is predicted, one is merely taking account of the causal conditions that are likely to cause that event later—it exists only as a potential and its course can be modified. If the causes and circumstances are prevented from coming together, nothing happens. Karma is only inevitable when it is not purified by certain specific practices, and for this reason Tibetan astrology includes a great many practices and rituals designed to confront these potential future threats.

# PART TWO

# *Practical Astrology*

# INTRODUCTION

## THE CALENDAR AND PRACTICAL ASTROLOGY

Astrology is inseparable in Tibet from the use of the calendar. All Tibetans are concerned to ensure that their everyday lives are in accordance with astrological circumstances in order to harmonize their existence as much as possible with natural cosmic rhythms. Once aware of the energies of the moment, humanity no longer acts blindly but in accordance with the universe.

For this purpose, the Tibetans use almanacs, known as *lotho*, which they consult regularly. These almanacs, compiled each year by the astrological colleges, consist of a calendar, some general predictions for the year and each lunar month, and daily and monthly astrological tables both general and applicable to the individual. Similar almanacs existed in the Middle Ages in the West and a few survive to this day, but rationalism has gradually reduced their use to checking dates. This is not the case in Tibet, where the calendar is still an expression of the cosmic cycles that set the rhythms of our lives.

The framework of the calendar is of Chinese origin: the years, the months, and the days are designated by an animal and an element. The year comprises twelve lunar months of thirty days each. Each day is divided into twelve double hours.

Astrological qualities, elements, trigrams, and Mewas are attributed to the years, months, days, and hours. To these are added the influence of the moon in its passage through the twenty-eight constellations, the planetary cycles, and the twelve links of interdependent origination, which latter derive from the Kālacakra. In order to determine whether a given day is auspicious, it is necessary to bear in mind all these elements and their harmonious or inharmonious combinations.

Chinese and Indian astrology are perfectly linked together in the Tibetan calendar, and have a common basis in the lunar cycle.

## THE IMPORTANCE OF THE LUNAR CYCLE

Western astrology is "solar": the twelve signs of the zodiac are determined by the apparent movement of the sun through the ecliptic in the course of a solar year. Each sign is an archetype of the various functions of the sun, reflecting the variations of solar influence as colored by its passage through the sky.

In the East, the year consists of twelve lunations. These twenty-seven or twenty-eight lunations or lunar mansions are a sort of "lunar zodiac," and daily life is linked to the phases of the moon. The tides, the growth of plants, the weather, the menstrual cycle, and the individual's psychic characteristics are all known to be affected by lunar cycles. At the full moon, psychic arousal is at its peak, and accidents, acts of violence, and mental crises seem to be more frequent. The power of this lunar influence can be used to advantage: in the Buddhist calendar, full-moon day is the day of the Buddha, and is devoted to the practice of meditation so that advantage can be taken of this intensity of energy.

Western astrology is not unaware of the importance of the

moon, but it neglects certain aspects of its influence, such as the lunar mansions, which nowadays are considered only in magic. The place accorded to the moon in Eastern astrology has no counterpart in Western practice. The Western preference for a solar astrology seems to correspond to a culture geared to expansion, concrete creation, an external orientation. The sun symbolizes the creative Self, personal will and ambition, the instinct of domination, all of which values are prized in our society. The moon, on the other hand, is the planet of impermanence, change, and fluidity. Its rapid course suggests the fleeting and transitory aspect of phenomena, and its light is a reflection, like the mirror of the mind in which the illusory images of the world are reflected. It symbolizes deep psychic phenomena, changing emotions, dreams, the unattainable and the changing, the subjective and relative aspects of the world.

In Buddhism, the moon is a favorite analogy for describing the world of appearances. In a Tibetan text, we read, "Hypnotized by the pure variety of perceptions, like the illusory reflection of the moon in water, beings wander without end, bewildered in the vicious circle of saṃsāra." This is a clear statement of lunar symbolism. Phenomena dance in infinite variations and fascinate our deluded mind—it is rather like mistaking the reflection of the moon in water for the moon itself.

The moon is also a symbol of contemplation and meditation: when a meditator is troubled by the agitation of the world, he calms his mind and there appears in him the clear and limpid mirror of the pacified mind that reflects everything without grasping. The moon is thus the signifier of wisdom and the "mind of enlightenment," *bodhicitta*.

In India, as in Tibet and China, the emphasis is on the fluctuating and impermanent nature of the phenomenal world. The effort to achieve realization is concerned more with awareness of oneself than with material conquest; and this perhaps explains the choice of a lunar astrology.

# 4

## THE
## MAIN COMPONENTS
## OF CHRONOLOGY
## AND THE CALENDAR

In this chapter I shall describe the essential components of Jung-tsi astrology, which is a Chinese-based system. These components provide the framework for Tibetan chronology, and as the most important interpretive elements in the study of astrology, they must be understood from the very beginning. These factors derive from interactions between cosmic or planetary energies and terrestrial energies. We are not dealing here with the planets as such but rather with their action in contact with the earth.

It has often been said that Chinese astrology is not so much an astrological system as a geomantic art; and it is terrestrial experience rather than metaphysical speculation that dominates Chinese astrology.

### THE FIVE ELEMENTS

The five Chinese elements are known in Tibetan as *jungwa*: Wood (*Shing*), Fire (*Me*), Earth (*Sa*), Metal (*Chak*), and Water (*Chu*). These elements should not be confused with the constituents of the universe (Earth, Water, Fire, Air, and Ether), which are also used in Indian astrology to designate the main components of material or subtle phenomena. Thus in the body, Earth denotes flesh and bones; Water denotes bodily fluids; Fire denotes body heat; Air denotes the Winds; and Ether or Space corresponds to consciousness.

The five Chinese elements, however, are a little different. They are, in fact, natural forces of transformation, in constant interaction with each other. The term "element" is to be understood as a dynamic principle, a principle of energy; and certain authors prefer to speak of "agents" rather than the more confusing "elements." However, it is possible to establish correspondences between the two systems, assimilating Wood to Air and Metal to Earth.

The names of the elements—Wood, Fire, Earth, Water, and Metal—are symbolic: they allow description of the elements by analogy, but have little to do with the objects of the same name. None of the elements is good or bad in itself. However, in contact with each other they react according to their affinities. There are therefore favorable, neutral, and harmful relations. An element can also become dangerous when there is too much or too little of it.

## Elements and Directions

Each element is associated with a direction and a season. In the *Jungtsi Men Ngak Dawe Öser*, we find a description of how the elements are located in space, with reference to the great cosmic turtle, the base of the universe:

> Here is the teaching on the five parts of the turtle (*rüpel*): this science has been established thanks to the method of representing the world of appearances as an illusory turtle. The profound meaning of this teaching must be understood.
>
> The base of the world is a turtle lying on its back. Its head denotes the south and the element of Fire; its right side indicates the direction East and the element Wood. Its left side

53

shows the West and the element Metal. Its tail indicates the North and the element Water. Finally, its four limbs in the four intermediate directions (Northeast, Northwest, Southeast, and southwest) correspond to the element Earth.

All the sciences of astrological calculation are established on this basis.

It will be noted that Earth occupies a place of particular importance. This can be interpreted in a number of ways: As the force that emanates from the Earth when it enters into contact with

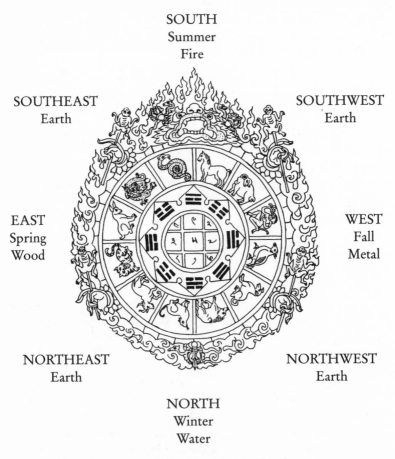

*The orientation of the Cosmic Turtle, the seasons, and the elements*

the four celestial elements, it is assigned the center as its direction, or alternatively the four intermediate points. According to other sources, the Earth element is composed of the four others and only appears as a result of their interaction. It is therefore not assigned any particular direction.

In the course of the year, each of the elements predominates in one of the seasons: in spring, Wood dominates; in summer, Fire; in autumn, Metal; and in winter, Water. However, at the end of each season, its characteristic element loses strength, and it is at this time that Earth, hitherto hidden, predominates; and then the following season supervenes, dominated by another element. Thus the Earth element only shows its strength between seasons; and since each season is connected with one of the cardinal directions, Earth is naturally associated with the intermediate points.

## The Characteristics of the Elements

Each of the elements embraces a number of meanings and correspondences: each has its inherent characteristics, activity, direction, season, color, planet, organ, etc. These allow the nature of each element to be defined, but it must not be forgotten that the elements never exist in isolation: they are dynamic and in constant interaction, and their characteristics derive all their value from this context. In the Tibetan text, we read: "Although the essence of the elements is one, different characteristics can be distinguished. None of the five activities can be understood in isolation." The essence of the elements is said to be unique because they are all a manifestation of pure cosmic energy. Each one represents a particular mode of action of that energy in the terrestrial realm. The text continues: ". . . the essential characteristics of the elements Wood, Fire, Earth, Metal, and Water are respectively mobility, destruction, solidification (coagulation), cutting, and permeation (humidification)."

The text also defines the elements in terms of activity. We shall describe each of them in turn.

WOOD

Wood is symbolized by a young tree with leaves of soft green; or by the wooden handle of the sword of Mañjuśrī, piercing the flank of the cosmic turtle. Wood corresponds to awakening, to morning, spring, and the direction East. As a symbol of vitality, its characteristics are growth, mobility, the power of inspiration and creativity. Its nature is soft and harmonious, but in excess it can become choleric. Its color is green, its organ is the liver, whose role is to transform and synthesize bodily constituents. Its flavor is acid and its planet is Jupiter. The associated trigrams are *Tsin*, the awakener, thunder, and *Zön*, softness, wind.

People born under Wood possess a vital attraction and remain in close touch with the life-giving earth, which makes them calm, balanced, and confident. Thanks to these traits, Wood natives attract the support of the group in their undertakings, which are usually successful. Their innovative ideas testify to a great openness of mind. Their greatest fault is scattered energy, which can spoil their chances of success. The voice is guttural.

FIRE

Fire is symbolized by brilliant, burning flames as well as by the visceral blood of the cosmic turtle. Fire is associated with the South, with the heat of midday and summer. Its qualities are eagerness, joy, fervor, and passion. It is full of sparkle and transforms everything it touches—to the point at which it burns. Its purificatory powers can easily become destructive. Its passion is violent and its character is a mixture of impatience, intolerance, and burning ambition—anything that resists it must be destroyed.

Its organ is the heart, its flavor is bitterness, and its color is red. In its qualities of clarity, perspicacity, and brilliance, Fire is associated with the Sun. Its warlike, intolerant, and destructive character relates it to the planet Mars. Its trigram is *Li*, which is attached to a corpse about to be burned.

Natives of Fire are small and dark, with aquiline noses and sibilant voices. Because of their violent and quick-tempered character, they are not people to be reasoned with. They are very perceptive and will not tolerate compromise. They are generous, warm, and idealistic and set high goals for themselves, achieving them through ambition and sweeping all obstacles aside. Others are attracted and magnetized by their brilliance, like butterflies drawn to a flame. They are mystic warriors with burning hearts and only hypocrites and the mediocre need fear them.

## EARTH

Earth is symbolized by a yellow square or by the four limbs of the cosmic turtle. It is the center of all things. It is connected with the beginning of the afternoon, the time of rest, and with the four intermediate periods between the seasons, as well as with the four intermediate points of the compass. It is a crystallizing force, and works slowly and powerfully, stabilizing and concretizing things. Its qualities are fertility and abundance. Its virtue is realism, a sense of the concrete.

Its organ is the spleen, its flavor is sweetness, and its planet is Saturn. The trigram of Earth is *Khön*, the receptive.

Earth natives are thickset with powerful limbs, and their features are thick, their voices deep, coming from the belly. They are practical people and think with wisdom and prudence. They work methodically, although slowly, and with concrete, solid objectives. They are enterprising and shrewd and can be possessive and selfish, attached to material things.

## METAL

Metal is represented by a rapier or the point of the sword of Mañjuśrī emerging from the left flank of the turtle. It corresponds to evening, decline, the direction West, and autumn. It has all the characteristics of a blade: coldness, dryness, clarity, purity, firmness, and sharpness. It is a symbol of integrity and justice and cuts through with resolution, but when rigid, it becomes destructive and impedes progress.

Its organ is the lung, its flavor is tart, its color is white, and its planet is Venus. It is associated with the trigram *Da*, the joyful—this may seem to contradict the foregoing, but Metal has two aspects: although rigid and cutting as an ideal of justice, it is nonetheless a magnetic and joyful element, drawn by earthly delights; and in this sense it symbolizes sexuality and pleasure.

People born under Metal have solid and well-proportioned bodies, nasal voices, and clear complexions. They are intellectuals, fond of novelty and of justice, resolutely pursuing their objectives and intolerant of any interference in their business. They are therefore strong individualists. However, they are constantly torn between their moral ideal and their attachment to the pleasures of the flesh, and take refuge in a rigid attitude in order to disguise their contradictions and their instability.

WATER

Water is symbolized by waves or by the urine of the cosmic turtle. It is associated with the North, the cold of winter, and night. It is more commonly considered in terms of its cold aspect than its fertility, another attribute frequently associated with it. Water is the principle of penetrating moisture, the total cessation of activity. Passivity and the absence of passion lead to calm and receptivity. Water also symbolizes the hidden, that which is at rest but potentially rich, the rest that is necessary before starting again.

Its colors are dark blue and black, its flavor is salt, and its organ is the kidney, the regulator of bodily fluids. It is associated with the Moon and the planet Mercury, and the trigram *Kham*, the unfathomable.

Water natives correspond to the lymphatic temperament. Their bodies are round and fat, their skin is soft and supple, and their complexion is dark. Their lips are thick, their faces round, and their mouths half-open. Their affable and easy manner makes them easy to communicate with. They are patient and placid, ready to listen to others; they are confidants, giving wise advice, guided by solid intuition. Although they are timid and fearful, their patience and adaptability allow them to wear down resistance and overcome obstacles. In excess, the calm that characterizes Water can become idleness and laxity. Its openness makes it easily influenced and dependent.

TABLE 1

## CHARACTERISTICS OF THE ELEMENTS

| Element | Symbol | Color | Direction | Period | Quality | Activity | Organ | Planet and Parkha |
|---------|--------|-------|-----------|--------|---------|----------|-------|-------------------|
| Wood | Tree | Green | East | Spring Dawn | Vitality | Mobility | Liver | Jupiter Tsin, Zön |
| Fire | Flames | Red | South | Summer Midday | Ardor | Destruction | Heart | Sun, Mars Li |
| Earth | Square | Yellow | Center | Interseasonal Afternoon | Fertility | Solidification | Spleen | Saturn Khön |
| Metal | Sword | White | West | Autumn Evening | Rigidity | Cutting | Lungs | Venus Da |
| Water | Waves | Blue-black | North | Winter Night | Rest | Impregnation | Kidneys | Mercury, Moon Kham |

## The Relations between the Elements

In nature, the elements come together and either harmonize or fight, according to their affinities. From these relations arise the natural cycles of transformation. In astrology, these interactions must be known perfectly: they constitute the basis of all calculations and predictions in the Jungtsi system.

We may refer here to the Tibetan text, which says: "The relations between elements are those of mother, son, friend, or enemy. The mother of Wood is Water; the mother of Water is Metal; the mother of Metal is Earth; the mother of Earth is Fire; and the mother of Fire is Wood."

The maternal relationship is also known as "the cycle of the production of the elements." This is the best type of relationship: the mother-element engenders, protects, and nurtures the son-element.

The correlative of the mother relationship is the son relationship: "The son of Wood is Fire; the son of Fire is Earth; the son of Earth is Metal; the son of Metal is Water; and the son of Water is Wood."

It will be noted that in the cycle of creation, the order of the son-relationships follows the seasons (Spring/Wood, Summer/ Fire, etc.). If Wood gives birth to Fire, this means that the potential of Fire is contained within Wood itself; in the same way, if Fire engenders Earth, the latter is latent in Fire. The five elements are therefore not different and distinct energies, but a single cosmic force that has five modes in the world of appearances.

Another approach to this cycle is based on analogy: wood is inflammable, and when it burns (Fire) it leaves ashes (Earth). From earth, metal (Metal) is extracted. The vapor of cold metal can be condensed into water (Water), which is necessary for vegetable growth (Wood).

"The enemy of Wood is Metal; the enemy of Metal is Fire; the enemy of Fire is Water; the enemy of Water is Earth; the enemy of Earth is Wood." This is the cycle of defeat: the enemy-elements dominate, use, and destroy the weaker elements. Thus the cutting property of metal enables it to cut and chop wood; while fire can make metal malleable and even melt it. Water extinguishes fire; earth absorbs water; and wood feeds on earth.

Conversely, the defeated element is the servant of the conqueror because it benefits it. This is the relationship of friendship: "The friend of Wood is Earth; the friend of Earth is Water; the friend of Water is Fire; the friend of Fire is Metal; the friend of Metal is Wood."

These relations are summarized in table 2.

These relations are binary, but if a third element is present it can intervene to modify the process. For example, Fire attacks Metal, but Water extinguishes Fire—it therefore comes to the aid of Metal. Water extinguishes Fire, but Earth absorbs Water, thus helping Fire, and so on. This is the relationship of control, in accordance with the logic "My enemy's enemies are my friends."

Again, by reinforcing another element, the son of a particular element prevents it from defeating that other element: Water attacks Fire, but Wood engenders Fire and therefore reinforces it, and the process is thus arrested, for Water can do nothing against Wood, its son. This is the process of interruption.

These "feedback" effects can be summarized as in table 3.

TABLE 2

RELATIONS BETWEEN ELEMENTS

| Element | Mother | Son | Friend | Enemy |
|---------|--------|-----|--------|-------|
| Wood | Water | Fire | Earth | Metal |
| Fire | Wood | Earth | Metal | Water |
| Earth | Fire | Metal | Water | Wood |
| Metal | Earth | Water | Wood | Fire |
| Water | Metal | Wood | Fire | Earth |

| enemy ↓ | | Fire | mother ← | |
|---------|------|-------|----------|-------|
| | | Water | | |
| Wood | Fire | Earth | Metal | Water |
| | | Wood | | |
| son → | | Metal | friend ↑ | |

There is a scale of affinity that allows the relationships between elements to be assessed. The symbols used are the "black and white pebbles," represented here respectively by crosses and circles:

| | | |
|---|---|---|
| Excellent relationship | O°O | (mother) |
| Very good relationship | O O | (friend) |
| Good relationship | O | (Earth-Earth, Water-Water) |
| Neutral relationship | OX | (son) |
| Bad relationship | X | (Fire-Fire, Metal-Metal, Wood-Wood) |
| Very bad relationship | XX | (enemy) |

## Polarity of the Elements

Each of the elements can have a masculine (*Pho*) or feminine (*Mo*) polarity. This *Pho-Mo* alternation is undoubtedly connected with the Chinese principles of Yin and Yang. *Pho* and *Mo* are not antagonistic but complementary: *Pho* denotes an ele-

TABLE 3

## INTERACTIONS OF THE ELEMENTS

| Control | | | Interruption | | |
|---|---|---|---|---|---|
| *The element* | *attacks* | *but is destroyed by* | *The element* | *attacks* | *which is reinforced by* |
| Wood | Earth | Metal | Wood | Earth | Fire |
| Fire | Metal | Water | Fire | Metal | Earth |
| Earth | Water | Wood | Earth | Water | Metal |
| Metal | Wood | Fire | Metal | Wood | Water |
| Water | Fire | Earth | Water | Fire | Wood |

ment's movement of expansion, growth, and expression, while *Mo* is the symbol of rest, receptivity, and passivity. Thus the Chinese symbolize Male Wood with a tree, and female Wood with a flexible bamboo. Male Fire is lightning, the living flame; while female Fire is the fire of the hearth. Male Earth is represented by a hill or by the Earth itself; while in its female aspect it is a valley or an earthenware vessel. Male Metal is a weapon; as female it is a cauldron. Water can be a wave or stagnant.

The native influenced by a male element is active and expresses elemental energy; while if dominated by a female element he or she is introverted and thoughtful.

## *Importance of the Elements*

The great importance of the elements is borne out by our text:

When the activities of the elements are not agitated, they produce good fortune. When they are imbalanced, they give rise to suffering, illness, and death.

When the elements come together in aggregates, discursive thought and karma are engendered. From this aggregation arise sickness and dangers caused by the Dön demons and the executioner spirits.

All good fortune and all suffering without exception arises from the activities of the elements—this is why the calculations are important.

We have now established the principles for determining the elements. As forces of transformation, the elements suffuse and sustain everything in the universe. They enter into the characteristics of all the components of Jungtsi astrology: animals, Mewas, Parkhas, etc., and govern the relations between them. A knowledge of the elements is therefore the key to all calculations and all combinations of Jungtsi astrology.

## THE TWELVE ANIMALS

The twelve animals are used to designate years, months, days, and hours. In China, a system of twelve branches was classically used to express the cycle of twelve years. The twelve animals are a later development, but they were quickly assimilated to the more abstract system of branches. The Tibetans use the cycle of twelve years only in this later form—there has never been any system of branches, only symbolic animals. The twelve animals are:

| Rat | (Chi) | Dragon | (Druk) | Monkey | (Tre) |
|------|-------|--------|--------|--------|--------|
| Cow | (Lang) | Snake | (Trül) | Bird | (Ja) |
| Tiger | (Tak) | Horse | (Ta) | Dog | (Khyi) |
| Hare | (Yö) | Sheep | (Luk) | Pig | (Phak) |

Each animal is associated with an element, which represents its life force. The Tiger and the Hare are Wood. The Horse and the Snake are Fire. The Monkey and the Bird are Metal. The Pig and the Rat are Water. The Cow, the Dragon, the Sheep, and the Dog are connected with the element Earth.

## The Directions of the Animals

The direction attributed to each animal relates to the associated element. Returning to the *Jungtsi Men Ngak Dawe Öser*, we read:

Here are described the natural directions of the animals:

In the first Eastern section is the Tiger and in the second the Hare. The dragon is found in the Southeast.

In the first Southern section is the Snake and in the second the Horse. The Southwest is the place of the Sheep.

In the first Western section is the Monkey and in the second the Bird. The Northwest is the realm of the Dog.

In the first Northern section is the Pig and in the second the Rat. The Northeast is the direction of the Cow.

## The Polarity of the Animals

In table 4, the male or female character inherent in each animal is distinguished, as well as the character attributed to them in the twelve-year cycle. The inherent polarity of an animal corresponds to its symbolism and also bears upon the composition of its psychological character.

The Rat is a nocturnal animal and a symbol of prosperity—it is therefore female, as is the Hare, which is associated with the

TABLE 4

POLARITY OF THE ELEMENTS

| Animal | Element | Direction | Own polarity | Polarity in the 12-year cycle |
|--------|---------|-----------|--------------|-------------------------------|
| Rat | Water | North | − | + |
| Cow | Earth | Northeast | − | − |
| Tiger | Wood | East | + | + |
| Hare | Wood | East | − | − |
| Dragon | Earth | Southeast | + | + |
| Snake | Fire | South | + | − |
| Horse | Fire | South | + | + |
| Sheep | Earth | Southwest | + | − |
| Monkey | Metal | West | + − | + |
| Bird | Metal | West | + | − |
| Dog | Earth | Northwest | − | + |
| Pig | Water | North | − | − |

Moon. The Dragon, by contrast, the symbol of thunder,[1] is male; and so on.

> Male animals (*Pho* = *Yang*): Tiger, Dragon, Snake, Horse, Sheep, Bird
> Female animals (*Mo* = *Yin*): Rat, Cow, Hare, Dog, Pig
> The monkey is considered to be both male and female.

This polarity is not the same in the twelve-year cycle but alternates male/female. It should be recalled here that originally the Chinese used the twelve branches, alternately Yin and Yang; when the animals were substituted, the same male/female alternation was retained.

Male and female years are distinguished: the years of the Rat, Tiger, Dragon, Horse, Monkey, and Dog are male. The years of the Cow, Hare, Snake, Sheep, Bird, and Pig are female.

## Personality Profile

According to legend, when the Buddha was about to attain the final liberation of *parinirvāṇa*, he wanted to meet with all the animals so that he could bless them, but only twelve came. In recognition of this, the Blessed One named the years of the twelve-year cycle in their honor, according to the order in which they appeared before him.

The animal associated with a year gives it its specific character and influences the life and the personality of those born under its aegis. This, however, is crude and general—more specific data (particulars of month, day, and hour of birth) is required in order to obtain a truly personalized profile.

### THE RAT

The Rat is full of charm, loves company and acts with flair, is direct in dealings with people, and is widely appreciated. How-

---

1. The Tibetan word *druk* (*'brug*) means both "thunder" and "dragon."

ever, although amiable and generous on the outside, the Rat is in reality egotistical, calculating, and manipulative.

The Rat is independent and careful, keenly aware of the need to protect its internal universe and accumulate wealth—the Rat likes money. The Rat's ambitions are realized in social contacts: the Rat must succeed at all costs. The Rat is selfish and readily abuses others, who must serve its plans. The Rat is discreet in matters that concern it and able to turn almost everything to its own advantage. It is therefore successful in most of its undertakings, provided it does not become scattered, as can happen. It can adapt itself to all situations, is a skilled organizer, and has excellent prospects.

The Rat is sensual and appreciates luxury. In its emotional life, it is sentimental and generous to those it likes, particularly its family. Once its confidence has been gained, it is excellent as an intimate friend.

Its outward behavior, at once brilliant and calm, conceals great interior aggression. A frustrated or crossed Rat becomes manipulative, aggressive, backbiting, vengeful, and obstinate.

### THE COW

The Cow is a real monolith. Stable, solid, tenacious, and obstinate, it is a great worker. Independent and discreet, it does not meddle in the affairs of others. It is incapable of frivolity and speaks only on the basis of sound knowledge—and can then display the qualities of a first-class orator.

The cow's quiet strength, its sober intelligence and logic, its competence and its sense of responsibility make it someone to be trusted. It is an excellent leader and demands as much of itself as of others.

In adversity, the Cow is impartial but at the same time does not easily change its mind. It is obstinate and traditionalist, materialistic and unemotional, and cannot be persuaded other than by its own weapon, logic.

On the outside, the Cow appears rough, surly, and reserved. When misunderstood and unsatisfied, it becomes rigid, authoritarian, conventional, and resistant to change. Although naturally patient, it should not be pushed, for it then displays a terrible anger that overturns everything in its path.

At the emotional level, the Cow is slow and naive and its fidelity can withstand any test. But if thwarted, it can play dirty.

## THE TIGER

The Tiger is a symbol of awakening to life, which it seizes enthusiastically and with determination. Unpredictable and daring, the Tiger dislikes monotony. It likes to put itself forward and command, but hates to obey and is a fierce enemy of hierarchy and convention.

The Tiger's fondness for independence leads it to an unconventional lifestyle. It has artistic imagination and keeps away from the beaten track. A noble and generous master, the Tiger meets challenges with audacity, but lacks moderation and has difficulty calming its emotions. When crossed, the bad side of its character appears and it can become violently enraged, for it is a superego and cannot bear to have its weak points touched.

The Tiger is a romantic and passionate lover, jealous but not very faithful, and always feels a need to pour out its heart. When its faults get the better of it, it is a hothead, a rebel, easy but quick tempered.

## THE HARE

The Hare is a model of calm, virtue, and prudence and is loved for its elegance, its good manners, and its kindness. Its speech is soft and its subtlety of judgment makes it an excellent diplomat and a good negotiator. The Hare is also worldly and enjoys luxury. However, despite these surface qualities, it hates the unexpected and the sudden: its principal concern is to maintain a life of calm and comfort in a peaceful environment. It is therefore discreet, sometimes indifferent, and dislikes confusion. It is not endowed with great bravery and seeks to avoid all difficulties, sidestepping them if need be without becoming involved. Nothing is more precious to the Hare than its own narcissistic comfort, and its main fear is the disturbance of its psychic balance and its private space. It is polite even to enemies—but beware!

The Hare is crafty and its attacks are subtle and devious. When threatened, it becomes suspicious and underhand, even cunning, in fear of being trapped or driven to the wall. It is very sensitive to criticism. In love, the Hare is sensual but not very faithful, and does not like to become involved in emotions. It hates intrusion in its private life and is distant to its own family.

## THE DRAGON

The Dragon is a flamboyant person, impetuous and lucky. The Dragon is said to be blessed with four things: wealth, virtue, harmony, and long life—as long as it is in control. The Dragon is full of energy and convinced of its own superiority. It is a natural leader and has great wisdom. In order to live to the full, it must feel itself as the object of destiny and have some special mission to perform. The Dragon is a "person of the moment" and likes big enterprises. It may be a little inclined to megalomania, but is always sincere.

The Dragon is full of enthusiasm, intuitutive, and endowed with a superior intelligence. It is widely admired, which allows it to exert its influence and express its manipulative tendencies. It follows only its own judgment and despises the opinions of others. The Dragon is full of its own idealism, but it can run aground and does not know how to cut corners.

The Dragon is very demanding and is never satisfied with those around it—they always lack breadth and never achieve the desired height. Nothing and nobody is good enough for the Dragon, which is why it is irritable, frustrated, unhappy, and always asking for more. If it meets strong opposition, it will fight bravely and will not mince its words. It speaks out frankly and has no tact. It is impatient and prone to attacking without guarding its retreat. Its anger is terrible and wounding, but it forgives easily once it has recovered its calm. The Dragon never accepts defeat, and nothing can overcome it.

In society, it likes pomp and is a born showman. It is a visionary and mocks at preachers and failed idealists. However, it is generous and energetic and a good friend whose advice is valuable. The Dragon is very open and cannot easily conceal its explosive feelings. It is a sincere but demanding lover.

## THE SNAKE

The Snake is a deep thinker endowed with innate wisdom. It also has a great talent for seduction, as well as good manners, natural grace, good humor, and a taste for refinement. The Snake attracts company, enjoys style and all the good things of life, for it is an elegant sensualist. The Snake talks little, keeps its own secrets, thinks a lot, and trusts only its own judgment. At times it can be headstrong and stubborn. It does not tolerate hardship or defeat and can become jealous and play dirty—it is then implacably calculating and coldly awaits the moment to strike, not hesitating to trick hypocrites. Although the Snake is sociable, it is touchy, untrustworthy, and easily angered. Its anger is violent and vengeful.

This sign must accept its karma, and cannot escape from it. However, a Snake knows how to change its skin and learns quickly from experience. The Snake is very fond of sex, exclusive, possessive, and jealous. It dominates its partner but is not always faithful.

## THE HORSE

The Horse has abundant energy and a lively mind, it is passionate, eager, and charming. It is adventurous and soon leaves the family to explore the world. It likes exercise and is always on the move, leading a life of excitement. It is very sociable, more brilliant than intelligent, and draws to itself inventive people who will help it to attain success. It is an eloquent leader, sometimes talks too much and cannot keep a secret. Its nature is changeable and unstable.

The Horse is falsely independent: it wishes to be free but has a gut fear of failure, and for this reason it needs a supportive environment and looks everywhere for props. Its family and friends must arrange themselves around the Horse and in order to secure this position, it uses charm and assurance. The Horse is an opportunist who cannot bear to be ignored.

Although the Horse is an egoist, it is neither jealous nor possessive, but its impatience can lead it to disaster. Its interest fades almost as soon as it is aroused.

## THE SHEEP

The Sheep is good-natured, gentle, and easy-going, with a warm and tender heart. The Sheep has a strong sense of justice, but is indulgent and easily forgives. It loves nature and is sensitive to art but never strays from the beaten track.

Independent by nature, the Sheep can adapt to circumstances and seeks the protection of powerful people. It follows the trend, is terrified by obstacles, and leaves it to others to take responsibilities. It is a first-class team member but has no initiative and cannot exercise leadership. In its desire to be protected, it can easily allow itself to be used.

The Sheep is a pessimist and a worrier, easily loses its practical sense, and takes refuge in dreams, becoming whimsical, eccentric, or even theatrical. In adversity, the Sheep sulks in a corner and its weakness is disarming. It gets what it wants without violence and by devious paths and does not hesitate to become a parasite.

The Sheep has a great deal of filial spirit. In love, it is superficial and unstable, but a protective partner is good for it.

## THE MONKEY

The Monkey is inventive and well-adapted to life, and likes movement and great undertakings. It is wily, lively, agile, and at home in any work. In company, it seems brilliant, good-humored, and pleasant, as well as playful and affable. However, the Monkey is a clever diplomat and a born strategist who never acts without a plan in mind. It solves problems easily and is good at everything. Nothing pleases the Monkey more than its own ingenuity, for the Monkey has a superiority complex. Its humor is always at the expense of others and it believes it is immune to criticism. The Monkey never allows itself to be trapped and escapes from difficulties by means of clever dances of which it alone knows the secret. It likes to strut and chokes itself with fine words.

The Monkey is an opportunist and seizes any chance that presents itself and profits from it. It is entirely amoral and performs good or bad acts with equal indifference as long as they are to its own benefit. It has little time for scruples.

It is cultured and has a great thirst for knowledge, but as soon as it has mastered something it abandons it and turns to something else. It may meet obstacles and difficulties but its lucidity and suppleness enable it to land on its feet. In love, the Monkey is still an adolescent, seductive and passionate.

THE BIRD

The Bird is endowed with a sparkling and honest nature and a great appetite for life. It hates routine, likes fantasy, and enthusiastically seeks novelty. The Bird has an inquiring mind and a lively intelligence. It is alert, organized, honest, and frank, and sometimes brutal in its criticisms.

These gifts make it see itself as out of the ordinary, and it likes to appear so. It enjoys witticism and display where it can use its colorful appearance. It is confident, amusing, joyful, and garrulous and loses no opportunity to talk about itself. It loves discussion provided the subject is itself, and it excels in controversy.

The Bird seems sure of itself but is really deeply anxious about its image. To ignore it is the worst insult. It is selfish and stubborn and thinks it is always in the right. It prefers to work for itself rather than be exposed to the criticisms of superiors. Its dreams are somewhat fantastic and ambitious, and if it fails, it always thinks it can do better next time. It is a perfectionist and a scientist, but it can get lost in detail. Nevertheless, it is a good organizer and manager with sound financial sense.

Although conceited and pedantic, it is generous and surrounds itself with many friends. Its flair assures it the attention of important people. In its emotional life, it knows the heights and the depths and it finds difficulty in achieving balance. If it learns how to calm itself, it can find happiness in simplicity.

THE DOG

The Dog is loyalty and honesty personified. It is intelligent, has a strong sense of justice, and is a conscientious worker. It is an obliging friend and cannot help itself from lending a helping hand. However, it is careful and analytic, takes a long time to make decisions, and avoids being in the forefront. Its judgment is sound, and it is trustworthy, devoted, and altruistic.

The Dog cannot tolerate hypocrisy or ill will, but its anger is brief, inspired by its sense of morality. The Dog is not playful, for life is too serious. The Dog moralizes and analyzes situations so much that it becomes pessimistic.

The Dog is intuitive. It scents danger and exaggerates it, which makes it a worrier. If cheated, the Dog can display bitter cynicism. It may be a little alarmist. Its life is a heavy burden, and if it persists in taking everything seriously, it will have few opportunities for happiness. The Dog's affections are lasting if it is able to master its pessimism.

THE PIG

The Pig is honest, simple, and good-natured. It is jovial and natural and comes straight to the point. Its heart is pure and without malice. It is a "good person" with stable and beneficial friendships, and can be trusted. It is sincere, amiable, and charitable, but it is also innocent and naive. Since it does not know how to say no, it is a favorite victim for con artists. It is tolerant, hates lies, and prefers silence. However, when crossed it can defend itself savagely.

Although it appears to be unselfish, the Pig is fond of money. It is generous to friends and likes to share but expects to be repaid when the occasion arises. If need be, it will help itself.

The Pig is known for its sensuality, and it pursues pleasure diligently, sometimes as far as depravity.

## Compatibility between Animals

The connections between animals can be favorable or unfavorable. An understanding of their affinities is important when human relationships are under consideration—partnerships, marriages, friendships, latent or open conflicts, and so on—as well as in predicting favorable or difficult years for a particular sign.

As a general rule, enemy-animals are those which have opposite directions: Rat and Horse, for example, or Dragon and Dog. The best affinities exist between animals separated by an equilateral triangle: for example, the Rat is in harmony with the Monkey and the Dragon.

Other types of favorable, unfavorable, or neutral relations are harder to determine definitively, and Chinese, Tibetan, and Western writers are not in complete agreement as to compatibility. However, the animal sign is always found together with other factors, such as the elements, and these modify their relationships. Although other influences also play a part, then, table 5 on page 74 shows the ideal affinities. (We use again the symbols for seven degrees of compatibility.)

## THE TWELVE-YEAR CYCLE

Each year of the cycle is designated by one of the symbolic animals, in the order given above. From the astronomical point of

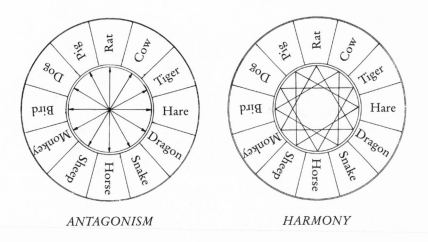

ANTAGONISM                    HARMONY

## TABLE 5

## RELATIONS BETWEEN ANIMALS

| Sign | Rat | Cow | Tiger | Hare | Dragon | Snake |
|---|---|---|---|---|---|---|
| Rat | O | OO | OX | OX | O OO | O |
| Cow | OO | OX | XX | O | OX | O OO |
| Tiger | OX | XX | X | OX | OX | XX |
| Hare | O | OX | X | O | XX | OX |
| Dragon | O OO | OX | XX | XX | O | O |
| Snake | O | O OO | XX | OX | O | OX |

| Sign | Horse | Sheep | Monkey | Bird | Dog | Pig |
|---|---|---|---|---|---|---|
| Horse | O | OO | X | OX | O OO | OX |
| Sheep | OO | O | OX | OX | X | O OO |
| Monkey | OO | OX | O | OX | OX | XX |
| Bird | OX | OX | OX | X | XX | OX |
| Dog | O OO | X | OX | XX | O | OX |
| Pig | OX | O OO | X | OX | OX | X |

Key  
O OO — Excellent    X — Intolerance  
OO — Very good    XX — Enmity  
O — Good    XXX — Total incompatibility  
OX — Neutral

view, the twelve-year cycle is known as the Jupiter Cycle. The planet Jupiter takes approximately twelve years to complete one revolution through the zodiac. It traverses on average one sign each year, and this has suggested to some writers a relationship between the animals and the signs of our zodiac. However, this correspondence is not very clear, since Jupiter's path is characterized by retrograde movement and its revolution does not correspond exactly to a complete revolution of the zodiac. The following table shows in general terms the mean position of Jupiter in the signs of the zodiac in a twelve-year cycle.

| Year | Rat | Cow | Tiger | Hare | Dragon | Snake |
|------|-----|-----|-------|------|--------|-------|
| Jupiter in | Sagittarius | Capricorn | Aquarius | Pisces | Aries | Taurus |

| Year | Horse | Sheep | Monkey | Bird | Dog | Pig |
|------|-------|-------|--------|------|-----|-----|
| Jupiter in | Gemini | Cancer | Leo | Virgo | Libra | Scorpio |

Of greater interest, however, are the general characteristics of each year of the cycle:

*The Year of the Rat* is a year of prosperity and plenty. It is quite tranquil and allows progress, growth, and investment. It is necessary, however, to beware of taking too many risks.

*The Year of the Cow* is a year of toil. Its fruits will grow from constant work and sustained effort. It is a bad year for the idle. One must be steadfast, attentive, and patient and keep one's cool in all undertakings.

*The Year of the Tiger* is an unpredictable year. Many dramatic developments can be expected: explosions, coups d'état, political unrest, catastrophes, heroic deeds, sudden and daring attacks, all are characteristic of this year. It is turbulent but hides its surprises well, whether they are good or bad, and a certain caution should be observed in all undertakings.

*The Year of the Hare* is a year of general relaxation, an easy life—so calm is it, indeed, that it leads to a certain degree of indolence.

*The Year of the Dragon* is energetic, giving rise to celebrations and grandiose projects. It is auspicious for marriage, birth, and new beginnings. It is a year of surprises, when an opportunity can be grasped or lost. There are also natural disturbances.

*The Year of the Horse* is a period of great activity of all sorts. It offers many freedoms and is good for energetic people. This is a year characterized by a life of excitement and daring. Powerful impulses allow projects to reach completion.

*The Year of the Sheep* is a year of rest after effort and is favorable for the flowering of emotion and interest in the arts—one

## TABLE 6

## CHARACTER OF YEAR AS FUNCTION
## OF NATAL ANIMAL

| ANIMAL Year | Rat | Cow | Tiger | Hare | Dragon | Snake |
|---|---|---|---|---|---|---|
| Rat | O OO | OO | X | O | OO | O |
| Cow | OX | OO | X | XX | OO | OX |
| Tiger | OX | XXX | OX | X | X | X |
| Hare | O | OX | OO | O OO | O | O |
| Dragon | O OO | OX | X | OX | O OO | X |
| Snake | X | OO | OX | OX | OX | OX |

| ANIMAL Year | Horse | Sheep | Monkey | Bird | Dog | Pig |
|---|---|---|---|---|---|---|
| Horse | XX | O | OX | XX | O | OO |
| Sheep | OX | X | O | O | OX | OX |
| Monkey | OO | OO | O OO | X | O | O |
| Bird | O | O to X | OX | O | X | OX |
| Dog | O | XX | XX | O | OO | X |
| Pig | XX | OX | X | XX | O | O |

| Key | | | | |
|---|---|---|---|---|
| O OO | Excellent | X | Intolerance | |
| OO | Very good | XX | Enmity | |
| O | Good | XXX | Total incompatibility | |
| OX | Neutral | | | |

should let oneself be guided by one's feelings during this year. Improvisation is advised.

*The Year of the Monkey* is extremely rich and holds many surprises—anything can happen. This is a year in which one must be cunning and seize new initiatives. All opportunities are open and one should be flexible enough to take advantage of them. This is a year of daring progress, not for the slow or timid.

*The Year of the Bird* is an energetic but scattered year. There are many opportunities, but concentration is necessary in order to enjoy their fruits. On the global scale, there is political hardening and repression.

*The Year of the Dog*, the sign of idealism and justice, brings generosity and reflection. It is a little overserious and favors those who have good intentions.

*The Year of the Pig* is more optimistic and indulgent than the preceding year, bringing security, prosperity, and a tendency to waste. The abundance of this year leads to sybaritic excess.

It is equally important to know how each sign travels through the twelve years of the cycle; thus for each individual, we will have an overview of favorable years and those in which obstacles may appear. As a general rule, the best years are those governed by animals that are in harmony with the native animal, while more difficult years correspond with enemy-signs.

## THE SIXTY-YEAR CYCLE

The cycle of twelve animals combined with the five elements of Chinese cosmology gives the cycle of sixty years, or great cycle of Jupiter. Each of the elements is associated with two successive animals, the first male and the second female—in other words, the odd years are male and the even female. The elements alternate in their order of generation: Wood, Fire, Earth, Metal, Water. (See table 7, pages 80–81.)

The first Tibetan sexagenary cycle begins in the year 1027, while the corresponding Chinese cycle (no. 62) begins in 1024, the year of the Wood Rat. This three-year shift may seem strange, but it can be explained by reference to Indian astrology. In the Kālacakra, a Jupiter cycle of sixty years is used, known as *Bṛhaspati Varṣa*, in which each year carries its own name in Sanskrit. The first year of the cycle is called *Prabhava* or "first," the second *Vibhava*, and so on. When the Kālacakra was introduced to Tibet, the Tibetan astrologers decided to adopt this cycle in parallel with the Chinese cycle, and they settled on 1027 as the starting date, which is the first year of an Indian cycle. Since the Chinese sexagenary cycle is a closed system, any year of the sixty-year cycle can be chosen as the starting year. Thus, by integrating the Kālacakra cycle, starting with 1027, the Tibetans were able to continue using the Chinese names of the years without any displacement.

The year 1027 is the Female Fire Hare year in the Chinese cycle, and Prabhava in the Kālacakra cycle. The correspondences are as follows:

|  | *China* |  |  |  | *Tibet* |  |  |
|---|---|---|---|---|---|---|---|
| 62nd cycle: | 1024 | – | 1083 | 1st cycle: | 1027 | – | 1086 |
|  | (Wood Rat) | | (Water Pig) |  | (Fire Hare) | | (Fire Tiger) |
| 63rd cycle: | 1084 | – | 1143 | 2nd cycle: | 1087 | – | 1146 |
| 77th cycle: | 1924 | – | 1983 | 16th cycle | 1927 | – | 1986 |
| 78th cycle: | 1984 | – | 2043 | 17th cycle: | 1987 | – | 2046 |

At the end of sixty years, the complete natural cycle of animals and elements is complete and a new one begins. On both the individual and the cosmic levels, the sixty-year cycle marks a completion, which is followed either by a radical change or by a sort of return to the original conditions. A new birth may occur.

## Relations between Natives of Different Years

The element-animal combination permits great refinement and precision in determining the types of relationship possible between natives of different years, and this aspect is frequently studied in matrimonial astrology or in order to determine the chances of good understanding between partners. (See table 8, pages 82–83.)

As a general rule, compatibility between both animals and elements is taken into consideration, although since the relations between elements seem to play a more decisive role, they are accorded greater importance.

The best relations are those between friend-animals and elements in a mother-relationship, such as Wood Rat–Fire Monkey or Fire Tiger–Earth Horse.

The relations between neutral or enemy-animals can be improved if the elements are in a mother-relationship: Tiger and Monkey are considered incompatible, but Water Tiger and Wood Monkey can enjoy friendly relations.

Harmonious relations between animals may be impaired by enemy-elements. Here there is an imbalance: the individual who has the conqueror-element will strongly dominate his or her partner. The defeated element is in fact the friend of the conqueror, and is therefore entirely under its control. For example, if a Metal Dog marries or associates with a Fire Horse, the latter will probably dominate completely. In the same way, a Metal Tiger will be stronger than a Wood Dog, and so on.

Relationships, contracts, and marriages between partners who have both enemy-elements and enemy-animals are highly inadvisable. Such a union risks disaster from two sides: the partner with the conqueror-element will not only experience deep disagreement but will also exercise tyrannical dominance over his or her partner. A Fire Tiger, for example, may not only disturb the stolid Metal Cow, but also wreck its defenses and its tranquillity. The wily Water Monkey, on the other hand, will make a fool of the Fire Tiger and take away his or her confidence and style.

## Characteristics of the Years of the Sixty-Year Cycle

Each animal sign is alternately combined with each of the five elements. The characteristics of each sign are therefore colored by the energy of the associated element. In judging the quality of a year or a native under its influence, it is necessary to form a synthesis that takes account of:

- The animal that rules the year and the corresponding element
- The element of the year
- The relationships between the element energy of the year and the element energy of the animal

TABLE 7

# THE TIBETAN SIXTY-YEAR CYCLES

| Sino-Tibetan Name | Indo-Tibetan Name | Translation | Tibetan Cycles | | | | | |
|---|---|---|---|---|---|---|---|---|
| | | | 1 … | 13 | 14 | 15 | 16 | 17 |
| 1. Fire Hare − | Rabjung | Initial | 1027 | 1747 | 1807 | 1867 | 1927 | 1987 |
| 2. Earth Dragon + | Namjung | Totally born | 1028 | 1748 | 1808 | 1868 | 1928 | 1988 |
| 3. Earth Snake − | Karpo | White | 1029 | 1749 | 1809 | 1869 | 1929 | 1989 |
| 4. Metal Horse + | Rabnyö | Totally drunk | 1030 | 1750 | 1810 | 1870 | 1930 | 1990 |
| 5. Metal Sheep − | Kyedak | Lord of birth | 1031 | 1751 | 1811 | 1871 | 1931 | 1991 |
| 6. Water Monkey + | Ang-gir | Name | 1032 | 1752 | 1812 | 1872 | 1932 | 1992 |
| 7. Water Bird − | Peldong | Glorious face | 1033 | 1753 | 1813 | 1873 | 1933 | 1993 |
| 8. Wood Dog + | Ngöpo | Substance | 1034 | 1754 | 1814 | 1874 | 1934 | 1994 |
| 9. Wood Pig − | Natsöden | Yellow | 1035 | 1755 | 1815 | 1875 | 1935 | 1995 |
| 10. Fire Rat + | Dzinche | Holder | 1036 | 1756 | 1816 | 1876 | 1936 | 1996 |
| 11. Fire Cow − | Wangchuk | Mighty Lord | 1037 | 1757 | 1817 | 1877 | 1937 | 1997 |
| 12. Earth Tiger + | Drumangpo | Much grain | 1038 | 1758 | 1818 | 1878 | 1938 | 1998 |
| 13. Earth Hare − | Nyöden | Mad, drunk | 1039 | 1759 | 1819 | 1879 | 1939 | 1999 |
| 14. Metal Dragon + | Namnön | Oppression | 1040 | 1760 | 1820 | 1880 | 1940 | 2000 |
| 15. Metal Snake − | Truchok | Perfect cube | 1041 | 1761 | 1821 | 1881 | 1941 | 2001 |
| 16. Water Horse + | Natsok | Varied | 1042 | 1762 | 1822 | 1882 | 1942 | 2002 |
| 17. Water Sheep − | Nyima | Sun | 1043 | 1763 | 1823 | 1883 | 1943 | 2003 |
| 18. Wood Monkey + | Nyidrölche | Liberating Sun | 1044 | 1764 | 1824 | 1884 | 1944 | 2004 |
| 19. Wood Bird − | Sakyong | Protector of Earth | 1045 | 1765 | 1825 | 1885 | 1945 | 2005 |
| 20. Fire Dog + | Mize | Inflexible | 1046 | 1766 | 1826 | 1886 | 1946 | 2006 |
| 21. Fire Pig − | Thamchedül | All-conquering | 1047 | 1767 | 1827 | 1887 | 1947 | 2007 |
| 22. Earth Rat + | Kündzin | Stopping all | 1048 | 1768 | 1828 | 1888 | 1948 | 2008 |
| 23. Earth Cow − | Galwa | Error | 1049 | 1769 | 1829 | 1889 | 1949 | 2009 |
| 24. Metal Tiger + | Namgyur | Custom | 1050 | 1770 | 1830 | 1890 | 1950 | 2010 |
| 25. Metal Hare − | Pongpu | Ass | 1051 | 1771 | 1831 | 1891 | 1951 | 2011 |
| 26. Water Dragon + | Gawa | Happiness | 1052 | 1772 | 1832 | 1892 | 1952 | 2012 |
| 27. Water Snake − | Namgyal | Totally victorious | 1053 | 1773 | 1833 | 1893 | 1953 | 2013 |

| No. | Element/Animal | Name | Meaning | | | | | |
|---|---|---|---|---|---|---|---|---|
| 28. | Wood Horse + | Gyalwa | Victorious | 1054 | 1774 | 1834 | 1894 | 1954 | 2014 |
| 29. | Wood Sheep + | Nyöche | Intoxicating | 1055 | 1775 | 1835 | 1895 | 1955 | 2015 |
| 30. | Fire Monkey + | Dong-ngen | Ugly face | 1056 | 1776 | 1836 | 1896 | 1956 | 2016 |
| 31. | Fire Bird – | Serchang | Gold pendant | 1057 | 1777 | 1837 | 1897 | 1957 | 2017 |
| 32. | Earth Dog + | Namchang | Hanging | 1058 | 1778 | 1838 | 1898 | 1958 | 2018 |
| 33. | Earth Pig – | Gyurche | Transformer | 1059 | 1779 | 1839 | 1899 | 1959 | 2019 |
| 34. | Metal Rat + | Künden | Having all qualities | 1060 | 1780 | 1840 | 1900 | 1960 | 2020 |
| 35. | Metal Cow – | Pharwa | Wild dog | 1061 | 1781 | 1841 | 1901 | 1961 | 2021 |
| 36. | Water Tiger + | Geche | Virtuous | 1062 | 1782 | 1842 | 1902 | 1962 | 2022 |
| 37. | Water Hare – | Dzeche | Beautiful | 1063 | 1783 | 1843 | 1903 | 1963 | 2023 |
| 38. | Wood Dragon + | Tromo | Terrible | 1064 | 1784 | 1844 | 1904 | 1964 | 2024 |
| 39. | Wood Snake – | Natsok yik | Varied wealth | 1065 | 1785 | 1845 | 1905 | 1965 | 2025 |
| 40. | Fire Horse + | Zilnön | Evil-crushing splendor | 1066 | 1786 | 1846 | 1906 | 1966 | 2026 |
| 41. | Fire Sheep – | Treu | Monkey | 1067 | 1787 | 1847 | 1907 | 1967 | 2027 |
| 42. | Earth Monkey + | Phurbu | Dagger, Jupiter | 1068 | 1788 | 1848 | 1908 | 1968 | 2028 |
| 43. | Earth Bird – | Zhiwa | Peaceful | 1069 | 1789 | 1849 | 1909 | 1969 | 2029 |
| 44. | Metal Dog + | Thunmong | Ordinary | 1070 | 1790 | 1850 | 1910 | 1970 | 2030 |
| 45. | Metal Pig – | Galche | Erroneous, contradictory | 1071 | 1791 | 1851 | 1911 | 1971 | 2031 |
| 46. | Water Rat + | Yongdzin | Guardian | 1072 | 1792 | 1852 | 1912 | 1972 | 2032 |
| 47. | Water Cow – | Bakme | Irreligious, impudent | 1073 | 1793 | 1853 | 1913 | 1973 | 2033 |
| 48. | Wood Tiger + | Künga | Total joy | 1074 | 1794 | 1854 | 1914 | 1974 | 2034 |
| 49. | Wood Hare – | Sinpu | Insects | 1075 | 1795 | 1855 | 1915 | 1975 | 2035 |
| 50. | Fire Dragon + | Me | Fire | 1076 | 1796 | 1856 | 1916 | 1976 | 2036 |
| 51. | Fire Snake – | Marser chen | Orange | 1077 | 1797 | 1857 | 1917 | 1977 | 2037 |
| 52. | Earth Horse + | Dükyi ponya | Messenger of time | 1078 | 1798 | 1858 | 1918 | 1978 | 2038 |
| 53. | Earth Sheep – | Döndrup | All-accomplishing | 1079 | 1799 | 1859 | 1919 | 1979 | 2039 |
| 54. | Metal Monkey + | Dragpo | Ferocious | 1080 | 1800 | 1860 | 1920 | 1980 | 2040 |
| 55. | Metal Bird – | Longen | Evil-minded | 1081 | 1801 | 1861 | 1921 | 1981 | 2041 |
| 56. | Water Dog + | Ngachen | Great drum | 1082 | 1802 | 1862 | 1922 | 1982 | 2042 |
| 57. | Water Pig – | Trak kyuk | Blood-vomiting | 1083 | 1803 | 1863 | 1923 | 1983 | 2043 |
| 58. | Wood Rat + | Mikmar | Mars | 1084 | 1804 | 1864 | 1924 | 1984 | 2044 |
| 59. | Wood Cow – | Trowo | Wrathful | 1085 | 1805 | 1865 | 1925 | 1985 | 2045 |
| 60. | Fire Tiger + | Zepa | Exhaustion | 1086 | 1806 | 1866 | 1926 | 1986 | 2046 |

(Handwritten annotations in left margin: "CATHERINE" and a checkmark beside 32; "Mark/David" and a checkmark beside 36; "Michael" and a checkmark beside 38.)

TABLE 8

AFFINITIES BETWEEN NATIVES

| Animal | Harmonious | Incompatible | Animal | Harmonious | Incompatible |
|---|---|---|---|---|---|
| Wood Rat | Fire, Water, Monkey, Cow, Dragon | Metal, Earth, Horse, Sheep | Wood Horse | Fire, Water, Tiger, Dog, Sheep | Metal, Earth, Cow, Rat |
| Wood Cow | Fire, Water, Rat, Bird, Snake | Metal, Earth, Sheep, Tiger, Horse | Wood Sheep | Fire, Water, Pig, Hare, Horse | Metal, Earth, Rat, Cow |
| Fire Tiger | Earth, Wood, Dog, Horse, Pig | Water, Metal, Monkey, Cow, Snake | Fire Monkey | Earth, Wood, Monkey, Dragon | Water, Metal, Tiger, Pig |
| Fire Hare | Earth, Wood, Pig, Dog, Sheep | Water, Metal, Bird, Dragon, Horse | Fire Bird | Earth, Wood, Cow, Snake, Dragon | Water, Metal, Hare, Dog |
| Earth Dragon | Metal, Fire, Rat, Monkey, Bird | Wood, Water, Dog, Tiger, Hare | Earth Dog | Metal, Fire, Tiger, Horse, Hare | Wood, Water, Dragon, Bird |
| Earth Snake | Metal, Fire, Cow, Bird | Wood, Water, Pig, Tiger | Earth Pig | Metal, Fire, Hare, Sheep, Tiger | Wood, Water, Snake, Monkey |
| Metal Horse | Water, Earth, Tiger, Dog, Sheep | Fire, Wood, Cow, Rat | Metal Rat | Water, Earth, Monkey, Cow, Dragon | Fire, Wood, Horse, Sheep |
| Metal Sheep | Water, Earth, Pig, Hare, Horse | Fire, Wood, Cow, Rat | Metal Cow | Water, Earth, Rat, Bird, Snake | Fire, Wood, Sheep, Tiger |
| Water Monkey | Wood, Metal, Rat, Dragon | Earth, Fire, Tiger, Pig | Water Tiger | Wood, Metal, Dog, Horse, Pig | Earth, Fire, Monkey, Cow, Snake |
| Water Bird | Wood, Metal, Cow, Snake, Dragon | Earth, Fire, Hare, Dog | Water Hare | Wood, Metal, Pig, Dog, Sheep | Earth, Fire, Bird, Dragon, Horse |
| Wood Dog | Fire, Water, Tiger, Horse, Hare | Metal, Earth, Dragon, Bird | Wood Dragon | Fire, Water, Rat, Monkey, Bird | Metal, Earth, Dog, Tiger, Hare |
| Wood Pig | Fire, Water, Hare, Sheep, Tiger | Metal, Earth, Snake, Monkey | Wood Snake | Fire, Water, Cow, Bird | Metal, Earth, Pig, Tiger |
| Fire Rat | Earth, Wood, Monkey, Cow, Dragon | Water, Metal, Horse, Sheep | Fire Horse | Earth, Wood, Tiger, Dog, Sheep | Water, Metal, Cow, Rat |

| Sign | | | Sign | | |
|---|---|---|---|---|---|
| Fire Cow | Earth, Wood, Rat, Bird, Snake | Water, Metal, Sheep, Tiger, Horse | Fire Sheep | Earth, Wood, Pig, Hare, Horse | Water, Metal, Rat, Cow |
| Earth Tiger | Metal, Fire, Dog, Horse, Pig | Wood, Water, Monkey, Cow, Snake | Earth Monkey | Metal, Fire, Rat, Dragon | Wood, Water, Tiger, Pig |
| Earth Hare | Metal, Fire, Pig, Dog, Sheep | Wood, Water, Bird, Dragon, Horse | Earth Bird | Metal, Fire, Cow, Snake, Dragon | Wood, Water, Hare, Dog |
| Metal Dragon | Water, Earth, Rat, Monkey, Bird | Fire, Wood, Dog, Tiger, Hare | Metal Dog | Water, Earth, Tiger, Horse, Hare | Fire, Wood, Dragon, Bird |
| Metal Snake | Water, Earth, Cow, Bird | Wood, Fire, Pig, Tiger | Metal Pig | Water, Earth, Hare, Sheep, Tiger | Fire, Wood, Snake, Monkey |
| Water Horse | Wood, Metal, Tiger, Dog, Sheep | Earth, Fire, Cow, Rat | Water Rat | Wood, Metal, Monkey, Cow, Dragon | Earth, Fire, Horse, Sheep |
| Water Sheep | Wood, Metal, Pig, Hare, Horse | Earth, Fire, Rat, Cow | Water Cow | Wood, Metal, Rat, Bird, Snake | Earth, Fire, Horse, Sheep |
| Wood Monkey | Fire, Water, Rat, Dragon | Metal, Earth, Tiger, Pig | Wood Tiger | Fire, Water, Dog, Horse, Pig | Metal, Earth, Monkey, Cow, Snake |
| Wood Bird | Fire, Water, Cow, Snake, Dragon | Metal, Earth, Hare, Dog | Wood Hare | Fire, Water, Pig, Dog, Sheep | Metal, Earth, Bird, Dragon, Horse |
| Fire Dog | Earth, Wood, Tiger, Horse, Hare | Water, Metal, Dragon, Bird | Fire Dragon | Earth, Wood, Rat, Monkey, Bird | Water, Metal, Dog, Tiger, Hare |
| Fire Pig | Earth, Wood, Hare, Sheep, Tiger | Water, Metal, Snake, Monkey | Fire Snake | Earth, Wood, Cow, Bird | Water, Metal, Pig, Tiger |
| Earth Rat | Metal, Fire, Monkey, Cow, Dragon | Wood, Water, Horse, Sheep | Earth Horse | Metal, Water, Tiger, Dog, Sheep | Wood, Water, Cow, Rat |
| Earth Cow | Metal, Fire, Rat, Bird, Snake | Wood, Water, Sheep, Tiger, Horse | Earth Sheep | Metal, Fire, Pig, Hare, Horse | Wood, Water, Rat, Cow |
| Metal Tiger | Water, Earth, Dog, Horse, Pig | Fire, Wood, Monkey, Cow, Snake | Metal Monkey | Water, Earth, Rat, Dragon | Fire, Wood, Tiger, Pig |

*Wood* gives an animal mobility and vitality, a supple and balanced creative power, and a quality of softness. Wood years are years of transformation.

*Fire* transmits a vital, brilliant, and transforming energy and enhances expression, extroversion, and the ability to make decisions; although it often brings about violence, intolerance, and destruction. Fire years are marked by rapid evolution, conflict, and drought.

*Earth* gives stability to the animal sign, along with realism and slowness of action. Earth years are calm, stabilizing, prosperous, and favorable for agriculture.

*Metal* makes an animal sign more rigid. The character is clear and cutting, or sometimes brittle and authoritarian. Metal years are energetic and positive but disturbed, and few compromises can be expected.

*Water* gives openness of mind, suppleness, reflection, communication, and intuition. The animal sign associated with Water becomes more thoughtful, lucid, and sensitive, but also more passive. Water years are auspicious for change and communication.

# 5

## INDIVIDUAL
## ENERGIES
## AND ELEMENTS

Here we are concerned with the application of the theory of the five elements to five human energy factors found in the ancient "nameless religion" of Tibet. This method is unique to Tibetan astrology, and is very important in working out yearly horoscopes. The five individual forces are the *La*, the *Sok*, the *Lü*, the *Wang thang*, and the *Lung ta*.

The *La* is the "soul," the "spirit"—to Tibetan Buddhists, this is chiefly a psychic principle connected with human vitality. The *La* is luminous and normally resides within the human body, through which it moves in accordance with a monthly cycle. According to the Kālacakra teachings, the cycle of movement occurs in the left side in males and on the right in females. At the new moon (30th and 1st days of the lunar month), the *La* is found in the soles of the feet, on the left or the right according to gender. During the period of the waxing moon, it moves as a luminous letter toward the crown of the head, which it reaches at the full moon (15th day). It then travels through the body again until it reaches its original position (see table 11, page 101).

According to Tibetan doctors, it is very important to avoid

any injury, bleeding, or surgery at the area where the *La* is located, or the *La-ne*—the life principle—would be damaged and life would be shortened or even destroyed. Tibetan doctors therefore take account of the cycles of the moon in order to ensure that even the most trivial operations do not present a threat to life.

The *La* is normally located in the body, but it can leave and wander in the external world when energy is low and when an individual faints or is in a coma. In such cases, a ritual is performed, the "recalling of the *La*" or *Laguk*, the object of which is to lead the *La* back to the body. When the *La* is weak, it can also be seduced and carried off by a class of demons known as *sri*—this is a case of possession, which can be remedied by the "repurchase of the *La*." Black magicians can summon an enemy's *La* by force and achieve mastery over the individual concerned—in attacks of this sort, the victim is weakened and falls ill. Here also there is an appropriate ritual to terminate this act of magic violence. At the time of death, it is said that the *La* will survive anywhere—in the grave, for example—but is not reincarnated. It is then able to visit the living.

Although it is connected with the body, the *La* often resides in an external object connected with the individual's life. This may be a hill or a mountain (*La ri*), a tree (*La shing*), or a stone such as the "turquoise of life" (*La yu*). In this case, the *La* is identified with the *Lha*, or god of the area. In Tibet, one must maintain harmonious relations with the environment, for local deities or external *La* influence the life force. Polluting or destroying the habitation of an external *La* will constitute a danger to the individual's own life.

There seem to be many points of similarity between the *La* on the one hand and the *Hun* soul of the Chinese and the *Ka* or double of the Egyptians on the other.

*Sok* refers to the vitality or "life force." It resides in the heart and sustains life, which lasts as long as the *Sok* remains vigorous. Death follows when it disappears. When the vitality is weakened, it is necessary to apply the ritual of "buying back the *Sok*" in order to strengthen it.

The *La* and the *Sok* are closely related. The *Jungtsi Men Ngak* states that "the mother of vitality is called *La*. Vitality and *La* are of the same essence." The *Sok* represents our life potential. It faces dangers similar to those which threaten the La, since it too can inhabit any object it pleases: when an individual is attacked by the *Dam sri* and *Dü chö* demons, who cut off life, he or she falls ill and dies.

The *Lü* or "body" is the energy of bodily health. On its strength depend our good health and our proneness to illness or injury.

The *Wang thang* is the "personal power," our capacity and ability to achieve our goals. This principle is connected with the individual's accumulation of merits and moral strength. When this force is strong, it favors prosperity, wealth, and plenty; enables the individual to avoid injury; and bestows the power to avoid deeds that are dangerous to the body's vitality. When it is weak, there is loss and ruin.

The *Lung ta* is the "Wind Horse." The symbolism of the horse is closely connected with the motive power that carries the energies in the subtle channels of the body, as well as with speed of action. In cosmology, the Wind Horse is one of the seven precious possessions of the *Cakravartin* or ruler of the world. According to the *Torch of Certainty*, "The excellent Horse, which is the same color as a peacock, can cover the four continents in a single instant." In another text, we read, "When the Cakravartin, the sovereign of the four elements, rides the Wind Horse, he departs in the morning and returns in the evening without feeling the slightest fatigue." If this legend is translated into terms of the cosmic man, the Wind Horse is none other than the body, the Cakravartin is the mind and the precious Horse is the mount of the winds, carrying the energies of the mind. The sovereign's journey performed in a single day symbolizes the daily circulation of the energies in the body. As a bearer of the vital airs, the Wind Horse can unify, harmonize, and strengthen Vitality, Health, and Personal Power. It symbolizes our fortune, our good luck, and our capacity to avoid bad situations. When the Wind Horse is weak, bad luck strikes—one dreams that one is descending a hill and sinking into a bog. When the Wind Horse is strong, one dreams of flying through the air or riding a white horse.

## ANIMALS, ELEMENTS, AND INDIVIDUAL FORCES

Each animal corresponding to the elements represents one of the five forces. According to our astrological text:

> The Vitality of the animals resides in the elements of the directions. The Vitality of the Tiger and the Hare is Wood, that of the Horse and the Snake is Fire. The Vitality of the Monkey and the Bird is Metal and that of the Rat and the Pig is Water. As for the Cow, the Sheep, the Dog, and the Dragon, all four have the Vitality of the Earth element.

This refers to working out the elements of the *Sok*. The text continues, "The mother of Vitality is called the *La*." The elements of the *La* are simply those that engender the elements of the *Sok*. For example, the *La* element of the Horse is Wood, because Wood produces Fire, which is the Vitality element of the Horse.

The *Wang thang* element is the same as the element that rules the year. For a person born in the year of the Metal Tiger, the Element of Personal Power is also Metal.

The elements of the *Lü* are arranged in a particular order over a thirty-year period, each one governing two successive years.

The *Lung Ta* elements are determined according to the following rules:

> The Tiger, the Horse, and the Dog all have the Wind of the Vitality element of the Monkey, namely Metal. The Rat, the

Dragon, and the Monkey all have the Wind of the Vitality element of the Tiger, namely Wood. The Bird, the Cow, and the Snake all have the Wind of the Vitality element of the Pig, namely Water. The Pig, the Sheep, and the Hare all have the Wind of the Vitality element of the Snake, namely Fire. These signs are grouped in harmonious sets of three. There is no Wind Horse of the Earth element.

This law brings to mind the rules of affinity for the animals: the animals that are grouped in a triad by the same Wind Horse are those that enjoy excellent relations. It should also be noted that enemy-animals are those whose Wind Horse elements are opposed. This is the case for the Dog (Metal), which has bad relations with Dragon (Wood)—Metal is the enemy of Wood.

Table 9 (pages 90–91) shows the elements of the five individual forces in the sixty-year cycle.

## YEARLY CALCULATION OF THE FIVE FORCES

In order to work out the state of one's personal energies from year to year throughout one's life, the element for the current year need only be compared with the element for the natal year. The rules of interpretation are as follows:

- When the element for the year is the mother of the natal element, the force in question will be excellent throughout the year.
- When the element for the year is the friend of the natal element, the force will be very good.
- When the element for the year and the natal element are both Earth, the force will be good. The same applies to Water-Water.
- When the element for the year is the son of the natal element, the force will be neutral.
- When one of the elements Fire, Metal, or Wood rules

TABLE 9

## ELEMENTS OF VITALITY, BODY, POWER, WIND HORSE, AND *LA* IN THE SIXTY-YEAR CYCLE

| Year | Vitality | Body | Power | Wind | La | | | |
|------|----------|------|-------|------|-----|---|---|---|
| Fire Hare − | Wood | Fire | Fire | Fire | Water | 1867 | 1927 | 1987 |
| Earth Dragon + | Earth | Wood | Earth | Wood | Fire | 1868 | 1928 | 1988 |
| Earth Snake − | Fire | Wood | Earth | Water | Wood | 1869 | 1929 | 1989 |
| Metal Horse + | Fire | Earth | Metal | Metal | Wood | 1870 | 1930 | 1990 |
| Metal Sheep − | Earth | Earth | Metal | Fire | Fire | 1871 | 1931 | 1991 |
| Water Monkey + | Metal | Metal | Water | Wood | Earth | 1872 | 1932 | 1992 |
| Water Bird − | Metal | Metal | Water | Water | Earth | 1873 | 1933 | 1993 |
| Wood Dog + | Earth | Fire | Wood | Metal | Fire | 1874 | 1934 | 1994 |
| Wood Pig − | Water | Fire | Wood | Fire | Metal | 1875 | 1935 | 1995 |
| Fire Rat + | Water | Water | Fire | Wood | Metal | 1876 | 1936 | 1996 |
| Fire Cow − | Earth | Water | Fire | Water | Fire | 1877 | 1937 | 1997 |
| Earth Tiger + | Wood | Earth | Earth | Metal | Water | 1878 | 1938 | 1998 |
| Earth Hare − | Wood | Earth | Earth | Fire | Water | 1879 | 1939 | 1999 |
| Metal Dragon + | Earth | Metal | Metal | Wood | Fire | 1880 | 1940 | 2000 |
| Metal Snake − | Fire | Metal | Metal | Water | Wood | 1881 | 1941 | 2001 |
| Water Horse + | Fire | Wood | Water | Metal | Wood | 1882 | 1942 | 2002 |
| Water Sheep − | Earth | Wood | Water | Fire | Fire | 1883 | 1943 | 2003 |
| Wood Monkey + | Metal | Water | Wood | Wood | Earth | 1884 | 1944 | 2004 |
| Wood Bird − | Metal | Water | Wood | Water | Earth | 1885 | 1945 | 2005 |
| Fire Dog + | Earth | Earth | Fire | Metal | Fire | 1886 | 1946 | 2006 |
| Fire Pig − | Water | Earth | Fire | Fire | Metal | 1887 | 1947 | 2007 |
| Earth Rat + | Water | Fire | Earth | Wood | Metal | 1888 | 1948 | 2008 |
| Earth Cow − | Earth | Fire | Earth | Water | Fire | 1889 | 1949 | 2009 |
| Metal Tiger + | Wood | Wood | Metal | Metal | Water | 1890 | 1950 | 2010 |
| Metal Hare − | Wood | Wood | Metal | Fire | Water | 1891 | 1951 | 2011 |
| Water Dragon + | Earth | Water | Water | Wood | Fire | 1892 | 1952 | 2012 |
| Water Snake − | Fire | Water | Water | Water | Wood | 1893 | 1953 | 2013 |
| Wood Horse + | Fire | Metal | Wood | Metal | Wood | 1894 | 1954 | 2014 |
| Wood Sheep − | Earth | Metal | Wood | Fire | Fire | 1895 | 1955 | 2015 |
| Fire Monkey + | Metal | Fire | Fire | Wood | Earth | 1896 | 1956 | 2016 |
| Fire Bird − | Metal | Fire | Fire | Water | Earth | 1897 | 1957 | 2017 |
| Earth Dog + | Earth | Wood | Earth | Metal | Fire | 1898 | 1958 | 2018 |
| Earth Pig − | Water | Wood | Earth | Fire | Metal | 1899 | 1959 | 2019 |
| Metal Rat + | Water | Earth | Metal | Wood | Metal | 1900 | 1960 | 2020 |
| Metal Cow − | Earth | Earth | Metal | Water | Fire | 1901 | 1961 | 2021 |
| Water Tiger + | Wood | Metal | Water | Metal | Water | 1902 | 1962 | 2022 |
| Water Hare − | Wood | Metal | Water | Fire | Water | 1903 | 1963 | 2023 |
| Wood Dragon + | Earth | Fire | Wood | Wood | Fire | 1904 | 1964 | 2024 |
| Wood Snake − | Fire | Fire | Wood | Water | Wood | 1905 | 1965 | 2025 |
| Fire Horse + | Fire | Water | Fire | Metal | Wood | 1906 | 1966 | 2026 |
| Fire Sheep − | Earth | Water | Fire | Fire | Fire | 1907 | 1967 | 2027 |
| Earth Monkey + | Metal | Earth | Earth | Wood | Earth | 1908 | 1968 | 2028 |
| Earth Bird − | Metal | Earth | Earth | Water | Earth | 1909 | 1969 | 2029 |
| Metal Dog + | Earth | Metal | Metal | Metal | Fire | 1910 | 1970 | 2030 |

| Year | Vitality | Body | Power | Wind | La | | | |
|------|----------|------|-------|------|-----|------|------|------|
| Metal Pig − | Water | Metal | Metal | Fire | Metal | 1911 | 1971 | 2031 |
| Water Rat + | Water | Wood | Water | Wood | Metal | 1912 | 1972 | 2032 |
| Water Cow − | Earth | Wood | Water | Water | Fire | 1913 | 1973 | 2033 |
| Wood Tiger + | Wood | Water | Wood | Metal | Water | 1914 | 1974 | 2034 |
| Wood Hare − | Wood | Water | Wood | Fire | Water | 1915 | 1975 | 2035 |
| Fire Dragon + | Earth | Earth | Fire | Wood | Fire | 1916 | 1976 | 2036 |
| Fire Snake − | Fire | Earth | Fire | Water | Wood | 1917 | 1977 | 2037 |
| Earth Horse + | Fire | Fire | Earth | Metal | Wood | 1918 | 1978 | 2038 |
| Earth Sheep − | Earth | Fire | Earth | Fire | Fire | 1919 | 1979 | 2039 |
| Metal Monkey + | Metal | Wood | Metal | Wood | Earth | 1920 | 1980 | 2040 |
| Metal Bird − | Metal | Wood | Metal | Water | Earth | 1921 | 1981 | 2041 |
| Water Dog + | Earth | Water | Water | Metal | Fire | 1922 | 1982 | 2042 |
| Water Pig − | Water | Water | Water | Fire | Metal | 1923 | 1983 | 2043 |
| Wood Rat + | Water | Metal | Wood | Wood | Metal | 1924 | 1984 | 2044 |
| Wood Cow − | Earth | Metal | Wood | Water | Fire | 1925 | 1985 | 2045 |
| Fire Tiger + | Wood | Fire | Fire | Metal | Water | 1926 | 1986 | 2046 |

both the current year and the natal year, the force will be in a bad condition.

• When the element of the year is the enemy of the natal element, the corresponding force will be in a very bad condition.

For example, individuals born in the year of the Fire Dragon will find that their Vitality is in very good condition during the year of the Wood Rat (Water is a friend of Earth). Their health will be average (Metal is the son of Earth), their personal power will be excellent (Wood is the mother of Fire). They must not rely on luck (bad Wood-Wood relation), but their physical condition will be very good (Metal is the friend of Fire).

Each year, Tibetan almanacs give tables that compare the elements of the five energies of the year with the natal elements. Table 10 (page 92) shows the degrees of harmony. The "little black and white pebbles," symbolized in the table by circles and crosses, indicate the degree of strength and harmony.

The Tibetans consider a child to be one year old at birth. If a child is born on the day after New Year's Day, it is considered to be two years old the next day. (As far as Tibetans are concerned, real birth takes place at the moment of conception.)

## DEGREES OF HARMONY

| Degree of Harmony | Symbol | Relation | Annual Element–Natal Element |
|---|---|---|---|
| Excellent | O OO | Mother | Earth-Metal, Metal-Water, Water-Wood, Wood-Fire, Fire-Earth |
| Very good | OO | Friend | Earth-Wood, Wood-Metal, Metal-Fire, Fire-Water, Water-Earth |
| Good | O | | Earth-Earth, Water-Water |
| Neutral | OX | Son | Earth-Fire, Fire-Wood, Wood-Water, Water-Metal, Metal-Earth |
| Bad | X | | Fire-Fire, Metal-Metal, Wood-Wood |
| Very bad | XX | Enemy | Earth-Water, Water-Fire, Fire-Metal, Metal-Wood, Wood-Earth |

# RITUALS CONCERNING THE FIVE
# PERSONAL FORCES

When the Vitality, the Health, the Power, the Wind, or the *La* become dangerously weak, the Tibetans have a great number of practices to strengthen their energies. In the almanacs, there is a short text entitled "Use of the *Kek Tsi* and the Results of the Little Pebbles":

> Comparing the year of birth and the current year gives the little pebbles of Vitality, the Body, personal Power, Winds, and *La*. The little white pebbles indicate good fortune and no demons or obstacles. As for the little black ones, we shall briefly indicate the ritual ceremonies that are to be performed.
>
> The black Vitality pebbles indicate irregular and accident-prone Vitality. Saving the lives of animals, performing the buying back of the *Sok*, building a bridge, doing a hundred thousand repetitions of the long-life mantra—these are the

*A page from the Tibetan* lo tho. *The translation appears below.*

| Age | 16 | 17 | 18 | 19 | 20 |
|---|---|---|---|---|---|
| Year of Birth | Earth Bird | Fire Monkey | Fire Sheep | Fire Horse | Wood Snake |
| Natal Mewa | 4 | 5 | 6 | 7 | 8 |
| Vitality | OX | OX | OO | XX | XX |
| Health | OX | OX | OO OO | OO OO | OO |
| Strength | XX | XX | OO OO | OO OO | X |
| Wind Horse | OX | X | OO OO | OO | OX |
| La | OX | OX | OO | XX | XX |

difficult ways of healing the Vitality. All the *Mamos*[1] then stop cutting off the Vitality thanks to the *Dö*.[2]

The black Body pebbles indicate the influence of diseases. It is necessary to invite monks of the four schools[3] to a feast, transform the energy of the Body by changing one's name, and then keep one's vows.

The black pebbles of personal Power indicate a decrease of good luck. The year will be full of calamities and the *Gong* demons will attack one's herds and one's riches. There will be loss and corruption and enemies will declare war. It is necessary to subdue the *Sri*[4] demons. Reciting the wealth *dhāraṇī*[5] and performing four hundred *To*[6] will restore good fortune by warding off the bad luck of Power and the Winds.

The black pebbles of the Winds show that the royal Wind Horse is hobbled. This leads to bad luck, misery, calamities, and hostile enemies. One is subject to unjust accusations. In order to increase the Wind Horse, one makes *tsatsa*[7] and performs oblations of consecrated water at the appropriate moment. To overcome enemies and slanders, one cures the Winds by the profound practice of *To*.

When Vitality, Body, Power, and Winds all have white pebbles, one is in an excellent position, without impurities or disputes. The *Lha* are favorable and take us to a celestial level. When all four are black, the divine tree is broken. In order to propitiate life, it is necessary to perform a hundred thousand repetitions of secret mantras in the marketplace.

When the pebbles are black, it is necessary to perform the buying back of the *Lü* and the recall of the *La*.

Of all the rituals designed to strengthen the personal energy of a sick person or animal, the most important are the Buying Back (*Lü*) and the Recall (*Kuk*), the *Dö*, and the *To*.

---

1. A class of ferocious female deity believed to cause various types of disease (see Appendix 1).
2. A wooden cross with threads of various colors bound around it, believed to entice certain spirits.
3. Nyingma, Sakya, Kagyü, and Gelug.
4. A class of demon believed to specialize in eating children.
5. A protective formula, similar to a mantra.
6. A rite for averting misfortune.
7. Figurines, usually made of clay, used in offering ceremonies.

The simplest practice for strengthening Vitality or prolonging life is saving the lives of animals intended for slaughter—because of the interdependence of all life, saving the lives of others prolongs our own lives.

Mantras are often used to attain longevity, or for healing or wealth. A mantra is a sacred formula whose sound energy is connected with a deity. We have in ourselves corresponding gross energies, and when the pure sound of the deity is pronounced, the internal energies are purified and transmuted. This activity takes us to higher states of consciousness and removes the obstacles to progress.

Buying back the Vitality or *La* is accomplished by means of the *Dö* ceremony. The object of *Dö* is to remove obstacles and hostile forces. When the demonic forces that cause illness, low energy, and obstacles are appeased by offerings, they give up their disturbing activities. The main offering is an effigy made of *tsampa*, representing the person to be protected. Other offerings for the demons are arranged around the person, all forming a ransom to the hostile forces in order to buy back life or good health. The ransom or *Lü* is placed in the center of a mandala representing the universe, and the central structure of the *Lü* is surmounted by a *namkha*, a diamond-shaped construction of colored threads wound around a cross. The tantric practitioner performing the ceremony consecrates the offerings, invites the demons to take their fill, and exhorts them to give up evil. The effigy of the buy-back is declared to be alive and the demon is requested to release the *La* or individual in its power and accept the effigy instead.

When this ceremony is not strong enough to dispel negative forces, exorcism or *To* is used. In this ritual, the yogi visualizes himself as a wrathful deity and offers the demons *tormas*, cone-shaped colored offerings made of *tsampa* and butter; and he exhorts the demons: "Malevolent forces in this place who create obstacles, take this torma offering and go! If you do not obey this order, you will be destroyed by the vajra (diamond scepter)." In some cases, a *torma* charged with the power of the protective deity is thrown in the direction of the demon in order to expel or destroy it.

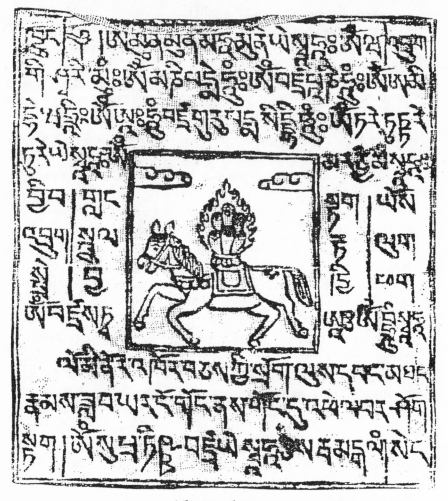

*The Wind Horse*

In exorcism properly so called, an effigy of the hostile force is made and placed in a triangular box. The demon is forced to enter this box by means of mantras, and is there imprisoned. The practitioner then destroys the effigy with a dagger (*phurba*) and liberates the mind of the demon to a pure buddha realm—in Buddhism, it is not permitted to kill a demon if one is able to liberate its consciousness.

## THE WIND HORSE

The Wind Horse, as we have seen, enables one to strengthen and group together Vitality, Health, Power, and Good Luck. There is a corresponding practice, which must be performed in the morning during the waxing moon, while the *La* and the energies are rising in the body. It is often accompanied by an offering of smoke or *sang*, where juniper branches are burned to purify the channels of the subtle body and the environment, and appease the local deities.

Here is the text of the ritual composed by Lama Mipham, a great Nyingma saint of the nineteenth century:

> To the assembly of the Three Jewels,[8] to the Three Roots,[9] to the gods and gurus,
> To the Three Mahāsattva Protectors,[10] to Jayadevī[11] *Pema Tötreng*[12] and the Vidyādharas[13] of India and Tibet,
> To the glorious protector Gāṇapati[14] and the divine armies of the warrior gods,
> To the five protective deities, to the great Gesar[15] and others . . .
> To all the deities of the cosmic lineage who rule over coincidence,
> To all these I make offerings of smoke and supplicate them to bestow their blessings upon us.
> Magic, charms, and sorcery of the dead, Döns, obstructive spirits, etc.
> May all the signs that testify to the weakening and corruption of the Wind Horse be pacified!

8. The three refuges (Skt. *triratna*): the Buddha, the Dharma, and the Sangha.
9. Guru, Deva, and Ḍākinī, the three tantric refuges.
10. The three bodhisattvas, Avalokiteśvara, Mañjuśrī, and Vajrapāṇi.
11. It has not been possible to identify this deity.
12. Padmasambhava.
13. Holders of the lineage of teachings.
14. The elephant-headed deity Gaṇeśa.
15. The semilegendary hero of Tibetan epic and protector of the teachings.

Battles, enmities, scandals, wars, and legal proceedings,
Recurrent calamities and so on,
May all this discord that creates obstacles be pacified!
Multiply strength and the force of virtue,
Wind Horse, four-footed miracle;
Accomplish siddhis[16] spiritual and temporal, supreme and
    ordinary,
And everything the mind desires without exception.

There follows a group of mantras, including the Kālacakra
mantra, the Padmasambhava mantra, the mantras of the Victors[17]
and the three bodhisattvas Mañjuśrī (wisdom), Avalokiteśvara
(compassion), and Vajrapāṇi (energy). Next comes the invocation to the four animals that protect the Wind Horse: the Tiger,
the Lion, the Garuḍa,[18] and the Dragon.
The text continues:

Come, all of you, come, come, Ho!
Make our life lift up, our virtue and our glorious
Wind Horse, higher and higher!
And by mantra put an end to interdependent origination.

When the practice is concluded, the Tibetans cry: "Ki Ki So So
Lha Gyal Lo" ("The gods have conquered").
    Gesar of Ling holds an important place among the deities in-
voked. Hero of the most popular Tibetan epic, Gesar is the warlike incarnation of Padmasambhava, who came to Tibet to
subdue four demon kings. Gesar personifies the ideal of the spiritual warrior. He is the chief of the warlike gods, tamer of
demons, and master of the flag of the glorious Wind Horse. He
is shown wearing armor and a helmet, riding the white charger
Kyang Gö Karkar, which is the Wind Horse itself. Indeed, be-

16. Supernormal powers. The "supreme siddhi" is realization.
17. The five Jinas, the buddhas of the five directions: Amogasiddhi, Akṣobhya,
Vairocana, Amitābha, and Ratnasambhava (these are often miscalled "Dhyāni
Buddhas").
18. A mythical bird associated with healing.

fore he took birth, Gesar asked for a horse "which death cannot overtake; it must be able to fly through the sky and travel the four continents of the world in an instant."

The name of Keser Khan is also invoked in Mongolia for the protection of warriors and soldiers, and for good luck. In the Shambhala tradition, it is said that when the great battle is fought against the forces of negativity, Gesar will be the general leading the armies of Shambhala. The *Dra Lha*, the two warrior deities whose chief he is, are ancient local gods.

The five protector deities mentioned in the text are the five *lha* guardians who dwell in the human body. These internal forces are concerned with protecting man against external dangers, as well as looking after his general well-being. These are familiar spirits who accompany man throughout his life and have charge of the harmony of the family.

The *Pho Lha,* or "male ancestral deity," lives under the right armpit. Invoking this deity gives long life and protection against injury. In women, it is replaced by the *Mo Lha*, or "female ancestral deity," which lives under the left armpit. The *Pho Lha* protects the outside of the house, while the *Mo Lha* under the name *Puk Lha* keeps watch over the inside. When moving house, care must be taken not to disturb the *Puk Lha*, otherwise the woman may fall ill. If this occurs, the new dwelling must be purified by ceremony.

The *Sok Lha* is the deity of the life force. It lives in the heart and protects the vitality. It is also known as *Zhang Lha*, "Deity of the Maternal Uncle."

The *Nor Lha* or "Deity of Wealth" lives under the left armpit in men and under the right in women. Invoking this deity brings wealth and prosperity.

The *Yül Lha* or "Deity of the Country" lives at the crown of the head. It protects reputation, property, and the links that tie one to one's native place.

The *Dra Lha* or "Warrior Deity" lives on the right shoulder and defends against enemies. In this role, it is invoked especially by warriors. It must be worshipped at least once a year to give protection against enemies and opponents. After death, in the

Bardo of Becoming, the *Dra Lha* joins the deceased before the Lord of Death, Yama, and defends him by tallying his good acts with white pebbles. The *Dra Lha* is therefore also called "the good conscience inside one" or "the innate good spirit," as opposed to the "innate evil spirit," who keeps a tally of bad acts with black pebbles.

The "gods of the cosmic lineage who rule over coincidence" are purely astrological deities, planetary spirits (*grāha*) and spirits of the stars and elements.

The Wind Horse has the power to eliminate the inauspicious influences of the constellations and planets, and thus to make circumstances favorable. When the Wind Horse is invoked, and also during the smoke purification rites, Tibetans make banners and prayer flags known as *Lung Ta*—these lengths of colored fabric can be seen fluttering in the wind throughout areas of Tibetan culture: on the roofs of houses and monasteries, around stūpas and in passes and all high places. Mantras and prayers of good omen are written on these banners, and the wind carries their positive energy. It is said that making and erecting Lung Ta in high places guarantees their protection against hostile forces and assists in the growth of vitality and good fortune; and at the tops of high passes they protect travelers against the dangers of the road.

There are numerous different types of *Lung Ta*, but most of them follow a general pattern. At the four corners are placed the four protecting animals: the Tiger; the Snow Lion or *Senge,* which is white with flowing mane and tail; the *Garuḍa* (*khyung*), a mythical bird, chief of the air spirits and enemy of the Nāgas, the underground serpent gods; and the Dragon. These animals symbolize victory over the four fears.[19] The Wind Horse is placed in the middle of the flag, proudly bearing the triple or sextuple flaming jewel on its back, symbolizing "the gem that satisfies all desires" or wish-fulfilling jewel (*cintāmaṇi*).

---

19. The Buddhist scriptures enumerate a number of sets of four fears (see, e.g., *Anguttara Nikāya*, 119), the most common probably being birth, decay, disease, and death.

The rest of the flag is occupied by mantras in great variety and profusion—among the most commonly used are those of the three bodhisattvas (Mañjuśrī, Avalokiteśvara, and Vajrapāṇi), those of the three deities of long life (Amitāyus, Vijaya, and White Tārā), the mantra of Guru Rinpoche (Padmasambhava), the Kālacakra mantra, and the mantras of the Victorious Gods of the Wind Horse. These are invariably followed by the invocation to the four animals and the exhortation to summon life, virtue, and Wind Horse "so that they will grow like the waxing moon." The text ends with the Mantra of Interdependent Origination and the expression *Lha gyal lo*, "The gods are victorious." There are also victory flags bearing the image of the king Gesar of Ling.

TABLE 11

## MONTHLY MOVEMENT OF THE *LA*
### *(after Namkhai Norbu Rinpoche)*

| Day | Site of La | Day | Site of La |
|-----|------------|-----|------------|
| 1 | Soles of feet | 16 | Sternum |
| 2 | Calves | 17 | Neck (left side) |
| 3 | Thighs | 18 | Stomach and insides of thighs |
| 4 | Waist | 19 | Outsides of thighs |
| 5 | Mouth (interior) | 20 | Face (both sides) |
| 6 | Palms | 21 | Soles of feet |
| 7 | Ankles | 22 | Hips |
| 8 | Elbows (medial) | 23 | Calves |
| 9 | Sexual organs | 24 | Palms |
| 10 | Waist | 25 | Tongue |
| 11 | Ears | 26 | Neck |
| 12 | Forehead | 27 | Shoulders |
| 13 | Teeth | 28 | Sexual organs |
| 14 | Heart | 29 | Pupils |
| 15 | Crown of head | 30 | Soles of feet |

The days are those of the Tibetan lunar month. The La is located at the soles of the feet, the lowest part of the body, at new moon (30th and 1st days of month), and at the crown of the head at full moon (15th day). Between these points, its movement does not seem coherent.

# 6

# MEWAS AND PARKHAS

The Mewas and Parkhas, important factors in Jungtsi astrology, are reminiscent of Chinese numerology and the *I Ching*. The two systems are complementary and offer scope for horoscopic and geomantic interpretation.

## THE NINE MEWAS

*Mewa gu* means "the nine moles." They are also known as *Ling gu,* or "nine colored islands." These nine Mewas are figures arranged in a magic square with base three. This is the design of the River Lo, which appeared on the belly of the turtle and gave rise to the magic square.

The figures in the magic square, whether added diagonally, horizontally, or vertically, always give a sum of 15. This magic square is found in the middle of most Tibetan astrological diagrams, on the belly of the cosmic turtle. It is therefore oriented with regard to space: the 5 is in the Center, 9 at the South, 3 at the East, 7 at the West, 1 at the North, 2 at the Southwest, 8 at the Northeast, 4 at the Southeast, and 6 at the Northwest.

South

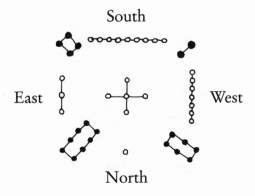

East

West

North

| 4 | 9 | 2 |
|---|---|---|
| 3 | 5 | 7 |
| 8 | 1 | 6 |

Each of the nine Mewas is associated with a color related to one of the five elements. According to our astrological text:

> The first is White, the second Black, the third Blue. The fourth is Green, the fifth Yellow, the sixth White, the seventh Red, the eighth White, and the ninth is Red.
> The three Whites (1, 6, 8) are Metal, the Black and the Blue (2, 3) are Water, the Green (4) is Wood, the Yellow (5) is Earth, and the Reds (7, 9) are Fire.

The correspondences are as shown in table 12 (page 104).

The system of the nine Mewas is dynamic: each year, each month, and each day, the Mewas move. The order of progression follows the increasing or decreasing figures, depending on the case. The course of movement across the magic square describes a diagram not unlike the seal of Saturn as used in Western magic.

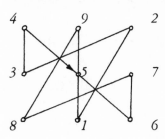

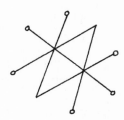

*The Seal of Saturn*

TABLE 12

## CHARACTERISTICS OF THE MEWAS

| Mewa | Color | Element | Direction |
|---|---|---|---|
| 1 | White | Metal | North |
| 2 | Black | Water | Southwest |
| 3 | Blue | Water | East |
| 4 | Green | Wood | Southeast |
| 5 | Yellow | Earth | Center |
| 6 | White | Metal | Northwest |
| 7 | Red | Fire | West |
| 8 | White | Metal | Northeast |
| 9 | Red | Fire | South |

The magic square of the Mewas is also known in this tradition as "The Magic Square of Saturn."

## THE ANNUAL MEWAS

Each year, a Mewa known as the "Natal Mewa" or *Kye Mewa* combines with the animal of that year. Since there are nine Mewas for twelve animals, each animal can only combine with three Mewas:

The White 8, the Black 2, and the Yellow 5 rule the Tiger, the Monkey, the Pig, and the Snake.

The Red 7, the Green 4, and the White 1 rule the Rat, the Horse, the Bird, and the Hare.

The Red 9, the White 6, and the Blue 3 rule the Cow, the Sheep, the Dog, and the Dragon.

The only Natal Mewas for a Rat year, therefore, are the Red 7, the Green 4, and the White 1—there are no other possibilities.

Each Mewa-number also forms the center of another magic square. If we develop each of these squares, we arrive at the system of nine magic squares oriented to the directions (see diagram).

**SE**

| 3 | 8 | 1 |
|---|---|---|
| 2 | 4 | 6 |
| 7 | 9 | 5 |

**S**

| 8 | 4 | 6 |
|---|---|---|
| 7 | 9 | 2 |
| 3 | 5 | 1 |

**SW**

| 1 | 6 | 8 |
|---|---|---|
| 9 | 2 | 4 |
| 5 | 7 | 3 |

**E**

| 2 | 7 | 9 |
|---|---|---|
| 1 | 3 | 5 |
| 6 | 8 | 4 |

| 4 | 9 | 2 |
|---|---|---|
| 3 | 5 | 7 |
| 8 | 1 | 6 |

**W**

| 6 | 2 | 4 |
|---|---|---|
| 5 | 7 | 9 |
| 1 | 3 | 8 |

| 7 | 3 | 5 |
|---|---|---|
| 6 | 8 | 1 |
| 2 | 4 | 9 |

| 9 | 5 | 7 |
|---|---|---|
| 8 | 1 | 3 |
| 4 | 6 | 2 |

| 5 | 1 | 3 |
|---|---|---|
| 4 | 6 | 8 |
| 9 | 2 | 7 |

**NE**            **N**            **NW**

Certain laws apply to the movements of the Mewas through the sixty-year cycle: it takes 180 years (three sixty-year cycles) to complete a full Mewa-animal-element cycle. These three cycles are known respectively as the upper, middle, and lower (see table 13). Our text explains the movement:

Here is the order of the (Natal) Mewas: the upper cycle begins with the White 1 (Wood Rat). When sixty years have passed, the Yellow 5 appears (Water Pig).

The middle cycle is reckoned from the Green 4 and ends with the White 8.

The lower cycle begins with the Mewa Red 7 and finishes with the Mewa Black 2. The garland of Mewas then begins to turn again, beginning with the first palace (White 1), and so on until the end of the kalpa.

It should be noted here that the cycles of annual Mewas begin in a Wood Rat year, like the Chinese sexagenary cycles.

In addition to the Natal Mewa, which is the same as the Body Mewa, each year also has a Mewa of Vitality, a Mewa of Power, and a Mewa of Wind Horse.

*The Mewas of Vitality and Power* can easily be determined by reference to the magic square of the yearly Natal Mewa:

If one studies the nine islands, with the Natal Mewa placed in the center, the Mewa of Vitality is found in the Southwest. The Mewa of Personal Power is found in the Northeast. As for the Body Mewa, that is found in the center.

For example, a person born in 1958 has the Natal Mewa White 6. Consulting the corresponding magic square (6 in the Center), we find 3 in the Southwest and 9 in the Northeast. The Mewa of Vitality is therefore Blue 3 and the Mewa of Power is Red 9. The Body Mewa is also the central 6.

*The Mewa of Wind Horse* is a little harder to work out—it corresponds to the Mewa of Vitality of the animal's Wind Horse. Thus if we want to find the Mewa of Wind Horse for the year of the Wood Rat 1984, (Natal Mewa Red 7), we first examine its Wind Horse, the Wood Tiger (see preceding chapter). We then find the Mewa of Vitality for the Wood Tiger in the same cycle. This Mewa, White 8, is thus the Mewa of Wind Horse for the year of the Wood Rat.

In their astrological diagrams, the Tibetans draw correspondences between three ranges of Mewa and the sixty-year cycle: the upper range gives the Natal Mewas for the upper cycle, the Mewas of Vitality for the middle cycle, and the Mewas of Power for the lower cycle. The middle range gives the Natal Mewas for the middle cycle, the Mewas of Power for the upper cycle, and the Mewas of Vitality for the lower cycle. The lower range gives the Natal Mewas of the lower cycle, the Mewas of Power for the middle cycle, and the Mewas of Vitality for the upper cycle. Thus the Natal Mewa for the Fire Tiger of the upper cycle is Red 8, its Mewa of Power is Black 2, and its Mewa of Vitality is Yellow 5. For the Fire Tiger of the middle cycle, however, the Natal Mewa (and the Body Mewa) is Black 2, the Mewa of Vitality is White 8, and the Mewa of Power is Yellow 5.

To work out your own Natal Mewas, see table 14 (page 110).

## THE EIGHT PARKHAS

*Parkha gye,* "The Eight Trigrams," are the Tibetan equivalents of the eight Chinese *pa-kua,* which form the basis of the *I Ching,* or "Book of Changes."

The origins of these trigrams show certain principles of ancient Chinese thought: Yin and Yang are the two modes in which energy manifests in constant interaction throughout the universe.

*Yin* means "the shaded side of a hill." This is the principle of passivity, receptivity, the feminine, even (as opposed to odd), darkness, night, the moon, winter, cold, wet, rest, the earth, and so on. The original meaning of *Yang* is "the sunny side of a hill." This is the active principle, expansion, masculinity, odd (as opposed to even), light, daytime, summer, warmth, dryness, activity, the sky, and so on.

The entire universe in all its varied manifestations arises from the interplay of these two forces. One is never found without the other. Without space, movement is impossible. In the Tibetan Tantras, the symbols of the vajra and the bell are a perfect ex-

TABLE 13

## NATAL MEWAS

| Upper Cycle | | Middle Cycle | | Lower Cycle | |
|---|---|---|---|---|---|
| 1864 | White 1 | 1924 | Green 4 | 1984 | Red 7 |
| 1865 | Red 9 | 1925 | Blue 3 | 1985 | White 6 |
| 1866 | White 8 | 1926 | Black 2 | 1986 | Yellow 5 |
| 1867 | Red 7 | 1927 | White 1 | 1987 | Green 4 |
| 1868 | White 6 | 1928 | Red 9 | 1988 | Blue 3 |
| 1869 | Yellow 5 | 1929 | White 8 | 1989 | Black 2 |
| 1870 | Green 4 | 1930 | Red 7 | 1990 | White 1 |
| 1871 | Blue 3 | 1931 | White 6 | 1991 | Red 9 |
| 1872 | Black 2 | 1932 | Yellow 5 | 1992 | White 8 |
| 1873 | White 1 | 1933 | Green 4 | 1993 | Red 7 |
| 1874 | Red 9 | 1934 | Blue 3 | 1994 | White 6 |
| 1875 | White 8 | 1935 | Black 2 | 1995 | Yellow 5 |
| 1876 | Red 7 | 1936 | White 1 | 1996 | Green 4 |
| 1877 | White 6 | 1937 | Red 9 | 1997 | Blue 3 |
| 1878 | Yellow 5 | 1938 | White 8 | 1998 | Black 2 |
| 1879 | Green 4 | 1939 | Red 7 | 1999 | White 1 |
| 1880 | Blue 3 | 1940 | White 6 | 2000 | Red 9 |
| 1881 | Black 2 | 1941 | Yellow 5 | 2001 | White 8 |
| 1882 | White 1 | 1942 | Green 4 | 2002 | Red 7 |
| 1883 | Red 9 | 1943 | Blue 3 | 2003 | White 6 |
| 1884 | White 8 | 1944 | Black 2 | 2004 | Yellow 5 |
| 1885 | Red 7 | 1945 | White 1 | 2005 | Green 4 |
| 1886 | White 6 | 1946 | Red 9 | 2006 | Blue 3 |
| 1887 | Yellow 5 | 1947 | White 8 | 2007 | Black 2 |
| 1888 | Green 4 | 1948 | Red 7 | 2008 | White 1 |
| 1889 | Blue 3 | 1949 | White 6 | 2009 | Red 9 |
| 1890 | Black 2 | 1950 | Yellow 5 | 2010 | White 8 |
| 1891 | White 1 | 1951 | Green 4 | 2011 | Red 7 |
| 1892 | Red 9 | 1952 | Blue 3 | 2012 | White 6 |
| 1893 | White 8 | 1953 | Black 2 | 2013 | Yellow 5 |
| 1894 | Red 7 | 1954 | White 1 | 2014 | Green 4 |
| 1895 | White 6 | 1955 | Red 9 | 2015 | Blue 3 |
| 1896 | Yellow 5 | 1956 | White 8 | 2016 | Black 2 |
| 1897 | Green 4 | 1957 | Red 7 | 2017 | White 1 |
| 1898 | Blue 3 | 1958 | White 6 | 2018 | Red 9 |
| 1899 | Black 2 | 1959 | Yellow 5 | 2019 | White 8 |
| 1900 | White 1 | 1960 | Green 4 | 2020 | Red 7 |
| 1901 | Red 9 | 1961 | Blue 3 | 2021 | White 6 |
| 1902 | White 8 | 1962 | Black 2 | 2022 | Yellow 5 |
| 1903 | Red 7 | 1963 | White 1 | 2023 | Green 4 |
| 1904 | White 6 | 1964 | Red 9 | 2024 | Blue 3 |
| 1905 | Yellow 5 | 1965 | White 8 | 2025 | Black 2 |

| Upper Cycle | | Middle Cycle | | Lower Cycle | |
|---|---|---|---|---|---|
| 1906 | Green 4 | 1966 | Red 7 | 2026 | White 1 |
| 1907 | Blue 3 | 1967 | White 6 | 2027 | Red 9 |
| 1908 | Black 2 | 1968 | Yellow 5 | 2028 | White 8 |
| 1909 | White 1 | 1969 | Green 4 | 2029 | Red 7 |
| 1910 | Red 9 | 1970 | Blue 3 | 2030 | White 6 |
| 1911 | White 8 | 1971 | Black 2 | 2031 | Yellow 5 |
| 1912 | Red 7 | 1972 | White 1 | 2032 | Green 4 |
| 1913 | White 6 | 1973 | Red 9 | 2033 | Blue 3 |
| 1914 | Yellow 5 | 1974 | White 8 | 2034 | Black 2 |
| 1915 | Green 4 | 1975 | Red 7 | 2035 | White 1 |
| 1916 | Blue 3 | 1976 | White 6 | 2036 | Red 9 |
| 1917 | Black 2 | 1977 | Yellow 5 | 2037 | White 8 |
| 1918 | White 1 | 1978 | Green 4 | 2038 | Red 7 |
| 1919 | Red 9 | 1979 | Blue 3 | 2039 | White 6 |
| 1920 | White 8 | 1980 | Black 2 | 2040 | Yellow 5 |
| 1921 | Red 7 | 1981 | White 1 | 2041 | Green 4 |
| 1922 | White 6 | 1982 | Red 9 | 2042 | Blue 3 |
| 1923 | Yellow 5 | 1983 | White 8 | 2043 | Black 2 |

pression of this principle: the vajra, the "diamond scepter," which is held in the right hand (masculine), symbolizes the indestructible energy of the mind of the buddhas, the active aspect of compassion, the practice of skillful means (the skillful utilization of situations and energies in order to attain realization). The bell, *ghaṇṭa*, is the complementary feminine principle of wisdom, the realization of emptiness, the mother of all things. These two are inseparable, for only through the union of wisdom and skillful means will perfect realization be attained.

*The law of change* is the dynamic aspect of the universe: all the cosmic and terrestrial rhythms, the lunations, the years, the seasons, the days, and the hours are a reflection of the interplay of Yin and Yang, where now one, now the other dominates. This continual process of the transformation of energy is symbolized by the eight trigrams and sixty-four hexagrams of the *I Ching*.

Yang is represented by an unbroken line: —; Yin by a broken line: – –. When three lines are combined, we have eight types of trigram, the *Parkha gye*, which symbolize the eight principal modes of combination of energy.

109

TABLE 14

## ANIMAL-MEWA CORRESPONDENCES

| Rat | Cow | Tiger | Hare | Dragon | Snake | Horse | Sheep | Monkey... |
|-----|-----|-------|------|--------|-------|-------|-------|-----------|
| Wood | Wood | Fire | Fire | Earth | Earth | Metal | Metal | Water |
| 1 | 9 | 8 | 7 | 6 | 5 | 4 | 3 | 2 |
| 4 | 3 | 2 | 1 | 9 | 8 | 7 | 6 | 5 |
| 7 | 6 | 5 | 4 | 3 | 2 | 1 | 9 | 8 |

*A page from the Tibetan* lo tho.
*The translation appears in table 14.*

The Tibetans use the allocation of space and the seasonal correspondences established by King Wen, using the river Lo as a
model. Occasional slight differences exist, such as the reversal of
the trigrams Chen and Sun.

According to our text:

Starting at the South and moving to the right, [these trigrams]
are found, in order: Li — Fire, Khön — Earth, Da — Metal,
Khen — Sky, Kham — Water, Kin — Mountain, Tsin —
Wood, and Zön — Wind. Although Sky, Mountain, and Wind
are new, they derive, in fact, from the five elements.

As the text suggests, the eight Parkhas are an extension of the
theory of the five elements. (See diagrams opposite.)

## Tibetan and Chinese Trigrams

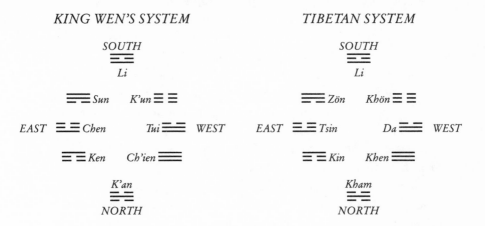

# The Symbolism of the Parkhas

Li ☲ is the Parkha of Fire, that which attaches itself to the flammable and consumes it. It therefore signifies attachment and passion. This is the light that gives all things their brilliance; and *Li* is therefore connected with perception. It symbolizes glory, brilliance, fame, and high capacity, as well as war, arms, and drought. Its animal is the Bird and its organ is the eye. Li is the younger daughter of the Sky and the Earth.

Khön ☷ is the Parkha of Earth. It is receptive, hides and protects things, but also represents abandon and beginnings. *Khön* symbolizes the cauldron, the vase, form and the soil ready to be fertilized by the sky. Its animal is the Cow and its organ is the belly. It is the mother of the other Parkhas.

Da ☱ is the Parkha of Metal. In China, it is called *Tui*, "The Lake," "The Joyous." *Da* is associated with pleasure, women, favorites, and children. It is therefore linked with the desire to reproduce. It is connected with the West and autumn, and signifies decline and death, collapse and breaking. Thus desire, the motive power of existence, is also the cause of our downfall. *Da's* animal is the Sheep and its organ is the mouth. It is the youngest daughter of the Sky and the Earth.

111

Khen ☰ is the Parkha of the Sky. It is the creator, masculine energy, force. It is the principle of superiority and symbolizes the chief, the prince, the ruler. Its animal is the Horse and its organ is the head. It is the father of the other trigrams.

Kham ☵ is the Parkha of Water. It signifies the cessation of activity, hibernation, and the danger of stagnation. Water penetrates and moistens, but it can also cause rotting. Its symbols are wells, traps, and ditches. The corresponding negative emotion is ignorance-stupidity, also symbolized by *Kham*'s animal, the Pig. Its organ is the ear. *Kham* is the younger son of the Sky and the Earth.

Kin ☶ is the Parkha of the Mountain. It is a symbol of immobility and stability, and is connected with sitting meditation. *Kin* signifies stopping, that is, protection against danger and invasions, but also against obstacles that hamper our progress. Its animal is the Dog and its organ is the hand. *Kin* is the youngest son of the Sky and the Earth.

Tsin ☳ is the Parkha of Wood. Its image is a young plant with green shoots. *Tsin* is a symbol of growth and movement. It is also called thunder, the awakener, suggesting a vital force that awakens and excites. Its energy is expressed in both love and work. Its animal is, of course, the Dragon. The feet are ruled by Tsin, which is the eldest son.

Zön ☴ is the Parkha of Wind. The wind is a gentle force that penetrates everywhere, but it can also be an agent of dispersion. It is not affected by anything it meets, although its changeable character and its dispersiveness affect its energy. Its animal is the Sheep and its organ the thigh. *Zön* is the eldest son of the Sky and the Earth.

## *The Annual Movement of the Parkhas*

There appear to be various types of movement of Parkhas in the succession of the years. The simplest rule for the calculation of the yearly Parkhas is based on the individual's sex:

For men, one starts with Li and moves toward Khön. For women, one starts with Kham and moves toward Khen.

The rotation of the Parkhas is therefore clockwise: Li—Khön—Da—Khen—Kham—Kin—Tsin—Zön—Li . . . , taken from the year of birth (*Li*). Thus, at two years old, a man will have the Parkha Khön, at three, Da, at eighteen, Khön, and so on. For women, the rotation begins with Kham at birth and moves counterclockwise: Kham—Khen—Da—Khön—Li—Zön—Tsin—Kin—Kham. . . . The male and female series meet in Da years.

This sort of rotation gives scope for a rather generalized interpretation, based only on sex and age.

Another account of the annual movement of the Parkhas is found also, but this is more closely linked to the annual movement of the Mewas. In fact, superimposing the magic square of Mewas on the arrangement of the Parkhas in accordance with the design of the river Lo gives a correspondence between Parkhas and Mewas.

Yellow 5 is concealed in the belly of the cosmic turtle. Red 9 corresponds to Li, Black 2 corresponds to Khön. Red 7 corresponds to Da, White 6 to Khen. White 1 is linked to Kham, White 8 to Kin. Tsin is connected with Blue 3 and Zön with Green 4.

As for progression, which is like the flight of a bird, this takes place from the center toward the Sky, followed by Metal, Mountain, Fire, Water, Earth, Wood, and Wind, and then returns to the center.

---

## ASTROLOGICAL INTERPRETATION
## OF THE MEWAS

Now that we have established the correspondence between Mewa and Parkha, we are in a position to approach the signifi-

## Orientation of the Parkhas around the Magic Square of the Mewas

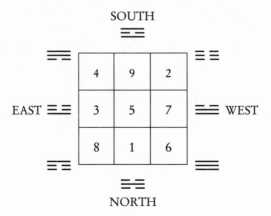

SOUTH

EAST

WEST

| 4 | 9 | 2 |
| 3 | 5 | 7 |
| 8 | 1 | 6 |

NORTH

---

*Order of Yearly Progression*

| Li | Kin | Da | Khen | | Zön | Tsin | Khön | Kham |
|----|-----|-----|------|---|-----|------|------|------|
| 9 | 8 | 7 | 6 | 5 | 4 | 3 | 2 | 1... |

The central Mewa, Yellow 5, is associated with:

Parkha ☱ for men     Parkha ☳ for women

---

cance of the Natal Mewas, which to a large extent hinges on the corresponding Parkha.

## White 1 (Metal) Parkha Kham (Water) ☵ North

A disturbed and pessimistic character—not very ambitious. Passive adaptation to situations. Externally open and friendly, internally stubborn. Difficult childhood, favorable middle age.

*Health.* Not very robust, sensitive, drug-dependent. Weakness of the kidneys, the bladder, and the genital organs. Depressive tendencies and fluctuating moods.

*Love.* Not very romantic but has great need of love. Possessive character.

114

*Fortune.* Mediocre, a modest existence.

*Occupations.* Requires calm and reflection, occupations in harmony with water.

## Black 2 (Water) Parkha Khön (Earth) ☷ Southwest

Amiable character, neither aggressive nor ambitious. Conventional mind, without initiative, obsession with detail. Excellent collaborator in the service of others. Best age: 45–47.

*Health.* Corpulent physique. Sweet tooth. Intestinal complaints and diseases of the skin, blood, and back.

*Love.* Very attentive to partner. More emotional than intelligent.

*Fortune.* Economical—neither rich nor poor. Catastrophic speculations.

*Occupations.* Relating to the public or a community. Work with nature, farming.

## Blue 3 (Water) Parkha Tsin (Wood) ☳ East

Independent character, optimistic, and young. Early maturity. Sociable and talkative. Positive and ambitious mind but impatient and obstinate, unwilling to put up with circumstances. Best age: 34–38. A life of movement, many ups and downs.

*Health.* Physically vigorous and active. Mental and nervous problems. Delicate feet.

*Love.* Early maturity, a direct and impulsive nature.

*Fortune.* What is earned is quickly spent. No accumulation.

*Occupations.* Those in which one can express oneself: orator, musician, teacher, writer; active work involving association with others.

## Green 4 (Wood) Parkha Zön (Wind) ☴ Southeast

Obedient and conventional character. Indecisive, little willpower. Changeable mind, but good common sense. Natural kindness, easily abused. Best age: youth until 38.

*Health.* Delicate constitution, large forehead. Irritable in the mornings. Respiratory and intestinal problems, proneness to epidemic. In the case of women, problems with the genital organs.

*Love.* Early maturity, physically seductive. Difficulty in stabilization.

*Fortune.* Regular income quickly spent. Vulnerable to theft.

*Occupations.* Communications, public relations, Master of Ceremonies, manufacture and trade in wool.

## Yellow 5 (Earth) Center: Beginning and End of Cycle

Extremist character: very positive or very negative, ambitious or lazy, ethical or depraved, etc. Critical age is 42, at which point life improves. Unusually high instinct for self-preservation.

*Health.* Vigorous and resistant constitution. Sensitive intestines, tumors and fevers, hypertension and blood problems.

*Love.* Strong need for love, passionate and dominating tendencies.

*Fortune.* Rapid recovery from loss. Mean. Tendency to disastrous gambling.

*Occupations.* High position for the ambitious and wise, lower jobs for others.

## White 6 (Metal) Parkha Khen (Sky) ☰ Northwest

Intuitive and spontaneous character. Spirituality, creativity, and innovation. Great innate leadership qualities, a spirit of conquest and high aims. Self-satisfaction and horror of failure. Favorable age: over 40.

*Health.* Lean and angular body. Tendency to overwork, fevers, headaches, and vertigo. Fragile lungs, heart, and bones.

*Love.* Spirit of conquest and domination.

*Fortune.* Skilled and daring financier.

*Occupations.* Managerial positions, law, teaching, priesthood.

# Red 7 (Fire) Parkha Da (Metal) ☰☰ West

Optimistic and demonstrative character. Excellent orator, manipulative tendencies. Sets store by external appearances, becomes angry when these are ignored. Quick mind, attentive to detail. Seeks happiness and freedom. Sensitive and emotional. Stable after age 40. Does not achieve much alone because lacks perseverance.

*Health.* Weak constitution. Problems with stomach, neurasthenia, belly, kidneys, and genital organs. Illnesses of the buccal cavity.

*Love.* Attractive power and sensuality. Innate love of freedom. Choice of partner very important.

*Fortune.* Money is made to be spent. No great fortune.

*Occupations.* Good orator, teacher, preacher, salesman.

# White 8 (Metal) Parkha Kin (Mountain) ☶☶ Northeast

Stubborn and opinionated character, holding views that are not easily changed. Strong and conservative mind that imposes its will on others. Placid appearance and inner strength. Lone wolf with a high opinion of itself.

*Health.* Large body, solid and heavy. Neurological problems, congestion of back and shoulders, arteriosclerosis, chronic constipation, hypochondria.

*Love.* Slow in relationships but unfailingly loyal. Marriage of trust.

*Fortune.* Early prosperity. Attracts money; investments.

*Occupations.* Stable positions requiring trust.

# Red 9 (Fire) Parkha Li (Fire) ☲☲ South

Extrovert character, sensitive, and emotional. Often has a brilliant but worthless life-style where appearances count for much.

Impulsive and impatient, hypercritical because expects too much of others. Frequent changes in relationships. Idealists scorn the material. Favorable middle age, and then deterioration in life-style.

*Health.* Medium build, strong and supple. Nervous problems, insomnia, diseases of the heart and eyes.

*Love.* Attractive and forward. Seduction by words and appearances. Fiery character, jealous and possessive. Amorous fantasies.

*Fortune.* Great need of money but lacks perseverance. No great fortune, neither rich nor poor.

*Occupations.* Artist, diplomat, actor, author, etc.

## THE PAPME

The Papme is a Mewa that changes as a function of the native's age. The Papme is derived from the Natal Mewa in accordance with a particular mode of movement. This movement depends in effect on the masculine or feminine character of the natal year, not on the gender of the native:

> This is the method of rotation: begin at the center and move toward the East. From the East, turn to the left if the [natal] year is masculine and to the right if the [natal] year is feminine. Then begin again at the center. . . .

## *Determining the Papme*

1. Find the Natal Mewa (*Kyeme*) and determine whether the natal year is masculine or feminine. To simplify, let us recall that even years are masculine, while odd years are feminine.

2. If the year of birth is masculine, the Papme is determined using the Natal Mewa according to the rule quoted: begin at the center and move toward the East, then turn left:

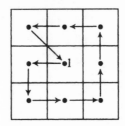

For example, a native of the Fire-Monkey year (1956) has White 8 as the Natal Mewa. For the first year of life, the Papme is the same as the Natal Mewa at the center, White 8. For the age of two, the Papme is White 6, at three Black 2, at four Green 4, and so on.

| 7 | 3 | 5 |
|---|---|---|
| 6 | 8 | 1 |
| 2 | 4 | 9 |

3. If the year of birth is feminine, the square for the Natal Mewa is used, starting at the center and moving toward the East, then turning right:

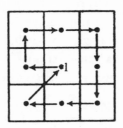

For example, for a native of the Fire-Bird year (1957), the Natal Mewa is Red 7. For the first year, the Papme is Red 7, for the second Yellow 5, for the third White 6, for the fourth Black 2, and so on.

| 6 | 2 | 4 |
|---|---|---|
| 5 | 7 | 9 |
| 1 | 3 | 8 |

## Interpretation of the Papme

A comparison of the Papme with the Natal Mewa shows the difficulties and obstacles met with during the year in question. There are two rules to be kept in mind:

- Every ten years, the Natal Mewa and the Papme are the same. A year in which this happens is regarded as critical and brings danger. This is a year in which the Natal Mewa must be strengthened, and for this purpose the Tibetans perform a special ritual known as "Warding off Evil through the Great Turtle." One must be particularly careful about one's health.
- In other years, the Papme element is compared with the Natal Mewa element from the point of view of the four possible relations of the elements. A mother-relationship means an excellent year, a friend-relationship a moderately good year, a son-relationship a mediocre year, and an enemy-relationship a difficult year.

## GEOMANTIC INTERPRETATION
## OF THE PARKHAS

As we have seen, each of the Parkhas has a fixed direction (see diagram below). Unlike the Mewas, the Parkhas do not change their direction.

## Orientation of the Parkhas

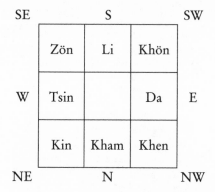

|    | SE | S | SW |    |
|----|------|------|-------|----|
|    | Zön | Li | Khön |    |
| W  | Tsin |  | Da | E |
|    | Kin | Kham | Khen |    |
|    | NE | N | NW |    |

There also exist different types of relationship between the Parkhas, some favorable and others unfavorable. Table 16 (page 123) shows these as given in the *Jungtsi Men Ngak Dawe Öser*.

The favorable and unfavorable directions for the year can be determined by placing the Parkha of the year in the center of a "geomantic house" whose eight directions are marked by the eight fixed Parkhas, and studying its relationship with each one of them. For example, the annual Parkha is Li. Comparing Li with the eight Parkhas assigned to the directions, we arrive at the following schemes.

## Example of the Relations between Parkhas

| Zön | Li | Khön |
|------|------|------|
| Tsin | Li | Da |
| Kin | Kham | Khen |

| Prosperity | Message of luck | Corporal punishment |
|------------|-----------------|---------------------|
| Life support | Li | Five demons |
| Injury | Sky medicine | Life-cutting demons |

Tibetan astrologers show the diagram of the eight geomantic houses on the belly of the Cosmic Turtle. We may simplify this diagram of the eight geomantic houses for our own use, as in table 17 (page 124).

TABLE 15

## THE PAPME

| Age Birth Mewa | Year | 1–10– 19–28– 37–46– 55–64– 73–82... | 2–11– 20–29– 38–47– 56–65– 74–83... | 3–12– 21–30– 39–48– 57–66– 75–84... | 4–13– 22–31– 40–49– 58–67– 76–85... | 5–14– 23–32– 41–50– 59–68– 77–86... | 6–15– 24–33– 42–51– 60–69– 78–87... | 7–16– 25–34– 43–52– 61–70– 79–88... | 8–17– 26–35– 44–53– 62–71– 80–89... | 9–18– 27–36– 45–54– 63–72– 81–90... |
|---|---|---|---|---|---|---|---|---|---|---|
| 9 | ♂ | 9 | 7 | 3 | 5 | 1 | 2 | 6 | 4 | 8 |
| 9 | ♀ | 9 | 7 | 8 | 4 | 6 | 2 | 1 | 5 | 3 |
| 8 | ♂ | 8 | 6 | 2 | 4 | 9 | 1 | 5 | 3 | 7 |
| 8 | ♀ | 8 | 6 | 7 | 3 | 5 | 1 | 9 | 4 | 2 |
| 7 | ♂ | 7 | 5 | 1 | 3 | 8 | 9 | 4 | 2 | 6 |
| 7 | ♀ | 7 | 5 | 6 | 2 | 4 | 9 | 8 | 3 | 1 |
| 6 | ♂ | 6 | 4 | 9 | 2 | 7 | 8 | 3 | 1 | 5 |
| 6 | ♀ | 6 | 4 | 5 | 1 | 3 | 8 | 7 | 2 | 9 |
| 5 | ♂ | 5 | 3 | 8 | 1 | 6 | 7 | 2 | 9 | 4 |
| 5 | ♀ | 5 | 3 | 4 | 9 | 2 | 7 | 6 | 1 | 8 |
| 4 | ♂ | 4 | 2 | 7 | 9 | 5 | 6 | 1 | 8 | 3 |
| 4 | ♀ | 4 | 2 | 3 | 8 | 1 | 6 | 5 | 9 | 7 |
| 3 | ♂ | 3 | 1 | 6 | 8 | 4 | 5 | 9 | 7 | 2 |
| 3 | ♀ | 3 | 1 | 2 | 7 | 9 | 5 | 4 | 8 | 6 |
| 2 | ♂ | 2 | 9 | 5 | 7 | 3 | 4 | 8 | 6 | 1 |
| 2 | ♀ | 2 | 9 | 1 | 6 | 8 | 4 | 3 | 7 | 5 |
| 1 | ♂ | 1 | 8 | 4 | 6 | 2 | 3 | 7 | 5 | 9 |
| 1 | ♀ | 1 | 8 | 9 | 5 | 7 | 3 | 2 | 6 | 4 |

## Using the Diagram

The diagram of the "four favorable and four inauspicious Par-khas" is used to determine an individual's good and bad directions each year. For this purpose, the individual's yearly Parkha is used as a basis, determined by age and sex (for men, starting with Li at birth and moving toward Khön, then Da, and so on; and for women, starting with Kham and moving toward Khen, Da, and so on).

Once the Parkha has been established, its geomantic house is studied in order to determine favorable directions and those which should be avoided. This study of directions is useful for establishing the best arrangement of furniture in a house—the

TABLE 16

RELATIONS OF PARKHAS

| Degree of Affinity | | Name | Corresponding Parkha Pairs |
|---|---|---|---|
| Favorable | High | Sky medicine | Li-Kham, Khen-Khön, Da-Kin, Tsin-Zön |
| | Medium | Life support | Li-Tsin, Kham-Zön, Da-Khen, Kin-Khön |
| | Low | Prosperity | Zön-Li, Khön-Da, Kin-Khen, Kham-Tsin |
| Medium | High | Message of luck | Da-Da, Li-Li, Khen-Khen, Kin-Kin |
| | Medium | Message of luck | Khön-Khön, Kham-Kham, Tsin-Tsin, Zön-Zön |
| | Low | Injury | Li-Kin, Zön-Khen, Da-Kham, Tsin-Khön |
| Bad | High | Five demons | Da-Li, Khön-Zön, Khen-Tsin, Kin-Kham |
| | Medium | Life-cutting demons | Li-Khen, Da-Tsin, Khön-Kham, Kin-Zön |
| | Low | Corporal punishment | Khen-Kham, Li-Khön, Zön-Da, Tsin-Kin |

bed, for example. It can also be used to determine the success or danger involved in a journey.

As a general rule, the Sky Medicine direction is very favorable for curing diseases and medical procedures, while Life Support is excellent for vitality—for the recuperation of vitality, for example. It is advised that the head of the bed should be oriented in this direction, particularly when one is ill or weak.

The direction Prosperity favors good luck and the increase of fortune. Message of Luck is a good omen for undertaking a journey. Injury or wounding must be avoided, otherwise accidents will be met with. Five Demons exposes us to demonic influences: it is advised to display a diagram of ransom (*Lü*) in this direction, representing the individual and his goods in order to deceive the demons. The direction Life-Cutting Demons threatens the individual's life, for the demons in question are those which steal the life force. It is recommended that one should lay a *phurba* facing in this direction, a ritual dagger with a three-faced blade, which removes hostile forces. The direction Corporal Punishment threatens a particular part of the body, depend-

TABLE 17

## THE EIGHT GEOMANTIC HOUSES

SOUTH

|  |  |  |  |  |  |  |  |  |
|---|---|---|---|---|---|---|---|---|
| Message of luck | Prosperity | Five demons | Prosperity | Message of luck | Corporal punishment | Five demons | Corporal punishment | Message of luck |
| Sky medicine | Zön | Corporal punishment | Life support | Li | Five demons | Injury | Khön | Prosperity |
| Life-cutting demons | Life support | Injury | Injury | Sky medicine | Life-cutting demons | Life support | Life-cutting demons | Sky medicine |
| Sky medicine | Life-support | Injury |  |  |  | Corporal punishment | Five demons | Prosperity |
| Message of luck | Tsin | Life-cutting demons |  |  |  | Life-cutting demons | Da | Message of luck |
| Corporal punishment | Prosperity | Five demons |  |  |  | Sky medicine | Injury | Life support |
| Life-cutting demons | Injury | Life support | Life support | Sky medicine | Life-cutting demons | Injury | Life-cutting demons | Sky medicine |
| Corporal punishment | Kin | Sky medicine | Prosperity | Kham | Injury | Five demons | Khen | Life support |
| Message of luck | Five demons | Prosperity | Five demons | Message of luck | Corporal punishment | Prosperity | Corporal punishment | Message of luck |

NORTH

ing on the Parkha, as well as the individual's *La*. In this case, it is necessary to perform the "repurchase of the *La*."

A man born in the Fire Dog year (1946), for example, will be entering his thirty-ninth year in 1984 (Wood Rat). His Parkha is therefore Tsin. During this year, his favorable directions are East, Southeast, South, and North. He must avoid Southwest, West, Northwest, and Northeast.

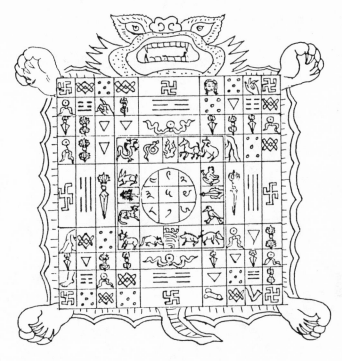

*The orientation of the Cosmic Turtle. The good or bad character of the directions is shown by the following symbols:*

*Sun: Sky Medicine*
*Vajra: Life Support*
*Knot of Eternity: Prosperity*
*Swastika: Message of luck*
*Triangle: Injury*
*Five points: Five demons*
*Phurba: Life-cutting demons*
*Body part: bodily punishment*

*The central circle contains the Mewas. It is surrounded by the twelve animals and the symbols of the four cardinal elements: tree (Wood), flames (Fire), sword (Metal), and waves (Water).*

*Tibetan xylograph illustrating the orientation
of the Parkhas and Mewas*

126

# 7

# KARTSI
# ASTROLOGY

As we have seen, Naktsi Chinese astrology is defined in terms of the observation of cycles of cosmic energy in time. White astrology, or *Kartsi*, which is of Indian origin, is quite different: this is an astrological system based on planetary movements in celestial space. In many particulars it approaches Western astrology, with which it shares a common origin.

## THE ZODIAC

The path that the sun follows through the celestial sphere in the course of a year is known as the ecliptic. This line determines both longitude 0° and latitude 0° of the zodiac.

The zodiac is a band 9° wide stretching across the ecliptic (from latitude +9° to −9°), across which the moon and the planets move.

In order to measure longitude in the zodiacal circle, the ancients defined the point of origin as 1° in the constellation of Aries. They then divided the zodiac into twelve equal segments of 30° each, the twelve signs. The twelve signs were established in terms of the stars and constellations that define the zodiac. After thousands of years of observation, a symbolic name was given to each of the twelve constellations that form the signs.

## THE TWO ZODIACS

The ecliptic forms an angle of approximately 23° with the celestial equator. The circles of the ecliptic and the equator intersect at two points, one of which is the *vernal point,* which the sun crosses at the spring equinox.

When the laws of Western astrology were fixed following Ptolemy, sometime during the second century, the vernal point coincided with 0° in the constellation of Aries. The West therefore assimilated 0° Aries to the vernal point, which was regarded as the definitive 0° point of the zodiac. However, the vernal point is not fixed: it shifts slowly through the skies at a rate of 50⅓ seconds retrograde per year. For this reason, a discrepancy has grown up over the centuries between the signs of the Western zodiac and the original constellations.

The Western system is known as the tropical zodiac and depends on the apparent movement of the sun through the seasons. Indian astrologers, aware of the movement of the vernal point, have preferred to adhere to a stellar or sidereal zodiac—this is the difference between Western astrology and the Indian system.

## Ayanaṃsa

*Ayanaṃsa* is the distance between the starting point of the sidereal zodiac and the vernal point for any given age. To calculate the ayanaṃsa, the following formula is used:

(present year − year of coincidence) × 0.014

The Indians consider that the exact coincidence between the two zodiacs occurred in the year A.D. 397. For 1984 this would give us an Ayanaṃsa of $(1984 - 397) \times 0.014 = 22°13'$. However, both our own calculations and Tibetan almanacs show that the ayanaṃsa should really be close to 24°. Western ephemerides show tropical longitude for planets (Sayana longitude). To convert these positions to sidereal longitude (Nirayana longitude), it is therefore necessary to subtract 24°.

## The Twelve Signs of the Indo-Tibetan Zodiac

Tibetan astrologers call the zodiacal band the *gola*, which they regard as a sphere rotating around the summit of Mount Meru once every twenty-four hours. The gola is divided into twelve *khyim* or houses, which are the twelve signs of the zodiac.

The names of the signs are the same as those used in the West, which demonstrates their common Mesopotamian origin. But as a result of the procession of the equinox, Aries in Tibet corresponds in our Western system to the last six degrees of Aries and the first twenty-four of Taurus.

Let us superimpose the two zodiacs (Indo-Tibetan in the in-

TABLE 18

### THE INDO-TIBETAN ZODIAC

| Tibetan name | Indian name | Translation | Nirayana longitude | Sayana longitude (occidental) |
|---|---|---|---|---|
| Luk | Meṣa | ♈ Aries | 0°–30° | 24°–54° |
| Lang | Vṛṣa | ♉ Taurus | 30°–60° | 54°–84° |
| Trik | Mithuna | ♊ Gemini | 60°–90° | 84°–114° |
| Karkata | Karka | ♋ Cancer | 90°–120° | 114°–144° |
| Senge | Siṁha | ♌ Leo | 120°–150° | 144°–174° |
| Pumo | Kanyā | ♍ Virgo | 150°–180° | 174°–204° |
| Sangwa | Tulā | ♎ Libra | 180°–210° | 204°–234° |
| Dikpa | Vṛścika | ♏ Scorpio | 210°–240° | 234°–264° |
| Zhu | Dhanus | ♐ Sagittarius | 240°–270° | 264°–294° |
| Chusin | Makara | ♑ Capricorn | 270°–300° | 294°–324° |
| Bumpa | Kumbha | ♒ Aquarius | 300°–330° | 324°–354° |
| Nya | Mīna | ♓ Pisces | 330°–360° | 354°–24° |

side, Western on the outside), as in the illustration. The meanings of the signs of the Indo-Tibetan zodiac are fairly close to those of the Western system. Among the more important differences, however, is the division of the signs into day and night—the day signs are at their maximum strength during the day and the night signs during the night; and a slightly different set of correspondences between sign and part of the body (see table 19).

## THE TWENTY-SEVEN LUNAR MANSIONS

Well before the Mesopotamian zodiac reached India, there was an ancient system of twenty-eight lunar constellations, which had existed since Vedic times. This lunar zodiac is common to China, Mesopotamia, India, and the Arab world, although certain variations are found.

This system divides the ecliptic into twenty-eight sectors, each marked by a characteristic star or group of stars. These sectors are known as "lunar mansions," and the moon passes through each of them in succession in the course of its monthly revolution, remaining approximately one day in each.

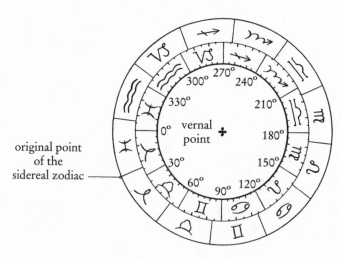

original point of the sidereal zodiac

*The two zodiacs superimposed*

130

TABLE 19

## DAY/NIGHT STRENGTH AND PART OF BODY GOVERNED ACCORDING TO THE INDIAN ZODIAC

| Sign | Day/Night Strength | Part of Body |
|---|---|---|
| ♈ Aries | Night | Head |
| ♉ Taurus | Night | Face |
| ♊ Gemini | Night | Arms, lungs |
| ♋ Cancer | Night | Heart |
| ♌ Leo | Day | Upper part of belly, stomach, and liver |
| ♍ Virgo | Day | Kidneys, stature |
| ♎ Libra | Day | Lower part of belly between navel and genitals |
| ♏ Scorpio | Day | Sexual organs |
| ♐ Sagittarius | Night | Thighs |
| ♑ Capricorn | Night | Knees |
| ♒ Aquarius | Day | Calves, ankles |
| ♓ Pisces | Day and night | Feet |

In Indian astrology, there are only twenty-seven lunar mansions or Nakṣatras, each one measuring 13°20′ on the ecliptic (13°20′ represents the moon's mean daily movement). However, one of the lunar mansions comprises two adjacent constellations and the system therefore has altogether twenty-eight constellations. For this reason, the Tibetan texts speak of twenty-eight lunar constellations, the *gyukar*.

## The Legend of the Moon

In the course of his monthly revolution, the Moon God Candra, riding his crystal chariot, pursues the twenty-eight beautiful goddesses of the stars, and each night he stays with one of them. These encounters give rise to different types of energy that influence our terrestrial world.

These twenty-eight goddesses are known as the daughters of the Four Guardian Kings of the Quarters of the Universe or

*Jigten Kyong* (Skt. *Lokapāla*). These guardians reside at the four cardinal doors of a palace on Mount Meru, at the foot of the divine realms. Their role is to defend the heavens and the universe against the assaults of demonic forces. *Yü Khor Sung* (Skt. *Dhritiraśtra*) is the guardian of the East and lord of the *Driza* (Skt. *Gandharva*), the celestial musician-deities who live on smells. *Pak Kyepo* (Skt. *Virudhaka*) rules in the South over the troops of Kumbhandas, the fire deities. *Mik Mizang* (Skt. *Virupakṣa*) protects the West and rules over the *Lu* or *nāgas*, deities of the water. *Nam Tö Se* (Skt. *Vaiśrāvana*), god of wealth, dwells in the North and governs the hordes of *Nödzin* (Skt. *Yakṣas*), the terrestrial spirits. Their twenty-eight daughters settled along the gola (ecliptic) above Mount Meru, and each of them thereafter governed a star.

## The Gyukar and the Divisions of the Zodiac

The Tibetans divide the gola into twelve *khyim* (signs) and twenty-seven *gyukar*, both systems having 0° Aries as their point of origin. There is thus an overlap between the gyukar and the gola, whose divisions do not correspond. The only possible common division is the "foot of the star," the *Gyukang* (Skt. *Pada*), which is one quarter of a lunar mansion.

We thus have the following subdivision:

Gola (360°) = 12 Khyim = 27 Gyukar = 108 Gyukang
    (*pada*)
1 Khyim = 9 Gyukang
1 Gyukar (13°20′) = 4 Gyukang

Therefore:

1 Khyim = 2 Gyukar + 1 Gyukang

There is also a smaller subdivision, the *Chu tsö*:

1 Chu tsö = ¹/₆₀ of a Gyukar = ¹/₁₅ of a Gyukang

The most interesting of these divisions is the *gyukang*, which constitutes ¹/₉ of a zodiacal sign and is identical to the Indian *navarasa*.

# The Characteristics of the Gyukar

Each gyukar is characterized by an Indian element (Wind, Fire, Water, and Earth). This Indian element indicates the energy tone of the lunar mansion. It is also governed by a particular planet, the order of the ruling planets being as follows:

|  |  |
|---|---|
| 1st mansion | Ketu |
| 2nd mansion | Venus |
| 3rd mansion | Sun |
| 4th mansion | Moon |
| 5th mansion | Mars |
| 6th mansion | Rāhu |
| 7th mansion | Jupiter |
| 8th mansion | Saturn |
| 9th mansion | Mercury |
| 10th mansion | Ketu |
| and so on | |

Nor is this all. In Tibet, Indian astrology came into contact with a system of Chinese origin and a number of interesting syntheses occurred. This is the case with the gyukar, which are divided according to the four directions and the four intermediate points, and which are also associated with the corresponding Chinese elements. According to the *Jungtsi Men Ngak*:

> Of the twenty-eight constellations, Mindruk, Narma, Go, Lak, Nabso, and Gyal are in the East. Kak is in the Southeast.
> Chu, Dre, Wo, Mezhi, Nak, and Sari are the stars of the South. Saga is in the Southwest.
> Lhatsam, Nrön, Nup, Chutö, Chume, and Drozhin are the Western group of stars. The star Jizhin is in the Northwest.
> Möndre, Möndru, Trumtö, Trume, Namdru, and Yugu are the stars of the North. Dranye is the star of the Northeast.
> The six constellations of the East are Wood, those of the South are Fire, those of the West are Metal, and those of the North are Water. The constellations of the intermediate points are Earth.

According to the Kālacakra, the twenty-seven gyukar are divided into three groups of nine: "the royal dwellings of the center" from the 1st to the 9th gyukar; "the royal dwellings of the South" from the 10th to the 18th gyukar; and "the royal dwellings of the North" from the 19th to the 27th. Each series is associated with nine symbols: Gem, Horse, Umbrella, Whip, Lion, Elephant, Sacred Text, Wheel of the Dharma, and Teaching Mudrā.

While the Indians number the Nakṣatras from 1 to 27, the Tibetans number them from 0 to 26. This detail must be borne in mind when consulting Tibetan almanacs.

## Calculating and Interpeting the Natal Gyukar

Any Western ephemeris can be used to work out the natal lunar mansion. First of all, the exact position of the moon is calculated for the hour of birth, working in tropical longitude. This position is then converted into a sidereal longitude, remembering that the ayanaṃsa varies in the course of the years. For example:

Native November 22, 1954, Paris, 13:00 (local time)
1. Convert local time to Greenwich Mean Time:

$$13h - 1 = 12h \text{ (solar)}$$
$$12h + 09m \text{ (Meridian Paris)} = 12:09$$

2. Determine the position of the moon:

Position of the moon at 0h: 20° ♎ 58′
Calculation for moon's daily movement:

Position 0h (day + 1) − 0h position (day) = 2° ♏ 51 − 20° ♎ 58′ = 32°51′ − 20°58′ = 11°53′

To work out the exact position of the moon for 12:09, the birth hour, it is best to use a table of proportional logarithms:

Log (birth hour GMT) + Log (daily movement) = Log (lunar movement)

*Illustration from an almanac showing the associations between the Gyukar and the nine symbols. The drawing on the turtle shows the distribution of the Gyukar among the belly and the limbs on the Cosmic Turtle. The planets in the Gyukar are also shown.*

$$\text{Log} (12h\ 09') + \text{Log} (11°53') = 2956 + 3053 = 6009$$
$$6009 = \text{Log} (6°01')$$

Thus 6°01' is the distance covered by the moon between 0h and 12:09. The exact position of the moon at birth is therefore:

$$20°58' + 6°1' = 26°\ \Omega\ 59'$$

3. Work out the Ayanaṃsa:
Taking the coincidence date for the two zodiacs as A.D. 285, the formula is:

$$(x - 285) \times 0.014 = \text{Ayanaṃsa}$$
$$(1954 - 285) \times 0.014 = 23.366 = 23°19'$$

The position of the moon in sidereal coordinates is therefore:

$$26°59' - 23°34' = 3°\ \Omega\ 25'$$

4. Natal gyukar:
This is between 23° ♍ 20' and 6° ♎ 40', i.e., Nakpa.

135

TABLE 20

THE CHARACTERISTICS OF THE 27 GYUKAR

| Gyukar | Nakṣatra | Sidereal Longitude and Star | Pada | Sign | Planet | Element | Chinese Element | Direction |
|---|---|---|---|---|---|---|---|---|
| 0 Takar, Yugu | 1 Aśvinī | 0°–13°20' β-Arietis (Scheratan) | 1 2 3 4 | ♈ | Khetu | Wind | Water | North |
| 1 Dranye | 2 Bharaṇī | 13°20'–26°40' 35 Arietis | | | Venus | Fire | Earth | Northeast |
| 2 Mindruk | 3 Kṛttikā | 26°40'–40° Pleiades | 1 2 3 4 | ♉ | Son | Fire | Wood | East |
| 3 Narma | 4 Rohiṇī | 40°–53°20' Aldebaran | | | Moon | Wood | Earth | East |
| 4 Go | 5 Mṛgaśirā | 53°20'–66°40' λ-Orionis | 1 2 3 4 | ♊ | Mars | Wind | Wood | East |
| 5 Lak | 6 Ārdrā | 66°40'–80° α-Orionis (Betelgeuse) | | | Rāhu | Water | Wood | East |

| | | | | | | | | | |
|---|---|---|---|---|---|---|---|---|---|
| 6 | Nabso, Gyaltö | 7 | Punarvasū | 80°–93°20' β-Geminorum (Pollux) | 1 2 3 4 | ♋ | Jupiter | Wind | Wood | East |
| 7 | Gyal, Gyalme | 8 | Puṣya | 93°20'–106°40' 5-Cancri | | | Saturn | Fire | Wood | East |
| 8 | Kak, Wa | 9 | Āśleṣa | 106°40'–120° α-Hydrae | | | Mercury | Water | Earth | Southeast |
| 9 | Chu, Ta chen | 10 | Maghā | 120°–133°20' α-Leonis (Regulus) | 1 2 3 4 | ♌ | Khetu | Fire | Fire | South |
| 10 | Dre, Ta chung | 11 | Purva-Phalgunī | 133°20'–146°40' δ-Leonis (Zosma) | | | Venus | Fire | Fire | South |
| 11 | Wo | 12 | Uttara-Phalgunī | 146°40'–160° β-Leonis (Denebola) | 1 2 3 4 | ♍ | Son | Wind | Fire | South |
| 12 | Mezhi | 13 | Hasta | 160°–173°20' δ-Corvi (Algorab) | | | Moon | Wind | Fire | South |
| 13 | Nakpa | 14 | Citrā | 173°20'–186°40' α-Virginis (Spica) | 1 2 3 4 | ♎ | Mars | Wind | Fire | South |

TABLE 20 (CONTINUED)

| Gyukar | Nakṣatra | Sidereal Longitude and Star | Pada | Sign | Planet | Element | Chinese Element | Direction |
|---|---|---|---|---|---|---|---|---|
| 14 Sari | 15 Svātī | 186°40'–200° α–Boötis (Arcturus) | | | Rāhu | Wind | Fire | South |
| 15 Saga | 16 Viśākhā | 200°–213°20' α–Librae | 1 2 3 4 | ♏ | Jupiter | Fire | Earth | Southwest |
| 16 Lhatsam | 17 Anurādhā | 213°20'–226°40' δ-Scorpii (Iridis) | | | Saturn | Earth | Metal | West |
| 17 Nrön, Deu | 18 Jyeṣṭhā | 226°40'–240° α-Scorpii (Antares) | | | Mercury | Earth | Metal | West |
| 18 Nup | 19 Mūla | 240°–253°20' λ-Scorpii (Schaula) | 1 2 3 4 | ♐ | Khetu | Water | Metal | West |
| 19 Chutö | 20 Purvāṣādhā | 253°20'–266°40' δ-Sagittarii | | | Venus | Water | Metal | West |

| | | | | | | | | | |
|---|---|---|---|---|---|---|---|---|---|
| 20 Chume | 21 | Uttarāṣāḍhā | 266°40'–280° σ-Sagittarii (Pelagus) | 1 2 3 4 | ♑ | Sun | Earth | Metal | West |
| 21 Drozhin + Jizhin | 22 | Uttara-Āṣāḍhā + Śravaṇa | 280°–293°20' α-Lyra (Vega) α-Aquilae (Altair) | | | Moon Moon | Earth Earth | Metal Earth | West Northwest |
| 22 Möndre | 23 | Dhaniāṣṭha | 293°20'– 306°40' β-Delphinium | 1 2 3 4 | ≈ | Mars | Water | Water | North |
| 23 Möndru | 24 | Satabhiṣak | 306°40'–320° λ-Aquarii | | | Rāhu | Earth | Water | North |
| 24 Trumtö | 25 | Purvabāad- rapada | 320°–333°20' α-Pegasi (Markab) | 1 2 3 4 | ⊬ | Jupiter | Fire | Water | North |
| 25 Trume | 26 | Uttara- bhādrapada | 333°20'– 346°40' γ-Pegasi α-Andromeda | | | Saturn | Water | Water | North |
| 26 Namdru, Shesa | 27 | Revati | 346°40'–0° Σ Piscum | | | Mercury | Water | Water | North |

Here are the meanings of the gyukar:

*0. Takar:* Goddess Ta Denma, the Equine or the Shining Daughter. Fine appearance, love of finery, jewels, and display. Great charm and elegance, loved by all. Intelligence and understanding. Impassive. Prosperity.

*1. Dranye:* Goddess Gekmo, the Dancer. Constant, faithful, and trustworthy. Happy and prosperous life, erudition. Good health, resistance to disease.

*2. Mindruk:* God Madrukpa (Skt. *Kārttikeya*), "He who has six mothers," youngest son of Mahādeva. Among the Hindus, Kārttikeya is a warrior god who rules the degenerate age of the Kāliyuga. Voracious, even gluttonous, a sensualist, susceptible to lechery and adultery. However, the native is famous and attractive and is introduced to royal or official circles.

*3. Narma:* Goddess Dalwe Lhadenma, the Peaceful Goddess, rules five star-gods in the form of a chariot. Connected with Kyegü Dakpo, the Lord of all Beings, or Brahmā. Faithful and beautiful, a fine speaker with a gentle voice. Amiable and calm. Clear and solid mind, charitable and moral, even religious. Has very large eyes.

*4. Go:* The Stag-Headed. Inferiority complex and shyness in youth. Later becomes optimistic, diligent but glib. Likes an easy life and baths. A sensualist, prosperous, and skillful.

*5. Lak:* Also known as Dragshul Chen, the Ferocious; Magpön Dra, the Hostile General; Goddess Nagmo, the Black. Incapable of sincerity, a cheat, proud, and selfish. Ungrateful, angry, cruel, and wicked.

*6. Nabso:* Goddess Jinme Lhamo, Goddess of Gifts. Reasonable and full of tact, content with little. Amiable character. Astute and intelligent but of weak physical constitution. Drinks too much water. Simple and retiring life.

*7. Gyal:* Goddess Tsinjema Jordenma, "She who Satisfies, She who Harmonizes." Good nature, erudition, perseverance. Masters passions and fulfills duty. Man of law. Popular and well-known, virtuous, rich, and charitable. Passive and sometimes obstinate.

8. *Kak:* Goddess Dengchen Lhamo, Dragon-Tailed Goddess. Joyful and strong appearance and speaks several languages. A cheat, ungrateful, selfish and a liar. Skill and learning. Will undergo various deceptions.

9. *Chu:* The Lord of the Eight Bonds, the Poet; Ta chen, the Great Horse. Very enthusiastic, a sensualist and entrepreneur. Respects power and has a religious mind. Likes flowers and perfumes. Much ability. Rich, with numerous servants.

10. *Dre:* Tau, Ta chung, the Little Horse; Tsokye, Lake-Born, the Lotus. Soft and eloquent of speech, perspicuity, and goodness. Likes travel, unstable. Official or prosperous merchant. Danger from fire.

11. *Wo*: Trawo, Multicolor; Chimo, Grandmother; Nyime Lhadenmo, Lady of the Sun. Sensualist, joyful and happy. Trustworthy, intellectual, mental health. Lively character, love and voluptuousness, popularity. Poor appetite.

12. *Mezhi:* Chama, Messenger; Rigje, Knowledge. When the moon is benefic: learned, courageous, enthusiastic, and endowed with an entrepreneurial spirit. Wealth in the second half of life. With a malefic moon: pitiless, shameless, cruel, and bibulous. Potential thief.

13. *Nakpa:* the Black; Ja nagpa, Black Bird. Good nature, fair of face, and charming eyes. Likes luxury and ornaments. Careful, indecisive, mind rather heavy, sordid.

14. *Sari:* Goddess Lunggi Lhamo, Goddess of the Wind; Lunggi, Mighty Lord of the Wind; Namthong Gong, High Celestial Vision. Charitable and generous, wise child, scholar, filial duty. Soft-spoken, in control of himself, fair-minded, and modest. Honest trader or state official. Suffers from thirst.

15. *Saga:* Goddess Wangpo Denma, She who has Power; Namthong Og, Lower Celestial Vision. Jealous, mean, indiscreet, quarrelsome, glib but prudent, lively temperament. Ability and good sense, business person. Religious fear in spite of everything.

16. *Lhatsam*: Lakpa, the Hand; Dzawö Lha, the Friendly God. Prosperous, honored by the great, risk-taker. Fond of

travel, high position in foreign country. Magnificent head of hair, red eyelashes. Attracted to the fair sex. Often dissatisfied and cannot tolerate hunger.

*17. Nrön:* Dubu, Bracelet; Lha Wangden, Divine Might. Charitable and contented with himself, but easily loses his temper and flies into violent rages. Hard words. Few friends, poverty. Juggles with words.

*18. Nub:* Tsawa, Root; Sokpa, Vitality. Pride, a firm mind, wealth. Likes luxury, comfort, and stability, hates insecurity. Good temperament but lively and sometimes coarse. Disciplined.

*19. Chutö:* Higher Water, Measure of Water. Very tall, proud, perspicuous, ambitious. Faithful friend, loves his mother. Loving spouse. Traveler, likes women and powerful friends.

*20. Chume:* Phul, Natsok, Perfect, Accomplished. Well-built and muscular, long nose. Humble, discreet, and virtuous, grateful and loved by parents. Popular, has many friends. Style and good manners.

*21. Drozhin:* Trokje, God of the Wind or Sun; and Jizhin, Ngag Nyen Pa, Pleasant-Voiced. Tsinjema, She Who Satisfies. The gyukar comprises two constellations. Famous and popular, learned, careful. Liked by the opposite sex. Appreciates perfumes. Contagious enthusiasm, perfect gentleman. Generous and rich.

*22. Möndre:* Thobden, He who Attains; Drog Tö, Higher Friend. Intrepid, independent, valiant, and noble. High ideals. Liked by his elders. Fond of music. Rich and generous.

*23. Möndru:* Goddess Chü Lhamo, Goddess of the Water; Drokme, Lower Friend. Sincere, faithful, legalistic. Can be deceived in business or love. Courageous, learned, sometimes coarse and implacable. Friend of kings.

*24. Trumtö:* Goddess Ri Lhamo, Goddess of the Mountains; Nema, Goddess of the Place; Palang Kang, Bull's Foot. Learned, good speaker but mean, jealous, pained, and sad. Loss of money due to women.

*25. Trume:* Trülching, Snake Net. Skilled and prolific speaker, but deceitful. Charitable, tactful, and good at study. Many children. Spiritual and sensitive.

26. *Namdru:* Shepa Gyeje, He who makes Knowledge Grow; Goddess Sowe Lhamo, She who Heals. Perfect body, courageous, even heroic. Scorns others' money. Subtle orator. Rich, has a weakness for women.

These are the traditional attributes of the lunar mansions. They must, however, be interpreted in conjunction with the planets that occupy them and their benefic or malefic character.

## THE PLANETS

Tibetan astrologers take account of the seven traditional planets: the Sun (*Nyima*), the Moon (*Dawa*), Mercury (*Lhakpa*), Mars (*Mikmar*), Venus (*Pasang*), Jupiter (*Phurbu*), and Saturn (*Penpa*), to which they add the Nodes of the Moon (*Rāhu* and *Ketu*) as shadow planets. The planets are represented by the symbols shown in the illustration on page 144, which can be found in all the astrological diagrams.

## The Legends of the Planets

In the Purāṇas, ancient Indian texts, there are a number of legends concerning the ten planets, and these legends are found in Tibet also.

The Sun, Sūrya, is known as Zadak, Lord of the Planets, or Namkhe Mik, Eye of the Sky, which is somewhat reminiscent of the Eye of Rā, the solar god of the Egyptians. As the provider of light and life, Sūrya has a chariot drawn by seven horses. He is accompanied by his eight wives and an entourage of servants. Although he is a symbol life, Sūrya is also the father of Yama, the Lord of Death. In astrology, Saturn is identified with Yama under the name Shinje Dakpo, Lord of Death. It is also known as Nyikye, Born of the Sun and Nyime Bu, Son of the Sun.

The planet Venus (Tārā) is the teacher of the *asuras*, the jealous gods. She is the wife of Jupiter who, under the name Vrihas-

Sun: Red disk

Moon: White crescent

Mars: Red and white eye

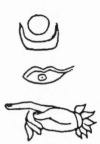

Mercury: Blue hand

Jupiter: Green phurba or ritual dagger

Venus: White arrowhead

Saturn: Yellow bundle of wood

Rāhu: Blue and gray bird's head

*The planetary symbols*

pati, teaches the gods. In this role, Jupiter is also known as the Guru, the Master of the Gods.

The god of the Moon, Candra, is famous for his intelligence, but is also a seducer and a dissolute. One day he seduced Tārā. Infuriated by his wife's pregnancy, Vrihaspati cursed Candra and condemned him to loss of power during the second half of the month. Thanks to the intervention of Sūrya, Vrihaspati was reconciled to Tārā. The son of adultery, Mercury (*Budha*), was then born. For this reason, Mercury is known as Dakye, "Born of the Moon."

These are the mythological links between the planets.

## The Legend of Rāhu

The legend of Rāhu exists in two versions, one Buddhist and the other Hindu. The Buddhist legend is as follows:

Once in ancient times, humanity was decimated by the poison Hala Hala, administered by demons. In order to cure human beings, the buddhas, moved by compassion, churned the Cosmic Ocean together with Mount Meru and thus made *amrita*, the water of immortality. When this amrita had been collected, it was given into the keeping of Vajrapāṇi, bodhisattva of energy. In spite of everything, however, th~ demon Rāhu was able to lay hands on the amrita, drank it all, and fled into space. In his flight, he threatened the Sun and Moon with reprisals if they betrayed him. Vajrapāṇi, starting off in pursuit, was able to catch him thanks to information received from the moon, and struck him with his vajra so violently that his head was separated from the rest of his body. Vajrapāṇi then had to drink Rāhu's poisonous urine so that it would not be spread among humans, and he thus lost his beautiful golden lustre and became totally black.

As for Rāhu, who had become immortal by drinking the amrita, he transformed himself into a monster with nine heads and the body of a snake. His wounds turned into eyes, which covered his body. In his hatred, he ceaselessly pursues the Sun and Moon in order to devour them. When he catches up with them, there is an eclipse, but he cannot destroy the stars because of the vigilance of Vajrapāṇi. Padmasambhava later subjugated the demon and made him a protector of the Dharma, Za Rāhula, chief of the planetary protectors.

In the very similar Hindu legend, it is the devas and āsuras who churn an ocean of milk in order to obtain the amrita. Despite the ruses of Viṣṇu, who wished to share the precious liquid only with the gods, the āsura Rāhu, disguised as a god, was able to drink some of it. Unmasked by Sūrya, the Sun, he fled. But Viṣṇu threw his disk and decapitated Rāhu. The deva then seized the gigantic head and body of Rāhu and hurled them into space. Ever since, the head, known as Rāhu, and the tail, known as Ketu, have occupied two opposite positions in the sky where the orbit of the moon crosses the ecliptic, trying to surprise the Sun and Moon and devour them. When Rāhu meets the Sun, he swallows it; but because his head is separated from his tail, the Sun immediately reappears—this is a solar eclipse. When the Moon meets the tail, Ketu, there is a lunar eclipse.

## Meanings of the Planets in Tibetan Astrology

Each of the planets signifies a number of particulars that can be used in interpretation:

> The Sun: The father, the mind, the will, courage, bravery, royalty, the right eye, gold, vitality, the direction East.
>
> The Moon: The mother, mental states, emotions, softness, water, agriculture, pearls, silver, clothing, the Northwest.
>
> Mars: The brother, activity, courage, violence, war, fire, blood, hatred, the animal nature, illicit love, weapons, wounds, lies, the South.
>
> Mercury: The uncle-nephew relationship, friendship, profession, study, truth, tact, human relations, commerce, sapphire, the North.
>
> Jupiter: Children, religion and high aspirations, the ministry, the priesthood, diplomacy, honor, education, the filial relationship and the elder brother, the well-being of the husband, the Northeast.
>
> Venus: The wife, the husband, music and the arts, perfume, incense, sense pleasures, poetry, clothing and ornaments, prosperity and treasure, the Southeast.
>
> Saturn: Longevity, limitations and obstacles, darkness, melancholy, the lack of spirituality, death, dishonor, sickness, poverty, accidents, imprisonment, sorrow, servants, iron, the West.
>
> Rāhu (rising node of the Moon): Maternal relationships, highly developed intellect, difficulties, and poison.
>
> Ketu (setting node of the Moon): Paternal relationships, the afterlife, torments, wisdom, and final liberation.

RELATIONS BETWEEN PLANETS

Planets can be friends, enemies, or neutral, either permanently or temporarily (see table on page 147). A planet becomes a provisional friend of another if it is in the 2nd, 3rd, 4th, 10th, 11th, or 12th sign counting from the planet in question. If it is in the 1st, 5th, 6th, 7th, 8th, or 9th, it becomes a provisional enemy.

| Planet | Friends | Neutral | Enemies |
|--------|---------|---------|---------|
| Sun | Moon, Mars, Jupiter | Mercury | Venus, Saturn, Rāhu |
| Moon | Sun, Mercury | Mars, Venus, Jupiter, Saturn | Ketu |
| Mars | Sun, Moon, Jupiter | Saturn, Venus | Mercury |
| Mercury | Sun, Venus | Saturn, Mars, Jupiter | Moon |
| Jupiter | Sun, Moon, Mars | Saturn | Mercury, Venus |
| Venus | Mercury, Saturn | Mars, Jupiter | Sun, Moon |
| Saturn | Venus, Mercury | Jupiter | Mars, Moon, Sun |

RULERSHIP OF THE PLANETS

The rulership of the planets is the same as in the Western system:

| | | |
|--|--|--|
| The Sun | rules | Leo |
| The Moon | rules | Cancer |
| Mercury | rules | Gemini and Virgo |
| Mars | rules | Aries and Scorpio |
| Venus | rules | Taurus and Libra |
| Jupiter | rules | Sagittarius and Pisces |
| Saturn | rules | Capricorn and Aquarius |

GENDER

| | |
|--|--|
| The male planets | the Sun, Mars, and Jupiter |
| The female planets | Moon and Venus |
| The neuter planets | Mercury and Saturn |

BENEFIC OR MALEFIC CHARACTER

Benefic planets: Jupiter, Venus, Mercury if well aspected, Moon between the 8th and 16th days of the lunation
Malefic planets: Saturn, Mars, Sun, Mercury if badly aspected, Moon between the 17th and 7th days.

147

HOROSCOPES

Horoscopes showing the positions of the planets in the signs are drawn up in a simpler manner than in the West: the signs are placed in a box, as in Hindu astrology.

The planets are represented by the numbers from 0 to 9, omitting 7:

| | | | |
|---|---|---|---|
| 0 | Penpa (Saturn) | 5 | Phurbu (Jupiter) |
| 1 | Nyima (Sun) | 6 | Pasang (Venus) |
| 2 | Dawa (Moon) | 8 | Drachen (Rāhu) |
| 3 | Mikmar (Mars) | 9 | Jukring (Ketu) |
| 4 | Lhakpa (Mercury) | | |

*Horoscope for May 7, 1978*
*(new moon)*

*Same horoscope using*
*Western symbols*

## Positions of the Planets

| | Planet | Tropical | Sidereal |
|---|---|---|---|
| 0 | Saturn | 23° ♌ | 29° ♋ |
| 1 | Sun | 16° ♉ | 22° ♈ |
| 2 | Moon | 16° ♉ | 22° ♈ |
| 3 | Mars | 10° ♌ | 16° ♋ |
| 4 | Mercury | 20° ♈ | 26° ♓ |
| 5 | Jupiter | 4° ♋ | 10° ♊ |
| 6 | Venus | 11° ♊ | 16° ♉ |
| 8 | Rāhu | 5° ♎ | 11° ♍ |
| 9 | Ketu | 5° ♈ | 11° ♓ |

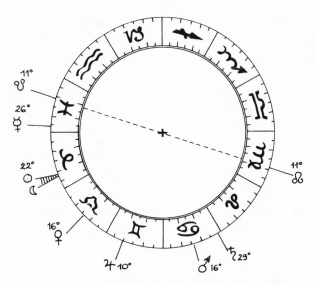

*Horoscope for May 7, 1978, in Western style*

The Tibetan horoscope strikes us as very imprecise: there is no notation for degrees, aspects, and so on. In this case there is also a gross error in the position of Venus (out by one sign). However, it must be borne in mind that the Tibetan horoscope is not used in the same way as its Western counterpart.

This type of horoscope, drawn for the full moon or the new moon, is found in the almanacs for each month.

## The Planets in Naktsi Astrology

The planets are also used in the Chinese-based system, in which they are related to the five elements and the twelve animals.

According to our text:

There are eight planets: the Sun, the Moon, Mars, Mercury, Jupiter, Venus, Saturn, and Rāhu.
    The Sun and Mars are Fire and rule the South; the Moon and Mercury are Water and rule the North; Jupiter is Wood

and rules the East; Venus is Metal and rules the West; Saturn is Earth and rules the four intermediate points.

As for Rāhu, the Head of the Dragon, it embraces all the elements. . . .

The 1st, 8th, 15th, 22nd, and 29th days of the month are linked to the same planet. The same applies to the other days.

There are outer, inner, and intermediate planets. The outer planets govern the sixty-year cycle: Earth and Metal years are ruled by Saturn, Wood years by Jupiter, Fire years by Mars, and the twelve Water years by Mercury.

The intermediate planets govern the twelve-year cycle: The Rat, the Dragon, and the Monkey are ruled by Mars; the Bird, the Cow, and the Snake are ruled by Jupiter; the Tiger, the Horse, and the Dog are ruled by Saturn; the Pig, the Sheep, and the Hare are ruled by Mercury.

The inner planets are connected with the eight Parkhas: male Li and Kham are linked to Mars, female to Saturn; male Da and Tsin are linked to Mars, female to Saturn; Male Khen and Zön are linked to Jupiter, female to Mercury; male Kin and Khön are linked to Mercury, female to Jupiter.

Every seven days, the same planet returns. In fact, the seven-day week is the same in China, India, and the West. We shall study the significance of this in daily astrology.

## Vital Forces, Planets, and Natal Stars

Each year in the twelve-year cycle has a ruling planet for Vitality, another for La, and a destroying planet. Similar categories are found in gyukar. If the natal moon falls in one of these, this has a meaning in the individual's life prognosis.

The figures in table 21 are for the planets of the gyukars, numbered in Tibetan style. Here is a brief explanation taken from a short almanac text:

> The planets of Vitality bring virtue and good fortune, while the destructive planets provoke obstacles and errors.
>
> The La planet brings about the defeat of enemies and the destructive planet reinforces them.

TABLE 21

## VITAL FORCES, PLANETS, AND NATAL STARS

| YEAR | Rat | Cow | Tiger | Hare | Dragon | Snake |
|---|---|---|---|---|---|---|
| La planet | 4 | 0 | 5 | 5 | 1 | 3 |
| Vitality planet | 3 | 4 | 0 | 0 | 4 | 6 |
| Destruction | 0 | 5 | 6 | 6 | 5 | 4 |
| La star | 19 | 16 | 4 | 10 | 2 | 12 |
| Vitality star | 5 | 13 | 26 | 26 | 23 | 11 |
| Power star | 2 | 11 | 8 | 11 | 16 | 5 |
| Kek star | 25 | 1 | 13 | 25 | 7 | 7 |
| Demon star | 9 | 7 | 11 | 24 | 8 | 8 |
| Destruction star | 22 | 4 | 1 | 17 | 10 | 5 |

| YEAR | Horse | Sheep | Monkey | Bird | Dog | Pig |
|---|---|---|---|---|---|---|
| La planet | 3 | 6 | 6 | 6 | 2 | 4 |
| Vitality planet | 6 | 2 | 5 | 5 | 4 | 3 |
| Destruction | 4 | 5 | 3 | 3 | 5 | 0 |
| La star | 16 | 7 | 7 | 13 | 8 | 1 |
| Vitality star | 11 | 0 | 0 | 6 | 26 | 7 |
| Power star | 5 | 1 | 1 | 24 | 4 | 10 |
| Kek star | 14 | 14 | 8 | 2 | 10 | 15 |
| Demon star | 4 | 4 | 4 | 10 | 2 | 2 |
| Destruction star | 26 | 26 | 16 | 23 | 11 | 11 |

The stars of the La, Vitality, and Power are excellent and quickly bring power and ability. Moreover, when the natal (moon) is conjunct the Power star, this means great merits. The natal moon in the destructive star brings about a short life, for the destructive star is then the same as the Death star.

Thus, if the planets of La or Vitality or the natal moon are conjunct the gyukar of the La, Vitality, or Power, this is a good sign for longevity, health, and prosperity. If the planets of the La or Vitality or the natal moon are in the gyukar Kek (inauspicious), "destruction," or "demon," this means many obstacles or a short life. If the destructive planet is in a malefic gyukar, this is a very bad omen. For example, a person born on September 9, 1957, at 12:00 is a Bird. The Vitality planet is 5, Jupiter. The *La* planet is 6, Venus, and the destructive planet is 3, Mars. The natal moon falls in gyukar 24, *Trumtö*. For that year, *Trumtö* is the Power star. This indicates that the native will have high capacity and the facility to achieve his or her aims. Enterprises will be crowned with success. Jupiter is in gyukar 12, neutral, and Venus is in gyukar 13, the *La* star. The conjunction of the *La* planet and the *La* star means a long life. Mars is in gyukar 10, "Demon." This operates to some extent against the rest of the prognosis and will bring obstacles and the risk of accidents.

# 8

## LUNAR TIME AND
## THE TIBETAN YEAR
## AND MONTH

### THE TIBETAN YEAR

The Tibetan year consists of twelve lunar months or lunations. It is not, therefore, the same length as the solar year. A lunation lasts approximately 29½ mean solar days. The lunar year thus has an average length of 354 solar days, as opposed to 365¼ solar days in a solar year.

In order to avoid too much of a lag between the lunar and solar years, a 13th lunar month has to be added in certain years. This occurs on average every thirty months—in a period of nineteen years, there are therefore seven intercalary months or *da shol*. An intercalary month takes the name and number of the preceding month; thus, if it follows the 5th month, it becomes 5b and the 5th month is known as a "double month."

The lunar month is the period that elapses between two new moons. It begins on the first day after the new moon and ends on the following new moon.

The official Tibetan year beings on the new moon of the first month of spring. The Tibetan spring begins roughly a month before ours, the equinox corresponding to the middle of the season. The date of New Year, known as *Losar*, fluctuates between the beginning of February and the end of March.

The Tibetan year is very close to the Chinese lunar year but it is not always the same: once every three years on average, the Chinese year begins a month before the Tibetan. Chinese astrologers also use a system of intercalary months, but these are not calculated in the same way: when the Chinese year has thirteen months, the Tibetan year does not necessarily have the same number; and vice versa. Tables showing the dates of Chinese years are therefore of no use in Tibetan astrology.

## THE TIBETAN MONTH

The lunar month normally comprises thirty lunar days and sometimes twenty-nine; or five mean solar days. A lunar day or *tse zhag* is the time required for the moon to travel 12° from the sun. If $D$ stands for the distance between the moon and the sun, the first lunar day is the period between $D = 0°$ (new moon) and $D = 12°$. The second day begins at $D = 12°$ and ends at $D = 24°$, and so on.

Two points should be borne in mind:

1. The lunar day is not equal to the solar day or *nyin zhag*—1 mean lunar day = 0.984 solar days.
2. The moon's speed varies throughout the month. Lunar days, therefore, are not of equal length: most of them are shorter than solar days, but some are longer. The situation is, therefore, more complex than would be the case if all lunar days were of equal length.

Tibetan astrologers fix the correspondences between solar and lunar days as follows. As we have seen, the lunar year has twelve months of 30 lunar days, or 360 lunar days altogether. However, in the same period, the sun rises 354 times, thus giving 354 solar days. The difference is $(360 - 354) = 6$ days per year. In order to determine the correspondence between the two systems, therefore, 6 lunar days per year must be left out.

In the Tibetan calendar, the situation is rather more complicated. Lunar days are of variable length, longer or shorter than solar days:

- When a lunar day begins after sunrise and ends before the following sunrise, it is left out, or *che*.
- When a long lunar day includes two sunrises, it is doubled, or *lhak*.

This is the astronomical rule, but Tibetan astrologers do not apply it rigorously: sometimes the days left out are those that are inauspicious, and auspicious days are doubled.

In any month, 1 or 2 days may be left out for 0 or 1 doubled day. For the whole year, it is only necessary that the difference between the number of days left and those doubled should be 6.

## Using the Table of Correspondences

The Table of Correspondences (table 22) shows:

- The Tibetan name of the year and the approximate corresponding Western year (it must be remembered that the Tibetan year overlaps two Western years, beginning in February).
- The Western date for the first day of each lunar month.
- The number of days left out or doubled.

To convert a Western date into a Tibetan date:

1. Find the corresponding Tibetan year.
2. Find the number of the lunar month.
3. Calculate the lunar day, bearing in mind that the Tibetan month, although it may contain 29 or 30 days, is always numbered from 1 to 30. When a day is left out, its number

is skipped. When a day is doubled, its number is used twice:

| Western Date (1884) | 6/24 | 6/25 | 6/26 | 6/27 | 6/28 | 6/29 | 6/30 | 7/1 | 7/2 |
|---|---|---|---|---|---|---|---|---|---|
| Tibetan Date | 5/1 | 5/2 | 5/4 | 5/5 | 5/6 | 5/7 | 5/8 | 5/9 | 5/10 |

| Western Date | 7/3 | 7/4 | 7/5 | 7/6 | 7/7 | 7/8 | 7/9 | 7/10 | 7/11 |
|---|---|---|---|---|---|---|---|---|---|
| Tibetan Date | 5/11 | 5/12 | 5/13 | 5/14 | 5/15 | 5/15 | 5/16 | 5/17 | 5/18 |

| Western Date | 7/12 | 7/13 | 7/14 | 7/15 |
|---|---|---|---|---|
| Tibetan Date | 5/19 | 5/20 | 5/21 | 5/22 |

For example: date of birth 12/12/1888. The Tibetan year is Earth Rat. December 12 falls in the 11th lunar month, which begins on December 4. Since there is no 4th day in that month, 12/12 falls on the 10th day. The Tibetan equivalent for this date is therefore Male Earth Rat year, 10th day, 11th month.

## The Names of the Tibetan Months

Since there are a number of parallel naming systems, it is not always easy to orient oneself. (See table 23, page 173.)

1. In one system, the months are named in numerical order: *Dawa Dangpo* or First Month, *Dawa Nyipa* or Second Month, *Dawa Sumpa*, or Third Month, and so on.
2. In the Indian system, the months take the name of the constellation in which the full moon occurs: *Chu Dawa* is the first month, since the full moon falls in the gyukar *Chu.*
3. In another system, the months are named after the twelve animals of the Chinese cycle; but here there are three different systems used. Suffice it to say that in the first system, the most common, the first month is the Month of the Dragon, the second is the Month of the Snake, and so on. This is the system used in Jungtsi astrology.

## TABLE 22

## CORRESPONDENCES BETWEEN THE TIBETAN AND WESTERN CALENDARS†

| Month / Year | 1 | 2 | 3 | 4 | 5 | 6 | 7 | 8 | 9 | 10 | 11 | 12 |
|---|---|---|---|---|---|---|---|---|---|---|---|---|
| Metal Dragon 1880 | 2/11<br>−28 | 3/11<br>+4<br>−21 | 4/10<br>+8<br>−15 | 5/10<br>−19 | 6/8<br>+3<br>−11 | 7/8<br>−14<br>+30 | 8/7<br>−7 | 9/5<br>−10<br>+26 | 10/5<br>−3 | 11/3<br>−7<br>+20 | 12/2<br>−1<br><br>1/1<br>−6<br>+12<br>−30 | 1/30<br>+15<br>−24 |
| Metal Snake 1881 | 3/1<br>−28 | 3/30<br>+8<br>−22 | 4/29<br>−26 | 5/28<br>+2<br>−19 | 6/27<br>−22<br>+29 | 7/27<br>−14 | 8/25<br>−17<br>+25 | 9/24<br>−10 | 10/23<br>−15<br>+19 | 11/22<br>−8<br>+23 | 12/22<br>−2 | 1/20<br>−7<br>+15 |
| Water Horse 1882 | 2/18<br>−1<br>+18<br>−25 | 3/20<br>−29 | 4/18<br>+11<br>−23 | 18/5<br>−26 | 6/16<br>+7<br>−19 | 7/16<br>−21 | 8/14<br>+4<br>−14 | 9/13<br>−17<br>+29 | 10/13<br>−11 | 11/11<br>−15<br>+23 | 12/11<br>−9<br>+26 | 1/10<br>−3 |
| Water Sheep 1883 | 2/8<br>−8<br>+18 | 3/10<br>−2<br>+22<br>−24 | 4/8<br>−7<br>+10<br>−30 | 5/7<br>+16<br>−23 | 6/6<br>−26 | 7/5<br>+12<br>−18 | 8/4<br>−21<br><br>9/2<br>+8<br>−14<br>−26 | 10/2<br>−18 | 10/31<br>+3<br>−11 | 11/30<br>−15<br>+26 | 12/30<br>−10<br>+29 | 1/29<br>−3 |
| Wood Monkey 1884 | 2/27<br>−9<br>+21 | 3/28<br>−3 | 4/26<br>−7<br>+15<br>−30 | 5/25 | 6/24<br>−3<br>+10<br>−26 | 7/23<br>−29 | 8/21<br>+7<br>−21 | 9/20<br>−25 | 10/19<br>+3<br>−18 | 11/18<br>+7<br>−11 | 12/18<br>−17<br>+29 | 1/7<br>−11 |
| Wood Bird 1885 | 2/15<br>−17<br>+20 | 3/17<br>−10<br>+25 | 4/16<br>−3 | 5/15<br>−7<br>+19<br>−30 | 6/13 | 7/13<br>−3<br>+15<br>−26 | 8/11<br>−28 | 9/9<br>+12<br>−22 | 10/9<br>−25 | 11/7<br>+6<br>−19 | 12/7<br>−24<br>+28 | 1/6<br>−18 |
| Fire Dog 1886 | 2/4<br>+2<br>−12 | 3/6<br>−17<br>+24 | 4/5<br>−10<br>+28 | 5/5<br>−3<br><br>6/3<br>−7<br>+24<br>−30 | 7/2<br>−12<br>+13 | 8/1<br>−3<br>+21<br>−25 | 8/30<br>−6<br>+11<br>−29 | 9/28<br>+16<br>−22 | 10/28<br>−26 | 11/26<br>+10<br>−20 | 12/26<br>−25 | 1/24<br>+2<br>−19 |
| Fire Pig 1887 | 2/23<br>+5<br>−13 | 3/25<br>−17<br>+28 | 4/24<br>−11 | 5/23<br>−14<br>+23 | 6/22<br>−7 | 7/21<br>−10<br>+19 | 8/20<br>−3 | 9/18<br>−6<br>+15<br>−29 | 10/17 | 11/16<br>−3<br>+9<br>−27 | 12/15<br>+13<br>−21 | 1/14<br>−26 |

†The information in this table is based on Dieter Schuh, *Untersuchungen zur Geschichte der tibetischen kalenderrechnung* (Wiesbaden, 1973), for years 1880–1979; and Rigpa Fellowship, *Tibetan Calendar*, for years 1980–1997.

TABLE 22 (CONTINUED)

| Month / Year | 1 | 2 | 3 | 4 | 5 | 6 | 7 | 8 | 9 | 10 | 11 | 12 |
|---|---|---|---|---|---|---|---|---|---|---|---|---|
| Earth Rat 1888 | 2/12<br>+4<br>−20 | 3/13<br>+8<br>−14 | 4/12<br>−18 | 5/11<br>+2<br>−11 | 6/10<br>−14<br>+27 | 7/10<br>−7 | 8/8<br>−10<br>+24 | 9/7<br>−3 | 10/6<br>−6<br>+19<br>−30 | 11/4 | 12/4<br>−4<br>+13<br>−28 | 1/2<br>+16<br>−22 \| 2/1<br>−27 |
| Earth Cow 1889 | 3/2<br>+7<br>−21 | 4/1<br>−26 | 5/1<br>+1<br>−19 | 5/30<br>+6<br>−11<br>−23 | 6/29<br>−14 | 7/28<br>+3<br>−6<br>−18 | 8/27<br>−10<br>+30 | 9/26<br>−2<br>−14<br>+18 | 10/25<br>−7<br>+23<br>−30 | 11/23 | 12/23<br>−5<br>+15<br>−29 | 1/21<br>+19<br>−23 |
| Metal Tiger 1890 | 2/20<br>−28 | 3/21<br>+11<br>−22 | 4/20<br>−26 | 5/19<br>+5<br>−19 | 6/18<br>−22 | 7/18<br>+1<br>−14 | 8/16<br>−17<br>+28 | 9/15<br>−10 | 10/14<br>−14<br>+22 | 11/13<br>−7<br>+27<br>−30 | 12/12 | 1/11<br>−6<br>+18<br>−30 |
| Metal Hare 1891 | 2/9 | 3/11<br>−6<br>+10<br>−29 | 4/9<br>+14<br>−22 | 5/9<br>−26 | 6/7<br>+9<br>−19 | 7/7<br>−22 | 8/5<br>+6<br>−14 | 9/4<br>−17 | 10/3<br>+2<br>−10 \| 11/2<br>−14<br>+26 | 2/12<br>−8 | 12/31<br>−14<br>+18 | 1/30<br>−7<br>+21 |
| Water Dragon 1892 | 2/29<br>−2 | 3/29<br>−6<br>+14<br>−30 | 4/27<br>+19<br>−22 | 5/27<br>−4<br>+8<br>−26 | 6/25<br>+15<br>−17<br>−29 | 7/24<br>+5<br>−21 | 8/23<br>−25 | 9/22<br>+1<br>−18 | 10/21<br>+7<br>−10<br>−23 | 11/20<br>−15<br>+29 | 12/20<br>−9 | 1/18<br>−14<br>+21 |
| Water Snake 1893 | 2/17<br>−8<br>+24 | 3/19<br>−2 | 4/17<br>−6<br>+18<br>−30 | 5/16 | 6/18<br>−3<br>+13<br>−26 | 7/14<br>−29 | 8/12<br>+10<br>−22 | 9/11<br>−25 | 10/10<br>+5<br>−18 | 11/9<br>−22<br>+29 | 12/9<br>−16 | 1/7<br>+2<br>−10 |
| Wood Horse 1894 | 2/6<br>−15<br>+24 | 3/8<br>−9<br>+28 | 4/7<br>−3 | 5/6<br>−7<br>+22<br>−30 | 6/4 \| 7/4<br>−3<br>+18<br>−26 | 8/2<br>−29 | 8/31<br>+15<br>−21 | 9/30<br>−25 | 10/29<br>+9<br>−19 | 11/28<br>−23 | 12/27<br>+2<br>−17 | 1/26<br>+5<br>−11 |
| Wood Sheep 1895 | 2/25<br>−16<br>+27 | 3/27<br>−10 | 4/25<br>−14<br>+21 | 5/25<br>−7 | 6/23<br>−11<br>+17 | 7/23<br>−3 | 8/21<br>−6<br>+14<br>−29 | 9/19 | 10/19<br>−3<br>+9<br>−26 | 11/17<br>+13<br>−19 | 12/7<br>−24 | 1/15<br>+5<br>−19 |

| Sign / Year | | | | | | | | | | | | |
|---|---|---|---|---|---|---|---|---|---|---|---|---|
| Fire Monkey 1896 | 2/14 +8 -12 | 3/15 -17; 4/3 -18 | 4/14 +1 -11 | 5/13 +14 -25 | 6/12 -8 | 7/11 -10 +22 | 8/10 -3 | 9/8 -6 +18 -29 | 7/10 | 11/6 -3 +12 -27 | 12/5 +17 -19 | 1/4 -25 |
| Fire Bird 1897 | 2/2 +8 -20 | 3/4 -25 +30 | 5/2 +4 -11 | 6/1 -15 +30 | 7/1 -7 | 7/30 -10 +27 | 8/29 -2 -14 +16 | 27/9 -6 +22 -29 | 10/26 | 11/25 -3 +16 -28 | 12/24 | 1 + 3/23 -27 +7 |
| Earth Dog 1898 | 2/21 +11 -21 | 3/23 -27 | 4/21 +4 -18 | 5/21 -22 +29 | 6/20 -15 | 7/19 -17 +26 | 8/18 -10 | 9/16 -13 +21 | 10/16 -7 +27 -29 | 11/14 -11 +15 | 12/14 -4 +19 -29 | 1/12 |
| Earth Pig 1899 | 2/11 -4 +10 -28 | 3/12 +14 -22 | 4/11 -25 | 5/10 +8 -19 | 6/9 -22 | 7/8 +4 -15 | 8/7 -17 +30 | 9/6 -10 | 10/5 -14 +25 | 11/4 -7; 12/3 -12 +19 | 1/2 -6 +22 -30 | 1/13 |
| Metal Rat 1900 | 3/1 -5 +13 -29 | 3/31 +18 -21 | 4/30 -4 +6 -26 | 5/29 +12 -19 | 6/28 -22 | 7/27 +9 -14 -25 | 8/26 -17 | 9/24 +5 -10 -22 | 10/24 -14 +29 | 11/23 -8 | 12/22 -12 +21 | 1/21 -7 +24 |
| Metal Cow 1901 | 2/19 -1 | 3/21 -6 +17 -29 | 4/19 | 5/19 -3 +11 -26 | 6/17 -29 | 7/16 +8 -22 | 8/15 -24 | 9/13 +4 -18 | 10/13 -21 +29 | 11/12 -15 | 12/12 +2 -9 | 1/10 -14 +24 |
| Water Tiger 1902 | 2/9 -8 +28 | 3/10 -1 | 4/9 -6 +21 -30 | 5/8 | 6/7 -3 +16 -26 | 7/6 -29; 8/4 +13 -22 | 9/3 -25 | 10/2 +8 -18 | 11/1 -22 | 11/30 +2 -16 | 12/30 +6 -9 | 1/29 -15 +27 |
| Water Hare 1903 | 2/28 -9 | 3/29 -14 +20 | 4/28 -7 +25 -30 | 5/27 -12 +14 | 6/25 -3 +21 -25 | 7/25 -7 +11 -29 | 8/23 +18 -20 | 9/22 -2 +7 -25 | 10/21 +12 -18 | 11/20 -23 | 12/19 +5 -17 | 1/18 -23 +27 |
| Wood Dragon 1904 | 2/17 -16 | 3/18 -30 | 4/16 -10 | 5/16 -14 +24 | 6/14 -7 | 7/14 -10 +19 | 8/12 -3 -29 | 9/10 -6 +16 | 10/10 -2 +12 -26 | 11/8 -30 | 12/7 +5 -24 | 1/6 +8 -18 |

TABLE 22 (CONTINUED)

| Month / Year | 1 | 2 | 3 | 4 | 5 | 6 | 7 | 8 | 9 | 10 | 11 | 12 |
|---|---|---|---|---|---|---|---|---|---|---|---|---|
| Wood Snake 1905 | 2/5<br>-23<br>+30 | 3/7<br>-17 | 4/5<br>+4<br>-10 | 5/5<br>-14<br>+28   6/4<br>-8 | 7/3<br>-10<br>+24 | 8/2<br>-3 | 8/31<br>-6<br>+21<br>-29 | 9/29 | 10/29<br>-3<br>+15<br>-26 | 11/27 | 12/26<br>-1<br>+8<br>-25 | 1/25<br>+11<br>-19 |
| Fire Horse 1906 | 2/24<br>-24 | 3/25<br>+3<br>-18 | 4/24<br>-22<br>+27 | 5/24<br>-15 | 6/22<br>+3<br>-7<br>-18 | 7/22<br>-10 | 8/20<br>-13<br>+20 | 9/19<br>-6<br>+26<br>-28 | 10/18<br>-10<br>+14 | 11/17<br>-3<br>+19<br>-27 | 12/16 | 1/15<br>-2<br>+11<br>-26 |
| Fire Sheep 1907 | 2/13<br>+14<br>-20 | 3/15<br>-25 | 4/13<br>+7<br>-18 | 5/13<br>-22 | 6/11<br>+2<br>-15 | 7/11<br>-17<br>+28 | 8/10<br>-10 | 9/8<br>-13<br>+24 | 10/8<br>-6 | 11/6<br>-10<br>+18 | 12/6<br>-4<br>-28<br>+22 | 1/4   2/3<br>-3<br>+14<br>-27 |
| Earth Monkey 1908 | 3/3<br>+18<br>-20 | 4/2<br>-3<br>+5<br>-25 | 5/1<br>+11<br>-19 | 5/31<br>-22 | 6/29<br>+6<br>-15 | 7/29<br>-17 | 8/27<br>+3<br>-10 | 9/26<br>-13<br>+28 | 10/26<br>-7 | 11/24<br>-11<br>+22 | 12/24<br>-5<br>+25<br>-28 | 1/22 |
| Earth Bird 1909 | 2/21<br>-4<br>+17<br>-28 | 3/22 | 4/21<br>-3<br>+10<br>-26 | 5/20<br>+16<br>-17<br>-30 | 6/18<br>+5<br>-22 | 7/18<br>-25 | 8/16<br>+2<br>-17 | 9/15<br>-21<br>+28 | 10/15<br>-14 | 11/13<br>+2<br>-7 | 12/13<br>-12<br>+25 | 1/12<br>-6 |
| Metal Dog 1910 | 2/10<br>-12<br>+16 | 3/12<br>-5<br>+20<br>-29 | 4/10 | 5/10<br>-3<br>+14<br>-26 | 6/8<br>-29 | 7/7<br>+10<br>-22 | 8/6<br>-24 | 9/4<br>+6<br>-18   10/4<br>-21 | 11/2<br>+2<br>-15 | 12/2<br>-20<br>+24 | 1/1<br>-13<br>+27 | 1/31<br>-8 |
| Metal Pig 1911 | 3/1<br>-12<br>+20 | 3/31<br>-6<br>+24<br>-29 | 4/29 | 5/29<br>-3<br>+18<br>-26 | 6/27<br>-29 | 7/26<br>+15<br>-21 | 8/25<br>+25 | 9/23<br>+5<br>-18 | 10/23<br>-22 | 11/21<br>+5<br>-15 | 12/21<br>-20<br>+27 | 1/20<br>-14<br>+30 |
| Water Rat 1912 | 2/19<br>-9 | 3/19<br>-13<br>+23 | 4/18<br>-7 | 5/17<br>-11<br>+17 | 6/16<br>-3 | 7/15<br>-6<br>+14<br>-29 | 8/13 | 9/12<br>-2<br>+10<br>-25 | 10/11<br>-29 | 11/9<br>+5<br>-22 | 9/12<br>+8<br>-16 | 1/8<br>-21<br>+30 |

| Year | 2/7 | 3/8 | 4/7 | 5/7 | 6/5 | 7/5 | 8/3 | 9/1 | 10/1 | 10/30 | 11/28 | 12/28 | 1/27 |
|---|---|---|---|---|---|---|---|---|---|---|---|---|---|
| Water Cow 1913 | 2/7<br>−16 | 3/8<br>+3<br>−9 | 4/7<br>−14<br>+27 | 5/7<br>−5 | 6/5<br>−10<br>+22 | 7/5<br>−3 | 8/3<br>−6<br>+19<br>−29 |  | 10/1<br>−2<br>+14<br>−25 | 10/30<br>−29 | 11/28<br>+8<br>−23 | 12/28<br>+11<br>−17 | 1/27<br>−23 |
| Wood Tiger 1914 | 2/25<br>+3<br>−17 | 3/27<br>−22<br>+26 | 4/26<br>−14 | 5/26<br>+1<br>−7 | 6/24<br>−11<br>+27 |  | 7/24<br>−3<br>−15<br>+17 | 8/22<br>−6<br>+24<br>−28 | 9/20<br>−10<br>+13 | 10/20<br>−2<br>+18<br>−26 | 11/18<br>−30 | 12/17<br>+11<br>−25 | 1/16<br>+15<br>−18 |
| Wood Hare 1915 | 2/15<br>−24 | 3/16<br>+6<br>−18 | 4/15<br>−21<br>+30 | 5/15<br>−15 | 6/13<br>−18<br>+26 |  | 7/13<br>−11 | 8/11<br>−13<br>+28 | 9/10<br>−6 | 10/9<br>−10<br>+18 | 11/8<br>−3<br>+23<br>−26 | 12/7 | 1/5<br>−1<br>+14<br>−26 |
| Fire Dragon 1916 | 2/4<br>[3/4<br>−1<br>+6<br>−25] | 4/3<br>+10<br>−18 | 5/3<br>−22 | 6/1<br>+4<br>−15 | 7/1<br>−18 |  | 7/31<br>+1<br>−10 | 8/29<br>−13<br>+27 | 9/28<br>−6 | 10/27<br>−10<br>+21 | 11/26<br>−4 | 12/25<br>−9<br>+14 | 1/24<br>−3<br>+17 |
| Fire Snake 1917 | 2/22 | 3/24<br>−2<br>+9<br>−25 | 4/22<br>+4<br>−18<br>−30 | 5/21<br>+3<br>−22 | 6/20<br>+9<br>−14<br>−26 |  | 7/20<br>−18 | 8/18<br>+7<br>−9<br>−21 | 9/17<br>−13 | 10/17<br>+1<br>−6 | 11/15<br>−11<br>+25 | 12/15<br>−5 | 1/13<br>−10<br>+17<br>−27 |
| Earth Horse 1918 | 2/12<br>−4<br>+20<br>−28 | 3/13 | 4/12<br>−2<br>+13<br>−26 | 5/11<br>−29 | 6/9<br>+8<br>−22 |  | 7/9<br>−25 | 8/7<br>+5<br>−18 | 9/6<br>−20 | 10/6<br>+1<br>−14 | 11/4<br>−18<br>+25<br>[12/4<br>−12<br>+28] | 1/3<br>−6 |  |
| Earth Sheep 1919 | 3/3<br>−5<br>+23<br>−29 | 4/1 | 5/1<br>−3<br>+17<br>−26 | 5/30<br>−29 | 6/28<br>+13<br>−22 |  | 7/28<br>−25 | 8/26<br>+9<br>−17 | 9/25<br>−21 | 10/24<br>+5<br>−14 | 11/23<br>−19<br>+28 | 12/23<br>−13 | 1/22<br>+1<br>−7 |
| Metal Monkey 1920 | 2/20<br>−12<br>+23 | 3/21<br>−6 | 4/19<br>−10<br>+16 | 5/19<br>−3<br>+21<br>−26 | 6/17<br>−7<br>+11<br>−29 |  | 7/16<br>+19<br>−20 | 8/15<br>−2<br>+8<br>−25 | 9/13<br>−29 | 10/12<br>+4<br>−21 | 11/11<br>+8<br>−15 | 12/11<br>−20 | 1/10<br>+1<br>−14 |
| Metal Bird 1921 | 2/8<br>+4<br>−7 | 3/10<br>−14<br>+30 | 4/28<br>−7 | 5/27<br>−11<br>+25 | 6/26<br>−4 |  | 7/25<br>−6<br>+22<br>−29 | 8/23 | 9/22<br>−2<br>+17<br>−25 | 10/21<br>−29 | 11/19<br>+11<br>−23 | 12/19<br>−28 | 1/17<br>+3<br>−22 |

TABLE 22 (CONTINUED)

| Month / Year | 1 | 2 | 3 | 4 | 5 | 6 | 7 | 8 | 9 | 10 | 11 | 12 |
|---|---|---|---|---|---|---|---|---|---|---|---|---|
| Water Dog 1922 | 2/27<br>-20<br>+25 | 3/29<br>-14<br>+30 | 4/28<br>-7 | 5/27<br>-11<br>+25 | 6/26<br>-4 | 7/25<br>-6<br>+22<br>-29 | 8/23 | 9/22<br>-2<br>+17<br>-25 | 10/21<br>-29 | 11/19<br>+11<br>-23 | 12/19<br>-28 | 1/17<br>+3<br>-22 |
| Water Pig 1923 | 2/16<br>+6<br>-16 | 3/18<br>-21<br>+29 | 4/17<br>-14 | 5/16<br>-18<br>+24 | 6/15<br>-11 | 7/14<br>-14<br>+20 | 8/13<br>-6 | 9/11<br>-9<br>+17 | 10/11<br>-2<br>+22<br>-25 | 11/9<br>-7<br>+10<br>-30 | 12/8<br>+14<br>-24 | 1/7<br>-29 |
| Wood Rat 1924 | 2/5<br>+6<br>-23 | 3/6<br>+9<br>-17<br>[4/5<br>-21] | 5/4<br>+3<br>-15 | 6/3<br>-18<br>+28 | 7/3<br>-11 | 8/1<br>-13<br>+25 | 8/31<br>-6 | 9/29<br>-9<br>+21 | 10/29<br>-3 | 11/27<br>-7<br>+14 | 12/26<br>-1<br>+17<br>-25 | 1/25<br>-30 |
| Wood Cow 1925 | 2/23<br>+9<br>-24 | 3/25<br>+13<br>-17 | 4/24<br>-22 | 5/23<br>+7<br>-15 | 6/22<br>-18 | 7/21<br>+3<br>-10 | 8/20<br>-13<br>+30 | 9/19<br>-6 | 10/18<br>-10<br>+24 | 11/17<br>-3 | 12/16<br>-8<br>+17 | 1/15<br>-2<br>+20<br>-26 |
| Fire Tiger 1926 | 2/13 | 3/14<br>-1<br>+12<br>-25 | 4/13<br>-29 | 5/12<br>+6<br>-22 | 6/11<br>-25 | 7/10<br>+2<br>-18 | 8/9<br>-21<br>+29 | 9/8<br>-13 | 7/10<br>-17<br>+24 | 11/6<br>-11<br>+28 | 12/6<br>-4 | 1/4<br>-9<br>+20<br>+24<br>[2/3<br>-3<br>-27] |
| Fire Hare 1927 | 3/4 | 4/3<br>-2<br>+16<br>-26 | 5/2<br>-29 | 5/31<br>+11<br>-22 | 6/30<br>-25 | 7/29<br>+7<br>-18 | 8/28<br>-21 | 9/26<br>+3<br>-14 | 10/26<br>-17<br>+28 | 11/25<br>-11 | 12/24<br>+2<br>-4 | 1/23<br>-10<br>+23 |
| Earth Dragon 1928 | 2/22<br>-5 | 3/22<br>-9<br>+15 | 4/21<br>-3<br>+20<br>-26 | 5/20<br>-29 | 6/18<br>+15<br>-22 | 7/18<br>-25 | 8/16<br>+12<br>-17<br>-29 | 9/14<br>+2<br>-21 | 10/14<br>+7<br>-14 | 11/13<br>-18 | 12/13<br>+1<br>-12 | 1/11<br>-18<br>+23 |
| Earth Snake 1929 | 2/10<br>-11<br>+26 | 3/12<br>-6 | 4/10<br>-10<br>+19 | 5/10<br>-3 | 6/8<br>-7<br>+14<br>-29 | 7/7 | 8/6<br>-2<br>+11<br>-25<br>[9/4<br>-28] | 10/3<br>+7<br>-21 | 11/2<br>-26<br>+30 | 12/2<br>-19 | 12/31<br>+4<br>-14 | 1/30<br>-19<br>+26 |

| Year | | | | | | | | | | | | | | | |
|---|---|---|---|---|---|---|---|---|---|---|---|---|---|---|---|
| Metal Horse 1930 | 3/1<br>-13<br>+29 | 3/31<br>-6 | 4/29<br>-10<br>+23 | 5/29<br>-4 | | 6/27<br>-6<br>+19<br>-29 | 7/26 | 8/25<br>-2<br>+16<br>-25 | 9/23<br>-28 | 10/22<br>+11<br>-22 | | 11/21<br>-26 | 12/20<br>+4<br>-20 | | 1/19<br>+7<br>-15 |
| Metal Sheep 1931 | 2/18<br>-19<br>+29 | 3/20<br>-13 | 4/18<br>+3<br>-6<br>-18<br>+22 | 5/18<br>-11<br>+28 | | 6/17<br>-3<br>-15<br>+17 | 7/16<br>-6<br>+24<br>-28 | 8/14<br>-10<br>+15 | 9/13<br>-2<br>+21<br>-24 | 10/12<br>-7<br>+9<br>-29 | | 11/10<br>+14<br>-23 | 12/10<br>-27 | | 1/8<br>+7<br>-22 |
| Water Monkey 1932 | 2/7<br>+10<br>-16 | 3/8<br>-20 | 4/6<br>+2<br>-14 | 5/6<br>-18<br>+26 | 6/5<br>-11 | 7/4<br>-14<br>+23 | 8/3<br>-6 | 9/1<br>-9<br>+19 | 10/1<br>-2 | 30/10<br>-6<br>+14<br>-30 | | 11/28<br>+18<br>-23 | 12/28<br>-28 | | 1/26<br>+9<br>-23 |
| Water Bird 1933 | 2/25<br>+13<br>-16<br>-29<br>+30 | 3/27<br>-21 | 4/25<br>+6<br>-15 | 5/25<br>-18 | | 6/24<br>+1<br>-11 | 7/23<br>-14<br>+28 | 8/22<br>-6 | 9/20<br>-9<br>+24 | 10/20<br>-3 | | 11/18<br>-7<br>+17 | 12/17<br>-1<br>+22<br>-23 | | 1/16<br>-30 |
| Wood Dog 1934 | 2/14<br>+12<br>-24 | 3/16<br>-28 | 4/14<br>+5<br>-22 | 5/14<br>+10<br>-14<br>-26<br>+30 | | 6/13<br>-18 | 7/12<br>+7<br>-10<br>-21<br>+27 | 8/11<br>-13 | 9/9<br>-17<br>+23 | 10/9<br>-10<br>+28 | | 11/8<br>-3 | 12/7<br>-8<br>+20 | 1/6<br>-2 | 2/14<br>-7<br>+12 |
| Wood Pig 1935 | 3/5<br>-1<br>+15<br>-25 | 4/4<br>-29 | 5/3<br>+9<br>-22 | 6/2<br>-25 | | 7/1<br>+5<br>-18 | 7/31<br>-21 | 8/29<br>+2<br>-14 | 9/28<br>-17<br>+27 | 10/28<br>-10 | | 11/26<br>-15<br>+20 | 12/26<br>-9<br>+23 | | 1/25<br>-3 |
| Fire Rat 1936 | 2/23<br>-8<br>+15 | 3/24<br>-2<br>+19<br>-25 | 4/22<br>-29 | 5/21<br>+13<br>-22 | | 6/20<br>-25 | 7/19<br>+10<br>-18 | 8/18<br>-21 | 9/16<br>+6<br>-14 | 10/16<br>-17 | | 11/15<br>+1<br>-11 | 12/14<br>-16<br>+23 | | 1/13<br>-10<br>+26 |
| Fire Cow 1937 | 2/12<br>-4 | 3/13<br>-9<br>+18 | 4/12<br>-3 | 5/11<br>-7<br>+12<br>-29 | | 6/9<br>+19<br>-21 | 7/9<br>-3<br>+9<br>-25 | 8/7<br>-28 | 9/5<br>+5<br>-21 | 10/5<br>-25<br>+30 | 11/4<br>-18 | 12/3<br>+4<br>-12 | 1/2<br>-17<br>+27 | | 2/1<br>-11<br>+29 |

TABLE 22 (CONTINUED)

| Month / Year | 1 | 2 | 3 | 4 | 5 | 6 | 7 | 8 | 9 | 10 | 11 | 12 |
|---|---|---|---|---|---|---|---|---|---|---|---|---|
| Earth Tiger 1938 | 3/3<br>−5 | 4/1<br>−9<br>+22 | 5/1<br>−3 | 6/30<br>−6<br>+17<br>−30 | 6/28 | 7/28<br>−2<br>+14<br>−25 | 8/26<br>−28 | 9/24<br>+10<br>−21 | 10/24<br>−25 | 11/22<br>+4<br>−19 | 12/22<br>+7<br>−13 | 1/21<br>−18<br>+29 |
| Earth Hare 1939 | 2/20<br>−12 | 3/21<br>+3<br>−5<br>−17<br>+21 | 4/20<br>−10<br>+26 | 5/20<br>−3 | 6/18<br>−7<br>+22<br>−29 | 7/17 | 8/16<br>−2<br>+18<br>−25 | 9/14<br>−28 | 10/13<br>+14<br>−22 | 11/12<br>−26 | 12/11<br>+7<br>−20<br>−13 | 1/10<br>+11 |
| Metal Dragon 1940 | 2/9<br>−19 | 3/9<br>+2<br>−13 | 4/8<br>−17<br>+25 | 5/8<br>−11 | 6/6<br>−14<br>+21 | 7/6<br>−7<br><br>8/4<br>−9<br>+17 | 9/3<br>−2 | 10/2<br>−5<br>+13<br>−29 | 10/31<br>+18<br>−22 | 11/30<br>−27 | 12/29<br>+10<br>−21 | 1/28<br>−27 |
| Metal Snake 1941 | 2/27<br>+1<br>−20 | 3/28<br>+5<br>−14 | 4/27<br>−18<br>+29 | 5/27<br>−11 | 6/25<br>−14<br>+25 | 7/25<br>−7 | 8/23<br>−9<br>+22 | 9/22<br>−2 | 10/21<br>−6<br>+17<br>−29 | 11/19 | 12/19<br>−4<br>+10<br>−28 | 1/17<br>+13<br>−22 |
| Water Horse 1942 | 2/16<br>−27 | 3/17<br>+5<br>−21 | 4/16<br>+9<br>−14 | 5/16<br>−18 | 6/14<br>+4<br>−11 | 7/14<br>−14 | 8/13<br>+1<br>−6<br>−18<br>+20 | 9/11<br>−9<br>+26 | 10/11<br>−2 | 11/9<br>−6<br>+20<br>−30 | 12/8 | 1/7<br>−5<br>+13<br>−29 |
| Water Sheep 1943 | 2/5<br>+15<br>−23 | 3/7<br>−28<br><br>4/5<br>+8<br>−22 | 5/5<br>−25 | 6/3<br>+3<br>−18 | 7/3<br>−21<br>+29 | 8/2<br>−14 | 8/31<br>−17<br>+26 | 9/30<br>−10 | 10/29<br>−14<br>+20 | 11/28<br>−7<br>+24 | 12/27<br>−1 | 1/26<br>−6<br>+15<br>−30 |
| Wood Monkey 1944 | 2/24<br>+19<br>−24 | 3/25<br>−29 | 4/23<br>+12<br>−22 | 5/23<br>−25 | 6/21<br>+7<br>−18 | 7/21<br>−21 | 8/19<br>+4<br>−14 | 9/18<br>−17<br>+30 | 10/18<br>−10 | 11/16<br>−14<br>+23 | 12/16<br>−8<br>+27 | 1/15<br>−2 |
| Wood Bird 1945 | 2/13<br>−7<br>+18 | 3/14<br>−1 | 4/13<br>−6<br>+11<br>−29 | 5/12<br>+16<br>−22 | 6/11<br>−25 | 7/10<br>+13<br>−17<br>−29 | 8/8<br>+3<br>−21 | 9/7<br>+9<br>−13<br>−25<br>+29 | 10/7<br>−17 | 11/5<br>+4<br>−11 | 12/5<br>−15<br>+26<br><br>1/4<br>−9<br>+30 | 2/3<br>−2 |

| Year | | | | | | | | | | | | |
|---|---|---|---|---|---|---|---|---|---|---|---|---|
| Fire Dog 1946 | 3/4 −8 +21 | 4/3 −2 | 5/2 −6 +15 −30 | 5/31 | 6/30 −3 +11 −25 | 7/29 −28 | 8/27 +8 −21 | 9/26 −24 | 10/25 +3 −18 | 11/24 +8 −10 −24 +25 | 12/24 −16 +29 | 1/23 −11 |
| Fire Pig 1947 | 2/21 −16 +21 | 3/23 −9 +25 | 4/22 −3 | 5/21 −7 +20 −30 | 6/19 | 7/19 −2 +16 −25 | 8/17 −28 | 9/15 +12 −21 | 10/15 −25 | 11/13 +7 −19 | 12/13 −24 +29 | 1/12 −17 |
| Earth Rat 1948 | 2/10 +2 −12 | 3/11 −16 +24 | 4/10 −10 +29 | 5/10 −2 −15 +28 | 6/8 −7 +25 −29 | 7/7 −10 +15 | 8/6 −2 / 9/4 −6 +11 −28 | 10/3 +17 −21 | 11/2 −3 +5 −25 | 12/1 +10 −20 | 12/31 −24 | 1/29 +2 −19 |
| Earth Cow 1949 | 2/28 +5 −13 | 3/30 −17 +28 | 4/29 −11 | 5/28 −14 +23 | 6/27 −7 | 7/26 −9 +20 | 8/25 −2 | 9/23 −5 +16 −29 | 10/22 | 11/21 −3 +10 −26 | 12/20 +13 −21 | 1/19 −26 |
| Metal Tiger 1950 | 2/17 +5 −20 | 3/19 +8 −13 | 4/18 −18 | 5/17 +2 −11 | 6/16 −14 +28 | 7/16 −7 | 8/14 −9 +25 | 9/13 −2 | 10/12 −6 +20 −29 | 11/10 | 12/10 −3 +13 −28 | 1/8 +16 −21 |
| Metal Hare 1951 | 2/7 −27 | 3/8 +8 −21 | 4/7 −25 / 5/7 +1 −18 | 6/5 +7 −10 −22 +27 | 7/5 −14 | 8/3 −17 +24 | 9/2 −9 | 10/1 −13 +19 | 10/31 −6 +24 −30 | 11/29 | 12/29 −4 +16 −29 | 1/27 +20 −22 |
| Water Dragon 1952 | 2/26 −28 | 3/26 +11 −21 | 4/25 +25 | 5/24 +5 −18 | 6/23 −21 | 7/22 +2 −14 | 8/21 −17 +28 | 9/20 −10 | 10/19 −13 +23 | 11/18 −7 +28 −29 | 12/17 −13 +15 | 1/16 −6 +19 −30 |
| Water Snake 1953 | 2/14 | 3/16 −5 +11 −28 | 4/14 +15 −22 | 5/14 −25 | 6/12 +10 −18 | 7/12 −21 | 8/10 +7 −13 | 9/9 −17 | 10/8 +3 −10 | 11/7 −14 +26 | 12/7 −8 | 1/5 −13 +18 / 2/4 −7 +21 |
| Wood Horse 1954 | 3/15 −1 | 4/4 −5 +14 −29 | 5/3 | 6/2 −3 +9 −25 | 7/1 −28 | 7/30 +6 −21 | 8/29 −24 | 9/27 +2 −17 | 10/27 −22 +26 | 11/26 −15 +30 | 12/26 −9 | 1/24 −14 +21 |

TABLE 22 (CONTINUED)

| Month / Year | 1 | 2 | 3 | 4 | 5 | 6 | 7 | 8 | 9 | 10 | 11 | 12 |
|---|---|---|---|---|---|---|---|---|---|---|---|---|
| Wood Sheep 1955 | 2/23<br>−8<br>+25 | 3/25<br>−2 | 4/23<br>−6<br>+18<br>−29 | 5/22 | 6/21<br>−3<br>+14<br>−25 | 7/20<br>−28 | 8/18<br>+11<br>+21 | 9/17<br>−24   10/5<br>−25 | 10/16<br>+6<br>−18 | 11/15<br>−22<br>+29 | 12/15<br>−16 | 1/13<br>+2<br>−10 |
| Fire Monkey 1956 | 2/12<br>−15<br>+24 | 3/13<br>−9<br>+29 | 4/12<br>−2<br>−14<br>+16 | 5/11<br>−6<br>+22<br>−29 | 6/9 | 7/9<br>−3<br>+19<br>−25 | 8/7<br>−7<br>+8<br>−28 | 9/5<br>+15<br>−20 | 11/3<br>+10<br>−18 | 12/3<br>−23 | 1/1<br>+2<br>−17 | 1/31<br>+5<br>−11 |
| Fire Bird 1957 | 3/2<br>−16<br>+27 | 4/1<br>−10 | 4/30<br>−14<br>+22 | 5/30<br>−7 | 6/28<br>−10<br>+18 | 7/28<br>−2 | 8/26<br>−5<br>+14<br>−28 | 9/24 | 10/24<br>−2<br>+9<br>−25 | 11/22<br>+13<br>−19 | 12/22<br>−24 | 1/20<br>+5<br>−18 |
| Earth Dog 1958 | 2/19<br>+9<br>−11<br>−24<br>+26 | 3/21<br>−17 | 4/20<br>+1<br>−10 | 5/19<br>−14<br>+26 | 6/18<br>−7 | 7/17<br>−10<br>+23 | 8/6<br>−2 | 9/14<br>−5<br>+19<br>−29 | 10/13 | 11/12<br>−2<br>+13<br>−26 | 12/11 | 1/10<br>−2<br>+4<br>−25 |
| Earth Pig 1959 | 2/8<br>+8<br>−19 | 3/10<br>−24 | 4/9<br>+1<br>−17 | 5/8<br>+5<br>−10 | 6/7<br>−14   7/7<br>+1<br>−6<br>−18<br>+21 | 8/5<br>−10<br>+28 | 9/3<br>−1<br>−13<br>+18 | 10/3<br>−6<br>+23<br>−19 | 1/11 | 12/1<br>−3<br>+16<br>−27 | 12/30 | 1/29<br>−2<br>+8<br>−26 |
| Metal Rat 1960 | 2/27<br>+11<br>−20 | 3/28<br>−24 | 4/26<br>+4<br>−18 | 5/26<br>−21<br>+30 | 6/26<br>−14 | 7/24<br>−17<br>+26 | 8/23<br>−10 | 9/21<br>−13<br>+22 | 10/21<br>−6 | 11/19<br>−11<br>+16 | 12/19<br>−4<br>+19<br>−28 | 1/17 |
| Metal Cow 1961 | 2/16<br>−3<br>+11<br>−27 | 3/17<br>+14<br>−21 | 4/16<br>−25 | 5/15<br>+8<br>−18 | 6/14<br>−21 | 7/13<br>+4<br>−14 | 8/12<br>−17 | 9/11<br>+1<br>−10 | 10/10<br>−13<br>+26 | 11/9<br>−7 | 11/8<br>−11<br>+19 | 1/7<br>−5<br>+22<br>−29 |
| Water Tiger 1962 | 2/5<br>+28   7/3<br>−4<br>−14 | 4/5 | 5/5<br>−3<br>+7<br>−25 | 6/3<br>+13<br>−18<br>−29 | 7/2<br>+3<br>−21 | 8/1<br>+10<br>−13<br>−24<br>+30 | 8/31<br>−17 | 9/29<br>+6<br>−9<br>−21<br>+25 | 10/29<br>−14<br>+30 | 11/28<br>−7 | 12/27<br>−12<br>+22 | 1/26<br>−6<br>+25<br>−30 |

| Year | | | | | | | | | | | | |
|---|---|---|---|---|---|---|---|---|---|---|---|---|
| Water Hare 1963 | 2/24 | 3/26 −5 +17 −29 | 4/24 | 5/24 −2 +12 −26 | 6/22 −28 | 7/21 +8 −21 | 3/20 −24 | 9/18 +5 −17 | 10/18 −21 +29 | 11/17 −14 | 12/16 +3 +8 | 1/15 −13 +25 |
| Wood Dragon 1964 | 2/14 −8 | 3/4 −13 +16 | 4/13 −6 +21 −29 | 5/12 | 6/11 −3 +16 −26 | 7/10 −28 | 8/8 +13 −21 | 9/7 −24 | 10/6 +9 −17 | 11/5 −21 | 12/4 +2 −15 −27 ‖ 1/3 −22 +23 | 2/2 −14 +27 |
| Wood Snake 1965 | 3/4 −9 | 4/2 −13 +20 | 5/2 −6 +26 −29 | 5/31 −10 +15 | 6/30 −3 +23 −24 | 7/29 −6 +12 −28 | 8/27 | 9/25 −1 +8 −25 | 10/25 +13 −17 | 11/24 −22 | 12/23 +6 −17 | 1/22 −22 +27 |
| Fire Horse 1966 | 2/21 −16 | 3/23 +1 −10 | 4/21 −13 +24 | 5/21 −7 | 6/19 −10 +20 | 7/19 −3 | 8/17 −5 +17 −28 | 9/15 | 10/15 −2 +12 −25 | 11/13 −30 | 12/12 +5 −23 | 1/11 +8 −18 |
| Fire Sheep 1967 | 2/10 −23 +30 | 3/12 −17 | 4/10 +4 −10 | 5/10 −14 +29 | 6/9 −7 | 7/8 −10 +25 | 8/7 −2 ‖ 9/5 −5 +22 −28 | 10/4 | 11/3 −2 +16 −26 | 12/2 −30 | 12/31 +8 −25 | 1/30 +11 −19 |
| Earth Monkey 1968 | 2/29 −24 | 3/29 +4 −17 | 4/28 −21 +28 | 5/28 −14 | 6/26 −17 +24 | 7/26 −10 | 8/24 −13 +21 | 9/23 −6 | 10/22 −10 +15 | 11/21 −3 +19 −27 | 12/20 | 1/18 −1 +11 −26 |
| Earth Bird 1969 | 2/17 +14 −20 | 3/19 −24 | 4/17 +7 −18 | 5/17 −21 | 6/15 +2 −14 | 7/15 −17 +29 | 8/14 −10 | 9/12 −13 +25 | 10/12 −6 | 11/10 −10 +19 | 12/10 −4 +22 −27 | 1/8 |
| Metal Dog 1970 | 2/7 −3 +14 −27 | 3/8 | 7/4 −2 +6 −25 ‖ 5/6 +11 −18 | 6/5 −21 | 7/4 +7 −14 | 8/3 −17 | 9/1 +4 −9 −21 +23 | 10/1 −13 +29 | 10/31 −6 | 11/29 −11 +22 | 12/29 −5 | 1/27 −11 +13 |
| Metal Pig 1971 | 2/25 −4 +17 −28 | 3/27 | 4/26 −2 +10 −25 | 5/25 −29 | 6/23 +6 −21 | 7/23 −24 | 8/21 +3 −17 | 9/20 −20 +28 | 10/20 −14 | 11/18 +3 −6 −19 +21 | 12/18 −12 +25 | 1/17 −6 |

TABLE 22 (CONTINUED)

| Month / Year | 1 | 2 | 3 | 4 | 5 | 6 | 7 | 8 | 9 | 10 | 11 | 12 |
|---|---|---|---|---|---|---|---|---|---|---|---|---|
| Water Rat 1972 | 2/15 * | 3/16 * | 4/14 * | 5/14 * | 6/12 * | 7/11 * | 8/10 * | 9/8 * | 10/8 * | 11/6 * | 12/6 * | 1/5 * / 2/4 * |
| Water Cow 1973 | 3/5 * | 4/4 * | 5/3 * | 6/2 * | 7/1 * | 7/30 * | 8/29 * | 9/27 * | 10/27 * | 11/25 * | 12/25 * | 1/24 * |
| Wood Tiger 1974 | 2/23 * | 3/24 * | 4/23 * | 5/22 * | 6/21 * | 7/20 * | 8/18 * | 9/17 * | 10/16 * | 11/14 * | 12/14 * | 1/12 * |
| Wood Hare 1975 | 2/12 * | 3/13 * | 4/12 * | 5/12 * | 6/10 * | 7/10 * | 8/8 * | 9/6 * / 10/6 * | 11/4 * | 12/3 * | 1/2 * | 2/1 * |
| Fire Dragon 1976 | 3/1 * | 3/31 * | 4/30 -14 | 5/30 * | 6/28 * | 7/28 * | 8/26 * | 9/24 * | 10/24 * | 11/22 * | 12/22 * | 1/20 * |
| Fire Snake 1977 | 2/19 * | 3/20 * | 4/19 * | 5/19 * | 6/17 * | 7/17 * | 8/15 * | 9/14 * | 10/13 -9 +18 -25 | 11/12 -3 +24 | 12/11 -8 +11 +14 | 1/10 -1 +14 -25 |
| Earth Horse 1978 | 2/8 * | 3/9 -1 +6 -24 | 4/8 +10 -18 | 5/8 -21 | 6/6 +5 -14 / 7/6 -17 | 8/4 +1 -10 | 9/3 -13 +28 | 10/3 -6 | 11/1 -10 +22 | 12/1 -3 | 12/30 -8 +14 | 1/29 -2 +17 -27 |
| Earth Sheep 1979 | 2/27 * | 3/29 -25 | 4/27 * | 5/27 * | 6/25 * | 7/25 * | 8/23 * | 9/22 * | 10/22 * | 11/20 * | 12/20 * | 1/18 * |
| Metal Monkey 1980 | 2/17 -3 +20 -27 | 3/17 | 4/16 -2 +13 -25 | 5/15 -29 | 6/13 +9 -22 | 7/13 -24 | 8/11 +5 -17 | 9/10 -20 | 10/9 +1 -13 | 11/8 -17 +25 | 12/8 -11 +28 | 1/7 -5 |
| Metal Bird 1981 | 2/5 -10 +20 | 3/7 -5 +24 -28 / 4/5 | 5/5 -2 +17 -26 | 6/3 -29 | 7/2 +13 -21 | 8/1 -24 | 8/30 +10 -17 | 9/29 -20 | 10/28 +5 -14 | 11/27 -18 +28 | 12/27 -12 | 1/25 +1 -6 |
| Water Dog 1982 | 2/24 -11 +23 | 3/26 -5 | 4/24 -10 +17 | 5/24 -3 | 6/22 -6 +12 -29 | 7/21 | 8/20 -1 +9 -24 | 9/18 -28 | 10/17 +4 -21 | 11/16 +9 -14 | 12/16 -19 | 1/14 +1 -14 |

*An asterisk denotes months for which details of doubled days are unavailable.

| Year | | | | | | | | | | | | | | | | |
|---|---|---|---|---|---|---|---|---|---|---|---|---|---|---|---|---|
| Water Pig 1983 | 2/13 −20 +22 | 3/15 −12 +26 | 4/14 −6 | | 5/13 −10 +21 | 6/12 −3 | 7/11 −6 +17 −29 | 8/9 | | 9/8 −1 +14 −24 | 10/2 −28 | 11/5 +8 −22 | 12/5 −27 +30 | 1/4 −20 | 2/2 +4 −15 | |
| Wood Rat 1984 | 3/3 −20 +26 | 4/2 −13 +30 | 5/2 −6 | | 5/31 −10 +25 | 6/30 −3 | 7/29 −6 +22 −28 | 8/27 −10 +11 | | 9/26 −1 +18 −25 | 10/25 −29 | 11/23 +12 −23 | | 12/23 −28 | 1/21 +4 −22 | |
| Wood Cow 1985 | 2/20 +7 −16 | 3/22 −20 +30 | 4/21 −14 | | 5/20 −17 +24 | 6/19 −10 | 7/18 −13 +21 | 8/17 −6 | | 9/15 −9 +17 | 10/15 −2 | 11/13 −6 +11 −30 | | 12/12 +15 −24 | 1/11 −29 | |
| Fire Tiger 1986 | 2/9 +6 −23 | 3/11 +10 −17 | 4/10 −21 | | 5/9 +3 −14 | 6/8 −17 +29 | 7/8 −10 | 8/6 −13 +26 | 9/5 −6 | 10/4 −9 +21 | 11/3 −2 | 12/2 −7 +15 | | 1/1 −1 +18 −25 | 1/30 −30 | |
| Fire Hare 1987 | 2/28 +9 −24 | 3/30 +14 −16 −29 | 4/28 +2 −21 | | 5/28 +8 −14 | 6/27 −17 | 7/26 +4 −9 −21 +24 | 8/25 −13 | | 9/23 +1 −5 −17 +20 | 10/23 −9 +25 | 11/22 −3 | | 12/31 −7 +18 | 1/20 −2 +22 −26 | |
| Earth Dragon 1988 | 2/18 | 3/19 −1 +13 −25 | 4/17 −28 | | 5/16 +7 −22 | 6/15 −25 | 7/14 +3 −17 | 8/13 −20 +30 | | 9/12 −13 | 10/11 −17 +24 | 11/10 −10 −29 | | 12/10 −3 | 1/8 −9 +20 | |
| Earth Snake 1989 | 2/7 −3 | 3/8 −9 +12 | 4/7 −2 +16 −25 | 5/6 −29 | 6/4 +11 −22 | 7/4 −25 | 8/2 +8 −17 | 9/1 −20 | | 9/30 +4 −13 | 10/30 −17 +28 | 11/29 −11 | | 12/28 −17 +20 | 1/27 −10 +23 | |
| Metal Horse 1990 | 2/26 −4 | 3/27 −9 +16 | 4/26 −2 +20 −25 | | 5/25 −7 +9 −29 | 6/23 +16 −21 | 7/23 −2 +6 −24 | 8/21 +14 −16 −28 | | 9/19 +3 −20 | 10/19 +8 −13 | 11/18 −18 | | 12/17 +1 −12 | 1/6 −17 +23 | |
| Metal Sheep 1991 | 2/15 −11 +26 | 3/17 −5 | 4/15 −9 +20 | | 5/15 −3 | 6/13 −6 +15 −29 | 7/12 | 8/11 −1 +12 −24 | | 9/9 −27 | 10/8 +7 −21 | 11/7 −25 | | 12/6 +1 −19 | 1/5 +4 −13 | 2/4 −18 +26 |

TABLE 22 (CONTINUED)

| Month / Year | 1 | 2 | 3 | 4 | 5 | 6 | 7 | 8 | 9 | 10 | 11 | 12 |
|---|---|---|---|---|---|---|---|---|---|---|---|---|
| Earth Monkey 1992 | 3/5<br>-12<br>+29 | 4/4<br>-6 | 5/3<br>-10<br>+24 | 6/2<br>-3 | 7/1<br>-6<br>+20<br>-29 | 7/30 | 8/29<br>-1<br>+16<br>-24 | 9/27<br>-28 | 10/26<br>+11<br>-21 | 11/25<br>-26 | 12/24<br>+4<br>-20 | 1/23<br>+7<br>-14 |
| Earth Bird 1993 | 2/22<br>-19<br>+29 | 3/24<br>-13 | 4/22<br>-17<br>+23 | 5/22<br>-10<br>+28 | 6/21<br>-2<br>-14<br>+18 | 7/20<br>-6 | 8/18<br>-9<br>+15 | 9/17<br>-2 | 10/16<br>-6<br>+10<br>-28 | 11/14<br>+15<br>-22 | 12/14<br>-27 | 1/12<br>+7<br>-21 |
| Wood Dog 1994 | 2/11<br>+10<br>-15 | 3/13<br>-20 | 4/11<br>+3<br>-14 | 5/11<br>-17<br>+27 | 6/10<br>+10 | 7/9<br>-13<br>+24 | 8/8<br>-6 | 9/6<br>-9<br>+20  10/6<br>-2 | 11/4<br>-6<br>+14<br>-29 | 12/3<br>+18<br>-23 | 1/2<br>-28 | 1/31<br>-22<br>+10 |
| Wood Pig 1995 | 3/2<br>-28 | 3/31<br>+2<br>-21 | 4/30<br>+6<br>-14 | 5/30<br>-17 | 6/28<br>+2<br>-10 | 7/28<br>-13<br>+29 | 8/27<br>-5 | 9/25<br>-9<br>+24 | 10/25<br>-2 | 11/23<br>-6<br>+18<br>-30 | 12/22 | 1/21<br>-6<br>+9<br>-29 |
| Fire Rat 1996 | 2/19<br>+13<br>-23 | 3/20<br>-28 | 4/18<br>+6<br>-21 | 5/18<br>+12<br>-13<br>-25 | 6/16<br>+1<br>-17 | 7/16<br>-20<br>+27 | 8/15<br>-13 | 9/13<br>-16<br>+23 | 10/13<br>-9<br>+28 | 11/12<br>-2<br>-15<br>+16 | 12/11<br>-7<br>+21 | 1/10<br>-1 |
| Fire Cow 1997 | 2/8<br>-7<br>+12<br>-30 | 3/9<br>+16<br>-24 | 4/8<br>-28 | 5/7<br>+10<br>-22 | 6/6<br>-25  7/5<br>+5<br>-17 | 8/4<br>-20 | 9/2<br>+2<br>-13 | 10/2<br>-16<br>+27 | 11/1<br>-10 | 11/30<br>-14<br>+20 | 12/30<br>-8<br>+24 | 1/29<br>-3 |

## THE ELEMENTS OF THE MONTHS

Although the year officially begins in the month of the Dragon (*Dawa Dangpo*, the 1st month), the Jungtsi astrological year begins in the Month of the Tiger, the 11th month of the previous year in the official calendar. This must be borne in mind when monthly elements are being calculated.

The rules are simple:

1. The element of the first astrological month (Tiger) is the son of the element of the year. Thus for a Fire Bird year, the son of Fire is Earth. However, caution is needed: the element Fire should not be attached to a Dragon month (1st month of the official calendar) but to the month of the Tiger (officially the 11th month of the previous year, Fire Monkey).

2. A given element goes with two successive months. In our example, Earth Tiger is followed by Earth Hare.

3. The elements follow each other in the order of production. The son of Earth is Metal, therefore the Earth Hare month is followed by the Metal Dragon month. Dragon, the 1st month of the official calendar is thus Metal, not Earth.

Since there are 5 elements and 12 animals, the same simple distribution is repeated every 10 years. Table 24 (page 173) can be used to calculate the element of a month, bearing in mind the final digit of the Western year.

For example, in 1978 (final digit 8), the Month of the Horse will be Wood. In 1984, it will be Metal. Naturally, it is important to remember the overlap between the Western and Tibetan years; for January 1978, the 12th month will be found in the 7 column.

TABLE 23

## THE TIBETAN MONTHS

| Month name | Period | Name/ Constellation | Indian Name | Common Animal | Tendrel |
|---|---|---|---|---|---|
| Dawa Dangpo 1st Month | February/March | Chu Dawa Tapa Dawa | Māgha | Druk Da Dragon | Consciousness |
| Dawa Nyipa 2nd Month | March/April | Wo Dawa | Phalguna | Trül Da Snake | Name and form |
| Dawa Sumpa 3rd Month | April/May | Nakpa Dawa | Caitra | Te Da Horse | Six senses |
| Dawa Zhipa 4th Month | May/June | Saga Dawa | Vaśākha | Luk Da Sheep | Contact |
| Dawa Ngapa 5th Month | June/July | Nrön Dawa | Jyeṣṭha | Tre Da Monkey | Feeling |
| Dawa Drukpa 6th Month | July/August | Chutö Dawa | Āṣādha | Ja Da Bird | Desire |
| Dawa Dünpa 7th Month | August/September | Droshin Dawa | Śrāvaṇa | Khyi Da Dog | Grasping |
| Dawa Gyepa 8th Month | September/October | Trume Dawa | Bhādra | Pak Da Pig | Becoming |
| Dawa Gupa 9th Month | October/November | Takar Dawa | Aśvinī | Chi Da Rat | Birth |
| Dawa Chupa 10th Month | November/December | Mindruk Dawa | Kārtika | Lang Da Cow | Old age and death |
| Dawa Chuchikpa 11th Month | December/January | Go Dawa | Mṛgaśirā | Tak Da Tiger | Ignorance |
| Dawa Chunyipa 12th Month | January/February | Gyal Dawa | Pauṣya | Yö Da Hare | Karmic formations |

TABLE 24

## MONTHLY ELEMENTS

| Official Month | | Final Digit of Year | | | | | | | | | |
|---|---|---|---|---|---|---|---|---|---|---|---|
| | | 0 | 1 | 2 | 3 | 4 | 5 | 6 | 7 | 8 | 9 |
| 1 | Wood | Dragon | Wood | Fire | Fire | Earth | Earth | Metal | Metal | Water | Water |
| 2 | Wood | Snake | Wood | Fire | Fire | Earth | Earth | Metal | Metal | Water | Water |
| 3 | Fire | Horse | Fire | Earth | Earth | Metal | Metal | Water | Water | Wood | Wood |
| 4 | Fire | Sheep | Fire | Earth | Earth | Metal | Metal | Water | Water | Wood | Wood |
| 5 | Earth | Monkey | Earth | Metal | Metal | Water | Water | Wood | Wood | Fire | Fire |
| 6 | Earth | Bird | Earth | Metal | Metal | Water | Water | Wood | Wood | Fire | Fire |
| 7 | Metal | Dog | Metal | Water | Water | Wood | Wood | Fire | Fire | Earth | Earth |
| 8 | Metal | Pig | Metal | Water | Water | Wood | Wood | Fire | Fire | Earth | Earth |
| 9 | Water | Rat | Water | Wood | Wood | Fire | Fire | Earth | Earth | Metal | Metal |
| 10 | Water | Cow | Water | Wood | Wood | Fire | Fire | Earth | Earth | Metal | Metal |
| 11 | Water | Tiger | Wood | Wood | Fire | Fire | Earth | Earth | Metal | Metal | Water |
| 12 | Water | Hare | Wood | Wood | Fire | Fire | Earth | Earth | Metal | Metal | Water |

# 9

## THE
## TIBETAN DAY
## OR
## "EVERYDAY ASTROLOGY"

### DAYS OF THE WEEK AND MONTH

One of the unique features of Tibetan astrology is the attention paid to the auspicious or inauspicious character of each day. All the factors of Nagtsi and Kartsi astrology so far described in yearly or monthly terms are also considered in determining the characteristics of days. The overall effect of these daily factors is considered before undertaking any activity—travel, work, ritual, and so on.

A distinction must be drawn between the collective and personal levels:

- Certain days are said to be auspicious or inauspicious for certain undertakings, and this applies universally. In this case, the daily energies are judged as either sufficiently good or sufficiently bad for all beings, whatever their personal astrological features.
- At a personal level, the auspicious or inauspicious character of a day is judged by comparing its astrological qualities with those of the individual's natal day.

## Characteristics of the Days of the Week

The seven-day week, in which each day is ruled by a particular planet, is found in Tibet as well as in India, China, and the West—this is an astrological feature common to all the continents of antiquity.

The ruling planet gives the day a particular character. It is also connected with one of the Indian elements representing the energy tone of each day. Days are also associated with the symbol of the ruling planet, with a color, and with advice regarding activities to be undertaken or avoided.

SUNDAY is the day of the Sun, "the planet of the gods" or "the planet of the royal soul." This is an important day for sovereigns and dignitaries.

*Favorable*: Sunday is favorable for royal and official ceremonies, for solemn exchanges, monastic ordination, festivals, art, ornaments, the birth of a son, war, the flying of flags and emblems, work related with fire, the preparation of medicines—and highway robbery!

*Unfavorable*: Sunday is unfavorable for judgments, peace treaties, setting off on a journey, founding a temple, moving house, parting with goods by sale or gift, marriage, funerals, sowing and planting seeds, surgical operations, beginning a piece of writing, and starting a new project.

In general, Sunday is not a very auspicious day and does not favor the success of any undertaking.

MONDAY is the day of the Moon, "the planet of the Nāgas" or "planet of the soul of women."

*Favorable*: Monday is favorable for planting and sowing seeds, irrigation and hydraulic works, the preparation of fermented drinks and medicines, purification, glorious deeds, adopting a child and hiring a servant, rituals, trade, feasts and sacraments, marriage, settling into a new dwelling, medical operations, making incense, building a temple, art, divination and astrology, and rites for driving away negativity and increasing positivity.

*Unfavorable*: Monday is unfavorable for setting off to war, judgments, separations, journeys, funerals, ordination, violent deeds, fire rituals, and physical exercise.

TUESDAY is the day of Mars, "the planet of the Āsuras" or "planet of the soul of men."

*Favorable*: Tuesday is favorable for military operations, conquest and wrathful rituals, sporting activities, banditry, beginning a reign, starting a family, moving house, borrowing money, magic, fire rituals and rituals for removing obstacles, rites such as *Metsa* or "points of fire," and games of chance.

*Unfavorable*: Tuesday is unfavorable for ordination, marriage, sacraments and purifications, giving a name or title, actions connected with death or with the transference of consciousness or *Phowa,* adopting a child, hiring servants, the arts, festivals, building, preparing medicines, sowing and planting, irrigation, trade, contracts, and acts of peace. It is a violent and warlike day and does not favor journeys.

WEDNESDAY is the day of Mercury, "the planet of the Yakṣas" or "planet of the soul of the prince." It is in general a positive day.

*Favorable*: Wednesday is favorable for undertaking journeys but not for ordination. It is favorable for sacraments and commerce, contracts, marriage, naming a son, the increase of glory, hiring servants, planting and irrigation, building a house, temple, or stūpa, digging a well, the arts, funerals and funeral ceremonies, the transference of consciousness (*Phowa*), divination, and astrology. Wednesday is an excellent day for finishing any undertaking, for surgical operations, for the accomplishment of positive actions, and the performance of rituals for dispelling negativities.

*Unfavorable*: Wednesday is unfavorable for disposing of important goods, for gifts, preparing medicines, war, banditry, cremations, and removing the remains of a dead person.

THURSDAY is the day of Jupiter, "the planet of the Bodhi-sattva" or "planet of the souls of Buddhists." It is a good day for spirituality.

*Favorable*: Thursday is favorable for monastic ordination, initiations and sacraments, fire rituals, the practice of mantras and the construction of maṇḍalas, marriage, study and teaching, sowing and planting seeds, preparing medicines and medical practice, making fermented substances, building houses, acquiring a new residence, building stūpas and temples, giving names, activities connected with horses, trade, metal work, rituals of power and rituals for increasing glory, divination, and astrology.

*Unfavorable*: Thursday is unfavorable for armies departing for war, funerals, building or repairing a roof, imprisonment (the most negative of results are to be looked for if imprisonment begins on this day), art, and magical practices. One should not leave one's animals alone on a Thursday.

FRIDAY is the day of Venus, "the day of magic power" or "day of the soul of medicine."

*Favorable*: Friday is favorable for teaching, rituals for overcoming obstacles, making offerings to deities, building temples and stūpas, trade and contracts, agricultural work and the planting of trees, preparing medicines, surgical operations, making incense, astrology, work in stones and precious metals, architectural and hydraulic works, journeys, and entering into intimate relations.

*Unfavorable*: Friday is unfavorable for disputes and negotiating claims, banditry, burial and the disposal of the dead, slaughtering animals, and the transference of consciousness.

SATURDAY is the day of Saturn. It is known as "the lame day," "the neutral day," and "day of the souls of children."

*Favorable*: Saturday is favorable for building a house, taking up residence in a new place, magical operations, long-life rituals, agricultural and hydraulic work, acquiring animals, astrological calculations, and banditry.

*Unfavorable*: Saturday is unfavorable for setting off to war, work with fire, building walls, solemn declarations, giving names and titles, beginning a reign, ordination, ritual offerings and sacraments, medical operations and making medicines, long journeys, plowing, disposing of goods or animals, making expenditures and gifts of all sorts, divination, the construction of temples and stūpas, and exhibitions.

Saturday is a favorable day for all sorts of acquisitions, but one must never let them out of one's house or leave them unattended.

## Relation between Days of the Week and Natal Animal

This section is concerned with the relations that obtain between the native, represented by the animal of the natal year, and the planet of the day. Certain days of the week will be favorable and others unfavorable for any given sign.

There are three important combinations:

1. The Day of the La is the day on which the individual's vital spirit is at its best. This will be an excellent day for any sort of activity, particularly spiritual activity.
2. The Day of Vitality (*Sok*) is the day on which vital en-

TABLE 25

### THE DAYS OF THE WEEK

| Tibetan Day | Western Day | Planet | Symbol | Element | Color |
|---|---|---|---|---|---|
| 1. Za Nyima | Sunday | Nyima/Sun | Solar disk | Fire | Pink |
| 2. Za Dawa | Monday | Dawa/Moon | Crescent | Water | Pale yellow |
| 3. Za Mikmar | Tuesday | Mikmar/Mars | Red eye | Fire | Dark red |
| 4. Za Lhakpa | Wednesday | Lhakpa/Mercury | Hand | Water | Turquoise |
| 5. Za Phurbu | Thursday | Phurbu/Jupiter | Dagger | Wind | Gold |
| 6. Za Pasang | Friday | Pasang/Venus | Garter | Earth | Multicolored |
| 7. Za Penpa | Saturday | Penpa/Saturn | Faggot | Earth | Yellow/Dark red |

ergy is at its highest. This will be an excellent day, particularly if much energy has to be expended.

3. The Day of Obstacles (*Gek*) is the day on which planetary energy is against the individual and creates obstacles. It is best not to undertake important activities and not to travel on this day.

Each animal of the twelve-year cycle is thus connected with an excellent day and a day of obstructions (see table 26, page 180). If the day of birth corresponds with one of those three days, there is a particular meaning for the individual:

• If the individual was born on a La day, he or she will be intelligent and resourceful.
• If the individual was born on a Day of Vitality, his or her life will be well-omened. These are both signs of long life.
• If the individual was born on a Day of Obstacles, he or she will meet hindrances. This also sometimes indicates a short life.

If you are a Monkey born on a Friday or a Thursday, congratulations! These two days will be generally favorable for you. Tuesday, however, will be your worst day.

## General Character of the Thirty Days of the Month

The 30 days of the month are lunar days. In one lunar day, the moon travels 12° from the sun. The days of the month are therefore related to the different phases of the moon. In the course of the month, the moon makes different aspects to the sun, and these may be either favorable or unfavorable. This is what gives the days their particular character. In the Indian, Chinese, and Arab traditions, there are lists showing the characteristics of the phases of the moon and the lunar days, and similar lists are also found in Western magic.

The following list shows the sun-moon distance in degrees, the corresponding aspects in Western astrology, and the general characteristics of each day.

179

TABLE 26

## RELATIONS BETWEEN NATAL ANIMAL AND DAYS OF THE WEEK

| Quality of Day | NATAL ANIMAL | | | | | |
|---|---|---|---|---|---|---|
| | *Rat* | *Cow* | *Tiger* | *Hare* | *Dragon* | *Snake* |
| Excellent | Wednesday | Saturday | Thursday | Thursday | Sunday | Tuesday |
| Good | Tuesday | Wednesday | Saturday | Saturday | Wednesday | Friday |
| Bad | Saturday | Thursday | Friday | Friday | Thursday | Wednesday |

| Quality of Day | NATAL ANIMAL | | | | | |
|---|---|---|---|---|---|---|
| | *Horse* | *Sheep* | *Monkey* | *Bird* | *Dog* | *Pig* |
| Excellent | Tuesday | Friday | Friday | Friday | Monday | Wednesday |
| Good | Friday | Monday | Thursday | Thursday | Wednesday | Tuesday |
| Bad | Wednesday | Thursday | Tuesday | Tuesday | Thursday | Saturday |

**1st Day (0°–12°)**

Favorable day, excellent for offerings and petitions, for taking vows, for religious practices and obtaining what one desires. Excellent for marriage, acquisitions, teachings, blessings, initiations, and construction.

**2nd Day (12°–24°)**

Favorable day—the same qualities and activities as the first day, but unproductive. Nothing should be done between midnight and 3:00 A.M.

**3rd Day (24°–36°) Semisextile (30°) and semiquintile (36°)**

Favorable day for starting a building, for vigorous activities, and for obtaining a high position.

**4th Day (36°–48°) Semisquare (45°)**

A generally unfruitful day. There is a need to employ a great deal of skill and intelligence in order to avoid being defeated in competition.

**5th Day (48°–60°)**

This is a day of very bad reactions. Failure in moral and virtuous actions, immorality.

**6th Day (60°–72°) Sextile (60°)**

Inauspicious for journeys.

**7th Day (72°–84°) Quintile (72°)**

Auspicious for journeys.

**8th Day (84°–96°) Square (90°)**

This is a day of emotional disturbance, very bad reactions, violence, and anger. It is unfavorable to morality and promotes evil acts.

**9th Day (96°–108°)**

This is an excellent day for long journeys, marriage, blessings, teachings and transmissions of power (initiations), and all major undertakings. It is good for building and ceremonies.

**10th Day (108°–120°) Beginning of Trine (120°)**

This is a fruitful day for journeys and excellent for marriage, acquisitions, teaching, initiations, blessings, ceremonies, offerings, and construction. Masculine energy is at its strongest on this day.

**11th Day (120°–132°) Trine (120°)**

An excellent day for firm action, for beginning a building, or for obtaining a high position. Spiritual activities are favored.

**12th Day (132°–144°)**

This is a day of wisdom.

**13th Day (144°–156°) Quincunx (150°)**

This is a day of speed, clarity, skill, and intelligence. Skillful actions are successful.

**14th Day (156°–168°)**

This is not a favorable day for journeys.

**15th Day (168°–180°) Opposition (180°) = Full Moon**

This is a bad day for journeys. It is an unproductive day on which many expected developments fail to take place. Nothing should be attempted between midnight and 3:00 A.M. This is a powerful day for meditation.

**16th Day (180°–168°)**

This a day of competition, speed, clarity, skill, and intelligence. Generally, it is a good day.

**17th Day (168°–156°)**

This a dangerous day on which there are very bad reactions. Obstacles are placed before morality and virtue.

**18th Day (156°–144°) Quincunx (150°)**

This is also a dangerous day and unfavorable for morality.

**19th Day (144°–132°)**

This is a moderately good day for beginning anything. It is quite favorable for marriage, acquisitions, teachings, initiations, blessings, construction, and ceremonies.

**20th Day (132°–120°) Trine (120°)**

This is an excellent day for firm and vigorous actions, for starting a building, or for obtaining a high position. It is also favorable for contracts.

**21st Day (120°–108°)**

This is a bad day for journeys.

**22nd Day (108°–96°)**

This is a favorable day for journeys.

**23rd Day (96°–84°) Square (90°)**

This is a day on which to cultivate firm and careful action. It is favorable for beginning a construction or obtaining promotion.

**24th Day (84°–72°)**

This is an excellent day for journeys. Activities are fruitful on this day. It is favorable for marriage, acquisitions, teachings, initiations, and blessings. Construction and ceremonies are favored.

**25th Day (72°–60°) Sextile (60°)**

This is a fruitful day for journeys. On this day, feminine energy is at its strongest. It is a day of speed, clarity, skill, and intelligence and brings success in competitions.

**26th Day (60°–48°)**

This is a favorable day for offerings and making requests to high personages. It is good for taking vows and for spiritual practices and religious ceremonies. On this day, one obtains one's desires.

**27th Day (48°–36°) Semisquare (45°)**
This is a day of wisdom.
**28th Day (36°–24°) Semisextile (30°)**
This day brings success to activities.
**29th Day (24°–12°)**
This is not a favorable day for journeys.
**30th Day (12°–0°) Conjunction (0°) = New Moon**
This is not a favorable day for journeys.

## Favorable and Unfavorable Days for Haircuts

For the Tibetans, as for the Indians, there is a direct relationship between the hair and the vital energy. It is therefore necessary to choose an auspicious day for cutting the hair and to avoid certain other days:

- The 4th, 6th, and 17th days of the month should be avoided, as should the full moon, when the vital energy is at the crown of the head, and the new moon (30th day). Cutting one's hair on those days will bring a loss of vitality.
- Favorable days are the 8th for longevity; the 9th for attractive energy; the 10th for increasing one's magnetism; the 11th for intelligence; and the 26th and 27th for good luck.

## Auspicious and Inauspicious Days for the Individual

Certain days of the month are auspicious or inauspicious for the individual when considered in conjunction with the ruling animal of the birth year. For each sign, there are three favorable days each month (basis, power, and success) and three unfavorable days (obstacles, disturbances, and enemies). If one knows one's natal animal, one can consult table 27 (page 184) to determine these days.

The characteristics of the days indicate the successes or obstacles that one will meet in one's activities. New projects should

TABLE 27

## AUSPICIOUS AND INAUSPICIOUS DAYS BY ANIMAL

|  | Rat | Cow | Tiger | Hare | Dragon | Snake |
|---|---|---|---|---|---|---|
| Basis | 20 | 17 | 5 | 11 | 3 | 13 |
| Power | 6 | 14 | 27 | 27 | 12 | 12 |
| Success | 3 | 12 | 9 | 12 | 17 | 6 |
| Obstacle | 26 | 12 | 14 | 26 | 8 | 8 |
| Disturbance | 10 | 18 | 12 | 25 | 9 | 9 |
| Enemy | 23 | 5 | 3 | 18 | 11 | 6 |

|  | Horse | Sheep | Monkey | Bird | Dog | Pig |
|---|---|---|---|---|---|---|
| Basis | 17 | 8 | 8 | 14 | 9 | 2 |
| Power | 12 | 1 | 1 | 7 | 27 | 8 |
| Success | 6 | 2 | 2 | 25 | 5 | 11 |
| Obstacle | 20 | 20 | 9 | 3 | 11 | 26 |
| Disturbance | 5 | 5 | 10 | 11 | 3 | 3 |
| Enemy | 27 | 27 | 17 | 24 | 12 | 12 |

be started and important tasks finished on days of success, for accomplishment is assured. On enemy days, all discussion, competition, argument, or battle will be lost.

When the weekly and monthly cycles are contrary to each other on the same day for a given individual, the weekly cycle is considered stronger than the monthly (planetary energies are stronger than monthly energies). Nevertheless, the two influences are complementary, and both must be taken into account in fine-tuning one's judgment.

## DAILY ASTROLOGICAL CYCLES

### In Jungtsi Astrology

Tibetan almanacs give a number of factors for each day, some of them drawn from Jungtsi astrology and others from Kartsi. It is best to study both in coming to a full understanding of the character of a day, and then to create a synthesis.

Certain factors derive from daily combinations and others must be examined independently. Each day also possesses a general tone that can be felt at the collective level, as well as a negative or positive quality for each individual.

Clearly, it would be a tiresome business to perform such analyses every day—and there would be little time left for anything else. However, it is useful to perform these calculation for important days in our lives: choice of marriage day, the day for laying the foundations of a house, the best days for making important decisions, signing contracts, setting off on journeys, and so on.

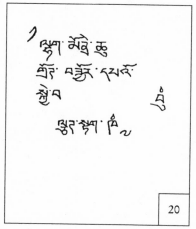

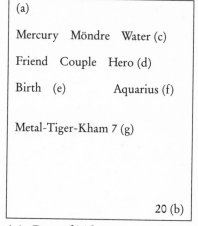

(a)

Mercury   Möndre   Water (c)

Friend   Couple   Hero (d)

Birth   (e)                    Aquarius (f)

Metal-Tiger-Kham 7 (g)

20 (b)

*Page of an almanac showing all the astrological configurations for 2/20/85 (Tibetan New Year). [Translator's note:* lags *in the above should be* lcags.]

(a) *Day of Tibetan month*
(b) *Western date*
(c) *Planet, constellation of day, and combined energy of both*
(d) *Key words for aspects and astrological junctures*
(e) *Nidana of day (link in the chain of interdependent origination)*
(f) *Sign where the moon enters*
(g) *Animal-element combination + Mewa + Parkha*

## Daily Animal-Element Combination

Each day is associated with an animal and an element. The daily animal is simple to work out: since there are 30 days in a month, it takes two months to complete a cycle of 60 animals (5 × 12). The animal for the 1st day of the 1st month is therefore the same as that for the 1st day of the 3rd month, and so on.

According to our text:

> The six male months (1st, 3rd, 5th, 7th, 9th, and 11th) begin with the Day of the Tiger. The full moon (15th day) falls on the Day of the Dragon, and the new moon (30th day) falls on the Day of the Sheep. The six female months (2nd, 4th, 6th, 8th, 10th, and 12th) begin on the Day of the Monkey, and the new moon falls on the Day of the Cow. The 1st, 13th, and 25th days (by twelves) have the same animal.

The daily element is also easily established. It depends on two simple rules:

1. The elements change each day in their order of production, i.e., Wood—Fire—Earth—Metal—Water, and so on.
2. The element of the 1st day of the month is the son of the element of that month. For example, in a Fire month the 1st day will be Earth, the 2nd Metal, the 3rd Water, and so on.

Because of the numerical rules that connect years, months, and days, the same cycle is repeated every ten years. When a day is doubled, it retains the same animal-element combination, whereas on missed days the cycle follows the normal course.

| Day | 1 | 2 | 3 | 4 | 4a | 5 | (6) |
|---|---|---|---|---|---|---|---|
| Cycle | Wood Tiger | Fire Hare | Earth Dragon | Metal Snake | — | Water Horse | Wood Sheep |
| | | | | Double day | | | Missed day |

Using table 28 (page 188), the animal-element combination for any day can quickly be determined. To use this table correctly, it is only necessary to consider the final digit—thus 1958, 1968, and 1978 have the same daily cycle. It must be remembered, however, that the Tibetan year overlaps the Western year: 1978 means February 1978 to January 1979. It is therefore important to check when the Tibetan year begins and ends.

For example, to find the combination for December 25, 1984, first convert the date to the Tibetan calendar—12/25/1984 = 3rd day of the 11th Tibetan month. Consulting the table for column 4 gives us Earth Tiger for the 1st day of the 11th month. Thus the 2nd day is Metal Hare, and the 3rd day, which is what we are looking for, is Water Dragon.

The characteristics of the days ruled by animal signs are as follows:

DAY OF THE RAT

Favorable for betrothals, the birth of a son, trade and important steps, the discovery of treasure, theft, and rituals for rain.

Fleshly contact should be avoided, as should eating meat, divination and exorcism, racing, and starting journeys.

DAY OF THE COW

Favorable for undertaking onerous tasks, roadworks or construction, battles, and efforts for the resolution of important problems. Good for journeys and the remarrying of widows.

Unfavorable for commerce and slander, spirituality and taking monastic vows, rituals for rain or rituals against negativities.

DAY OF THE TIGER

Favorable for prosperity rituals, art, building, fire rituals, and journeys toward the East or West.

Unfavorable for marriage and public ceremonies, medical treatment, ablutions, and theft.

DAY OF THE HARE

Favorable for funerals, royal coronations, and trade in animals.

TABLE 28

## ANIMAL SIGNS FOR DAYS

| Year with final digit | | | | 0 | 1 | 2 | 3 | 4 | 5 | 6 | 7 | 8 | 9 |
|---|---|---|---|---|---|---|---|---|---|---|---|---|---|
| Month | Day | Animal | | | | | | Element | | | | | |
| 1 | 1 | Tiger | | Fire | Fire | Earth | Earth | Metal | Metal | Water | Water | Wood | Wood |
| | 15 | Dragon | | Wood | Wood | Fire | Fire | Earth | Earth | Metal | Metal | Water | Water |
| | 30 | Sheep | | Wood | Wood | Fire | Fire | Earth | Earth | Metal | Metal | Water | Water |
| 2 | 1 | Monkey | | Fire | Fire | Earth | Earth | Metal | Metal | Water | Water | Wood | Wood |
| | 15 | Dog | | Wood | Wood | Fire | Fire | Earth | Earth | Metal | Metal | Water | Water |
| | 30 | Cow | | Wood | Wood | Fire | Fire | Fire | Earth | Metal | Metal | Water | Water |
| 3 | 1 | Tiger | | Earth | Earth | Metal | Metal | Water | Water | Wood | Wood | Fire | Fire |
| | 15 | Dragon | | Fire | Fire | Earth | Earth | Metal | Metal | Water | Water | Wood | Wood |
| | 30 | Sheep | | Fire | Fire | Earth | Earth | Metal | Metal | Water | Water | Wood | Wood |
| 4 | 1 | Monkey | | Earth | Earth | Metal | Metal | Water | Water | Wood | Wood | Fire | Fire |
| | 15 | Dog | | Fire | Fire | Earth | Earth | Metal | Metal | Water | Water | Wood | Wood |
| | 30 | Cow | | Fire | Fire | Earth | Earth | Metal | Metal | Water | Water | Wood | Wood |
| 5 | 1 | Tiger | | Metal | Metal | Water | Water | Wood | Wood | Fire | Fire | Earth | Earth |
| | 15 | Dragon | | Earth | Earth | Metal | Metal | Water | Water | Wood | Wood | Fire | Fire |
| | 30 | Sheep | | Earth | Earth | Metal | Metal | Water | Water | Wood | Wood | Fire | Fire |

| | | | | | | | | | | | | |
|---|---|---|---|---|---|---|---|---|---|---|---|---|
| 6 | 1 | Monkey | Metal | Metal | Water | Water | Wood | Wood | Fire | Fire | Earth | Earth |
| | 15 | Dog | Earth | Earth | Metal | Metal | Water | Water | Wood | Wood | Fire | Fire |
| | 30 | Cow | Earth | Earth | Metal | Metal | Water | Water | Wood | Wood | Fire | Fire |
| 7 | 1 | Tiger | Water | Water | Wood | Wood | Fire | Fire | Earth | Earth | Metal | Metal |
| | 15 | Dragon | Metal | Metal | Water | Water | Wood | Wood | Fire | Fire | Earth | Earth |
| | 30 | Sheep | Metal | Metal | Water | Water | Wood | Wood | Fire | Fire | Earth | Earth |
| 8 | 1 | Monkey | Water | Water | Wood | Wood | Fire | Fire | Earth | Earth | Metal | Metal |
| | 15 | Dog | Metal | Metal | Water | Water | Wood | Wood | Fire | Fire | Earth | Earth |
| | 30 | Cow | Metal | Metal | Water | Water | Wood | Wood | Fire | Fire | Earth | Earth |
| 9 | 1 | Tiger | Wood | Wood | Fire | Fire | Earth | Earth | Metal | Metal | Water | Water |
| | 15 | Dragon | Water | Water | Wood | Wood | Fire | Fire | Earth | Earth | Metal | Metal |
| | 30 | Sheep | Water | Water | Wood | Wood | Fire | Fire | Earth | Earth | Metal | Metal |
| 10 | 1 | Monkey | Wood | Wood | Fire | Fire | Earth | Earth | Metal | Metal | Water | Water |
| | 15 | Dog | Water | Water | Wood | Wood | Fire | Fire | Earth | Earth | Metal | Metal |
| | 30 | Cow | Water | Water | Wood | Wood | Fire | Fire | Earth | Earth | Metal | Metal |
| 11 | 1 | Tiger | Wood | Fire | Fire | Earth | Earth | Metal | Metal | Water | Water | Wood |
| | 15 | Dragon | Water | Wood | Wood | Fire | Fire | Earth | Earth | Metal | Metal | Water |
| | 30 | Sheep | Water | Wood | Wood | Fire | Earth | Earth | Earth | Metal | Metal | Water |
| 12 | 1 | Monkey | Wood | Fire | Fire | Earth | Earth | Metal | Metal | Water | Water | Wood |
| | 15 | Dog | Water | Wood | Wood | Fire | Fire | Earth | Earth | Metal | Metal | Water |
| | 30 | Cow | Water | Wood | Wood | Fire | Fire | Earth | Earth | Metal | Metal | Water |

Unfavorable for magic, rituals for prosperity, roadworks or irrigation works, festivals, wars, and the training of wild animals.

DAY OF THE DRAGON

Favorable for religious practice, consecrations and monastic ordination, the construction of religious buildings, rituals for the removal of negative forces, and the function of government.

Unfavorable for ploughing, rituals for rain, navigation and crossing mountain passes, journeys, surgical operations, war, mourning, and theft.

DAY OF THE SNAKE

Favorable for making gifts and loans, for ritual offerings to the Nāgas, for convalescents' first outings, and for journeys toward the South.

Unfavorable for felling trees, work connected with water and earth (which may provoke the Nāgas), funerals, medical care, marriage, mourning the dead, commerce, and journeys toward the North, East or West.

DAY OF THE HORSE

Auspicious for projects, festivals, friendly and international relations, war, judgments, and rituals for praising the gods.

Unfavorable for funerals and cutting the hair, trading in horses, marriage, important requests, racing, the manufacture of weapons, and litigation. Contact with blood should be avoided.

DAY OF THE SHEEP

Favorable for honorific ceremonies, household work, work connected with the earth, marriage, and the disposal of animals.

Unfavorable for medicine and operations, war, monastic ordination, rituals for rain, and important acts and petitions.

DAY OF THE MONKEY

Favorable for all sorts of amusement: festivals, sport, theatre, music, and games of chance; favorable also for marriage and funerals, rituals for rain and removing negativities, for planting trees and journeys toward the East or North.

Unfavorable for assuming important responsibilities, government acts, and theft.

DAY OF THE BIRD

Excellent for the preparation of medicines, lending aid, sales, important requests, the recitation of wrathful mantras, rituals for rain or fire, and growing plants.

Large festivals should be avoided, as should shows, gifts, magic rituals, and rituals for removing negativities, the manufacture of weapons, secret deliberations, and virtuous acts.

DAY OF THE DOG

Favorable for prosperity rituals, prayer, manufacture, the birth of a son, critics.

Bad day for cutting or washing the hair (such acts will become curses), marriage, sowing seeds, rituals for rain, household work, war, theft, violence, and important requests.

DAY OF THE PIG

Favorable for transmissions of power, welcoming ceremonies, and rituals for rain.

Contact with earth should be avoided, as should painting and rituals against negativity. Studies should not be commenced.

## Individual Interpretations

Each person can interpret this daily combination by relating it to the natal chart. This interpretation concerns two factors:

1.  In the natal horoscope, when the animal-element combination ruling the natal day has been determined, it is then compared with the animal-element combination for the natal year.

    • If the two animals are the same, the quality associated with the animal is strengthened.

191

- If the two animals are in harmony, this means there is a good balance between these two components of the personality. However, far greater importance attaches to the animal of the natal year than to the animal of the natal day. The latter indicates a certain nuance of personality and allows greater subtlety of judgment.
- If the two animals are not in harmony, this means a conflict in the personality, although the animal of the natal year still dominates.
- Elements are compared as follows: Their relationships are studied as elements in the natal day and natal year. If there is a mother-relationship, the element energy is excellent and gives strength to the individual. If there is a friend-relationship, the combination is again favorable. If there is an Earth-Earth or Water-Water connection, the relationship is good. If there is a son-relationship, the combination is neither good nor bad. The relationships Fire-Fire, Metal-Metal, and Wood-Wood are not good. An enemy-relationship denotes a bad element situation.

2. In order to determine the favorable or unfavorable prognostications of a certain day for a given person, both the animal and the element of that day are compared with those of the person's natal year. The interpretation follows the same reasoning:

- If the animals are harmonious, the day is favorable.
- If the animals are not harmonious, the day is not good and important activities should not be undertaken, nor important decisions made.
- If the animals are the same, judgment becomes a matter of subtlety and prudence is advised.
- The relations between elements follow the above rules. The individual will have more or less energy and will be more or less able to act successfully in accordance with this relationship.

## The Daily Mewa

Each day is associated with a particular Mewa. Here the Mewas follow the order White 1, Black 2, Blue 3, Green 4, and so on, rather than the opposite order as used in yearly calculations.

In a double day only one Mewa rules, but when a day is missed in the course of a month, it still has a Mewa:

Day:    1   2   3   4   4a   5   6   7   (8)   9   10   .   .   .
Mewa:   4   5   6   7   7    8   9   1    2    3    4   .   .   .

Working out the Mewa is simple. There are 30 days in a month and there are 9 series of Mewas. Every 90 days—that is, every 3 months—the same Mewa reappears. Since the year has 360 days, this rule applies to each year.

TABLE 29

### MEWAS OF DAYS

| Month | 1st Day | 15th Day | 30th Day |
|---|---|---|---|
| 2   5   8   11 | White 1 | White 6 | Blue 3 |
| 3   6   9   12 | Green 4 | Red 9 | White 6 |
| 1   4   7   10 | Red 7 | Blue 3 | Red 9 |

Returning to our example of 12/25/84, the 3rd day of the 11th Tibetan month, the 1st day of this month is White 1 and the 2nd day is Black 2. The Mewa of this day is therefore Blue 3.

INTERPRETING THE DAILY MEWA

The daily Mewa indicates certain activities that should be undertaken or avoided.

*White 1.* One should not teach small children to walk or let them out of the house to run. On the other hand, this Mewa is excellent for bathing, purification, and ritual offerings to deities, particularly the invocation and honoring of the Nāgas.

*Black 2.* One should avoid going out or traveling at night, weeping or mourning, marrying or engaging in ceremonies such as prayer rituals. However, this Mewa is good for performing magic rituals to dispel negative influences and obstacles, and offerings can be made to spirits of the *Düd, Mamo,* and *Shin* classes.

*Blue 3.* Negative day for felling trees, cutting wood, and all activities that disturb the Water element (irrigation, dams, and so on), as well as for marriage. Good for offering *tormas* (ritual cakes), offering medicines to the Nāgas, and performing medical rituals in connection with the local deities, such as the Nāgas, the *Sadak* or Lords of the Earth, the *Nyen,* and the *Tsen.*

*Green 4.* On this day it is advised that one should not let a young child out of the house, teach him to walk, or take him outside. A widow should not wash her hair. It is a good day for all medical activities: making medicines and giving medical treatments. Tormas can be offered to the eight Nāga families.

*Yellow 5.* One should not dig the soil, plough, participate in festivals, or buy dogs. One should not purchase goods in monasteries or from monks. This day is favorable for presenting petitions to authorities, repairing a religious building, consecrations, ordinations, and all sorts of virtuous acts. It is a good day to start teaching the Dharma.

*White 6.* One should not complain or lament on one's own account, sing the praises of others, fight, or reveal one's own weakness. One should avoid places where people are weeping and abstain from provoking conflicts and litigation. However, this is a good day for praying to the gods, for prosperity rituals, confession and purification, bathing, going out, traveling, moving house, and getting married.

*Red 7.* It is not good to cook red meat, to sell meat, or to take animals to slaughter. Belligerent acts should be avoided, as well as military action and theft. One should avoid using fire. It is a

favorable day for the propitiation of planetary forces, the invocation of the *Mu* spirits, and making ritual offerings to local
deities.

**White 8.** It is bad to burn food or foul refuse, or handle soiled
objects, for these acts will affect the vitality. One should not
mourn or allow oneself to become weak. It is a good day for
celebrating a wedding, bathing, purifying oneself, confessing the
breaking of vows (*samaya*), performing the smoke purification
(*sangchö*), reading prayers of blessing, and making offerings to
the Dharma Protectors.

**Red 9.** It is bad to entrust anyone with a mission, to send en-
voys, and to pay or lose money. An old dying man symbolizes
that the family's prosperity is exhausted. On the other hand, it
is good for recovering debts, receiving money, performing rituals for prosperity and longevity, and receiving initiation for
long-life practice.

INDIVIDUAL INTERPRETATION

In order to judge the value of the daily Mewa for a particular
individual, the element associated with the daily Mewa must be
compared with the element for the natal year. For this purpose,
the usual four types of relationship are used. For example, if the
daily Mewa is Black 2 and the individual's Natal Mewa is Red 7,
the Water-Water relationship should be studied. Since Water is
the enemy of Fire, this will be an unfavorable day for the individual. If, on the other hand, the Natal Mewa is Green 4, the day
will be very favorable, since Water is the mother of Wood.

The Tibetans make protective drawings to counteract the disturbing effects of the Mewas, and these are carried as talismans:

| | |
|---|---|
| White 1 | A white man and a white dog |
| Black 2 | A black dog and a masculine attribute |
| Blue 3 | A snake perching on an elephant |
| Green 4 | A white monkey surmounted by a red dog |
| Yellow 5 | A board pierced by a thorn |
| White 6 | A snake moving on its shadow |

Red 7      The medicine god riding a water buffalo

White 8    Four horns

Red 9      A king riding a pig

## The Daily Parkha

Each day has its own Parkha. The Parkhas follow each other in male order: Li-Khön-Da-Khen-Kham-Kin-Tsin-Zön. On a double day, the same Parkha applies, and missed days also have a Parkha.

| Day | 1 | 2 | 3 | 3a | 4 | 5 | 6 | 7 | (8) | 9 |
|-----|---|---|---|----|----|---|---|---|-----|---|
| Parkha | Li | Khön | Da | | Khen | Kham | Kin | Tsin | Zön | Li |
| | | | Double Day | | | | | | Missed Day | |

The rule for working out the daily Parkha is simple. There are 8 Parkhas and 30 days in a month. Every 4 months, therefore—every 120 days—the same Parkha rules. Since the year has 360 days (missing days are counted in the cycle), the same cycle is repeated each year.

TABLE 30

### DAILY PARKHAS

| Month | | | 1ˢᵗ Day | 15ᵗʰ Day | 30ᵗʰ Day |
|-------|---|---|---------|----------|----------|
| 3 | 7 | 11 | Li | Tsin | Kin |
| 12 | 4 | 8 | Tsin | Kham | Khen |
| 1 | 5 | 9 | Kham | Da | Khön |
| 2 | 6 | 10 | Da | Li | Zön |

For example, to determine the Parkha for 12/25/84, which is the 3rd day of the Tibetan 11th month, check the table for the 1st day of the 11th month, which is the Parkha Li. The 2nd day is therefore Khön and the 3rd day is Da.

INTERPRETING THE DAILY PARKHA

Like the Mewas, the daily Parkhas are good for certain activities and unfavorable for others.

*Li Day.* Smelting metal in a clay crucible, making fire offerings, painting, and playing chess are harmonious activities. One should avoid marrying, washing a corpse, and stealing.

*Khön Day.* Cutting wood and performing rituals of exorcism or the ceremony of the "door of the earth" are advised. On the other hand, one must not fight, bathe, lay the foundation stone of a building, or bury a corpse.

*Da Day.* It is good to travel toward the East, to work in that direction, to take oaths of friendship, to hunt, steal, and cut wood. However, it is inauspicious to invest money, lead troops, or burn a leper's corpse.

*Khen Day.* This is a favorable day for meeting important people, for performing virtuous acts, for the "door of the earth" ritual, and making a "Gyalpo demon trap." It is inauspicious for laying the foundation stone of a house, participating in a festival, and buying or selling a dog. If a person is ill, he or she should not go to the upper floor of a house, sleep in a temple, or invoke the Gyalpo spirits.

*Kham Day.* This is a good day for making offerings to the Nāgas and gods, for causing hailstorms, working in iron, and performing rituals to ward off negativities. It is strongly advised not to cross great rivers, go fishing, build canals or waterways, change the course of a river, make promises, fight, or settle in wild places.

*Kin Day.* It is good to pray to the local deities, to practice the Dharma and perform rituals from the Phurba cycle to ward off negativities, to train horses and cattle, build a house or lay its foundations. It is bad to recite texts, arrange an official interview, begin an inauguration ceremony, or buy or sell anything at all.

*Tsin Day.* It is good to invoke the local deities, plant trees, lay the foundations of a house, and take oaths of loyalty or friendship.

*Zön Day.* It is good to recite mantras, to perform wrathful rituals for warding off negativities, and to treat the insane. It is bad to make a mill wheel, to give a party or entertainment, and to amuse oneself. It is also bad to make promises of friendship.

As with the Mewas, most of the advice associated with the Parkhas is of a ritual nature. Each Parkha is connected with a class of deities or spirits who must not be disturbed, injured, or provoked. Thus, Tsin is the Parkha of the element Wood and the Nyen spirits who live in trees are associated with this Parkha. This is why it is not advisable to fell trees on a Tsin day, for this would provoke the vengeance of the Nyen, who are responsible for certain dangerous illnesses.

The following protective drawings are used as protective talismans to dispel the disturbances or bad energies of the Parkhas.

| | |
|---|---|
| Li Day | A *makara* or sea monster on the head of an elephant |
| Khön Day | A scorpion on the head of a carpenter |
| Da Day | A snake on the head of a murderer |
| Khen Day | A pig on the head of a leper |
| Kham Day | An elephant on the head of a thin barren woman |
| Kin Day | A man with a harelip and nails in his head |
| Tsin Day | A fox on the head of a blacksmith |
| Zön Day | A lizard on the head of a madman |

## In Kartsi Astrology

These are the elements of Indian astrology adopted in the Kālacakra system. The two main factors considered are the planets and the twenty-seven lunar constellations through which the moon travels in the course of its monthly journey. Kartsi astrology studies both the elements attributed to these and the relationships between planets and constellations, upon which are based various sets of predictions that determine the good or bad qualities of a day.

## THE PLANETARY ELEMENTS
## AND THE DAILY GYUKAR

As we have seen, each day of the week is ruled by a planet, which is associated with a particular element. At the same time, the moon travels through one or two gyukar each day, and these gyukar are also associated with particular elements. The relationship between the planetary element and the gyukar element can be more or less harmonious. This combination of elements is the most important factor in daily Kartsi predictions.

It will be recalled that the associations shown in table 31 hold between elements on the one hand and constellations and planets on the other. The three excellent combinations are as follows.

Earth-Earth, the Combination of Accomplishment. This portends perfection and acquisition. It indicates the realization of everything one thinks of or desires. It is excellent for laying the foundations of a house.

Water-Water, the Combination of Nectar. This portends the growth of vital energy and longevity. It is excellent for re-

TABLE 31

### ELEMENT CHARACTERISTICS
### OF PLANETS AND CONSTELLATIONS

| Element | Planet and day | Constellations |
|---------|----------------|----------------|
| Fire | Sun (Sunday) Mars (Tuesday) | Dranye, Mindruk, Gyal, Chu, Dre, Saga, Trumtö |
| Wind (Air) | Jupiter (Thursday) | Takar, Go, Nabso, Wo, Mezhi, Nakpa, Sari |
| Water | Moon (Monday) Mercury (Wednesday) | Lak, Kak, Nup, Chutö, Möndre, Trume, Namdru |
| Earth | Saturn (Saturday) Venus (Friday) | Narma, Lhatsam, Nrön, Drozhin/Jizhin, Chume, Möndru |

ceiving initiations or performing long-life practices. It also encourages the development of personal capacity (*wang thang*).

*Water-Earth*, the Combination of Youth. This brings great and lasting good luck.

The three good combinations are:

*Fire-Fire*, the Combination of Progress. This is favorable for growth and progress, and encourages the acquisition of the necessities of life, food and clothing.

*Air-Air*, the Combination of Perfection. This allows things to be concluded promptly and encourages the rapid realization of vows and intentions. It portends good luck.

*Fire-Air*, the Combination of Power. This favors the accumulation of energy and power. It indicates good luck.

The three bad combinations are:

*Air-Earth*, which portends failure, diminution, decline of prosperity, and impoverishment.

*Air-Water*, which indicates disagreement, disunity, and parting from friends.

*Fire-Water*, the Burning Combination. This brings suffering.

The worst combination is:

*Fire-Water*, the Combination of Death. This is unfavorable for all undertakings and weakens the vital energies.

The daily element combination is worked out on the basis of the day of the week corresponding to the date and the lunar position in the gyukar on that day. The respective elements can then be combined. For example, December 25, 1984, falls on a Tuesday (Mars—Fire); the moon is in *Chume* (Earth) and then in *Drozhin* (Earth). The daily combination is therefore Fire-Earth.

The reader is referred to the relevant chapter for determining the lunar position in the gyukar.

## THE TWENTY-EIGHT GREAT CONJUNCTIONS

The twenty-eight great conjunctions (table 32, pages 202–203) derive from the meeting of the daily planet and the gyukar (lunar constellation) in which the moon is located that day. Each of these great conjunctions has a meaning for the day:

*Beatitude* (**Kunga**). Very favorable for everything. Favors prosperity and the receiving of gifts.

*Time lapse* (**Düyuk**). Indicates something furtive. Sign of fear, dread of destruction. Unfavorable.

*Discipline* (**Dulwa**). Increase in possessions, wealth, and prosperity.

*Multitude or Lord of Birth* (**Kyedak**). Good luck and the love of a woman. Favorable for motherhood and children.

*Youth* (**Zhön**). Very positive for action. All tasks will be accomplished.

*Crow* (**Jarok**). Disagreements and disputes. War, destruction and famine, conflict, and impoverishment. Marriage should be avoided.

*Banner of Victory* (**Gyaltsen**). Very favorable, brings perfection. Abundance of wealth and possessions.

*Knot of Infinity* (**Pelpeu**). Accumulation of precious stones. Favorable.

*Diamond* (**Dorje**). Fear of natural phenomena such as lightning.

*Hammer* (**Thowa**). Bad, brings fear of imminent death.

*Parasol* (**Duk**). Good for energetic activities. Victory over enemies.

*Friendship* (**Drok**). Meeting with friends.

*Plenty or Mind* (**Yi**). Both necessities and luxuries are obtained. Pleasant surprise.

*Desire* (**Dö**). Fulfillment of vows, desires, and ideas.

*Firebrand* (**Kelme**). This sign portends war. There will be battles and conflict.

*Drawn Root* (**Tsatön**). Negative for vitality. Life expectancy may be diminished.

*Lord of Death* (**Chidak**). Death may occur.

TABLE 32

THE TWENTY-EIGHT GREAT CONJUNCTIONS

| Conjunction | Sun (Sunday) | Moon (Monday) | Mars (Tuesday) | Mercury (Wednesday) | Jupiter (Thursday) | Venus (Friday) | Saturn (Saturday) |
|---|---|---|---|---|---|---|---|
| Beatitude | Takar | Go | Kak | Mezhi | Lhatsam | Chume | Möndru |
| Time lapse | Dranye | Lak | Chu | Nakpa | Nrön | Drozhin | Trumtö |
| Discipline | Mindruk | Nabso | Dre | Sari | Nub | Jizhin | Trume |
| Multitude | Narma | Gyal | Wo | Saga | Chutö | Möndre | Namdru |
| Youth | Go | Kak | Mezhi | Lhatsam | Chume | Möndru | Takar |
| Crow | Lak | Chu | Nakpa | Nrön | Drizhin | Trumtö | Dranye |
| Banner | Nabso | Dre | Sari | Nub | Jizhin | Trume | Mindruk |
| Knot | Gyal | Wo | Saga | Chutö | Möndre | Namdru | Narma |
| Diamond | Kak | Mezhi | Lhatsam | Chume | Möndru | Takar | Go |
| Hammer | Chu | Nakpa | Nrön | Drozhin | Trumtö | Dranye | Lak |
| Parasol | Dre | Sari | Nub | Jizhin | Trume | Mindruk | Nabso |
| Friend | Wo | Saga | Chutö | Möndre | Namdru | Narma | Gyal |
| Abundance | Mezhi | Lhatsam | Chume | Möndru | Takar | Go | Kak |

| Desire | Nakpa | Nrön | Drozhin | Trumtö | Dranye | Lak | Chu |
|---|---|---|---|---|---|---|---|
| Firebrand | Sari | Nub | Jizhin | Trume | Mindruk | Nabso | Dre |
| Root | Saga | Chutö | Möndre | Namdru | Narma | Gyal | Wo |
| Lord of Death | Lhatsam | Chume | Möndru | Takar | Go | Kak | Mezhi |
| Arrow | Nrön | Drozhin | Trumtö | Dranye | Lak | Chu | Nakpa |
| Blow | Nub | Jizhin | Trume | Mindruk | Nabso | Dre | Sari |
| Lance | Chutö | Möndre | Namdru | Narma | Gyal | Wo | Saga |
| Ambrosia | Chume | Möndru | Takar | Go | Wo | Mezhi | Lhatsam |
| Club | Drozhin | Trumtö | Dranye | Lak | Mezhi | Nakpa | Nrön |
| Elephant | Jizhin | Trume | Mindruk | Nabso | Nakpa | Sari | Nub |
| Tiger | Möndre | Namdru | Narma | Gyal | Sari | Saga | Chutö |
| Exhaustion | Möndru | Takar | Go | Kak | Saga | Lhatsam | Chume |
| Ability | Trumtö | Dranye | Lak | Chu | Lhatsam | Nrön | Drozhin |
| Closure | Trume | Mindruk | Nabso | Dre | Nrön | Nub | Jizhin |
| Growth | Namdru | Narma | Gyal | Wo | Nub | Chutö | Möndre |

*Arrow* (**Da**). At the mental level, too much thought causes suffering. At the physical level, loss of the senses or limbs.

*Success* (**Drub**). Allows all things undertaken to succeed.

*Lance* (**Dung**). Brings disease or the fear of disease.

*Nectar* (**Dütsi**). Ruin of enemies.

*Club* (**Tunshing**). A sign of worry and fear, but also of understanding.

*Elephant* (**Langpo**). All projects are successful.

*Tiger* (**Tak**). Acquisition of a horse or vehicle. Favorable for journeys.

*Exhaustion* (**Ze**). Dwindling possessions, diminution of wealth. Decline of population.

*Skill or Movement* (**Yo**). One will fulfill the acts of a king. All rapid action will be successful.

*Firmness* (**Ten**). Taking power or governing may cause ruin. Not favorable to rapid action.

*Growth* (**Pel**). Prosperity increases.

In order to work out the twenty-eight great conjunctions, it is necessary to know only the daily planet and constellation. For example, for December 25, 1984, we have the conjunction Mars-*Chume,* which gives Abundance, and then the conjunction Mars-*Drozhin,* which is Desire.

The descriptions of the conjunctions indicate the tone of the day, the dangers and opportunities that it presents. It may be used in two distinct ways:

- In the natal horoscope, the conjunction that rules the day has a divinatory value for the native. In that role, the description must certainly be refined on the basis of its essence.
- In daily prognosis, the descriptions can be consulted before anything important is undertaken.

THE FIFTEEN CONJUNCTURES

The fifteen conjunctures (table 33) derive from the conjunction of the daily planet and certain lunar constellations. Unlike

TABLE 33

## THE FIFTEEN CONJUNCTURES

| Conjuncture | Sun | Moon | Mars | Mercury | Jupiter | Venus | Saturn |
|---|---|---|---|---|---|---|---|
| Obtaining | Mezhi | Drozhin | Takar | Lhatsam | Gyal | Namdru | Narma |
| Couple | Gyal | Go | Nabso | Möndre | Takar | Trume | Saga |
| Demon-King | Nub | Jizhin | Trume | Mindruk | Nabso | Dre | Sari |
| Practice | Chutö | Möndre Nakpa | | | Gyal | | |
| Luck | Trume | Mindruk Kak | Dre Sari | Nrön | Wo | Mindruk | Narma |
| Growth | Narma | Sari Chutö | Nabso Gyal | Lhatsam | Trume | Go | Möndre Trumtö |
| Accomplishment | Chu | Saga | | Nub | Trumtö | | Nrön |
| Harmony | | | | | | | |
| Union | Go | Nrön | | Chutö | Möndru | Takar Jizhin | Mezhi |
| Demon | Mindruk | Wo | Kak | Dre | Go | Gyal | Möndre Möndru |
| Death | Namdro | Mindruk | Möndru | Takar | Go | Narma | Mezhi |
| Bad meeting | Drozhin Möndre | Saga Lhatsam | Lhatsam | Nrön Nub | Drozhin | Narma | Chutö Dre |
| Disharmony | Möndru | Trume | Trumtö | Dranye | Takar Lhatsam | Gyal | Nakpa |
| Destruction | Saga Trumtö | Nrön Dre | Trumtö Namdru | Mezhi | Narma Nrön | Nabso | Dranye Kak |
| Burning | Chu | Saga | Lak | Nub | Möndre | Narma | Chutö |

the twenty-eight great conjunctions, which include all possible combinations, this system only considers certain particular conjunctions with certain special qualities. The fifteen conjunctures have both favorable and unfavorable consequences, which sometimes span several days. These characteristics may correspond with those of the twenty-eight great conjunctions, but sometimes they do not coincide.

Of these fifteen conjunctures, eight in particular are important. These are known as the "Eight Special Combinations," and often they are the only ones studied. However, the table shows all but one, Harmony, for which I have not been able to ascertain details.

The meanings of the conjunctures are as follows:

*1. Obtaining* (Drubjor): This is a positive combination where things or results are obtained. It is favorable for the accomplishment of activities of all sorts. During the seven days following, everything is generally excellent, but it is necessary to clarify the mind and observe the following:

- On Sunday, household tasks must be avoided, otherwise the house will be destroyed.
- On Monday, war may break out in the next two days.
- On Tuesday, it is bad to let cattle out to graze.
- On Wednesday, marriage should be avoided, for the spouse will die.
- On Thursday, working in wood will endanger future prosperity.
- On Friday, if one marries there will be no children.
- On Saturday, it is bad to send children on errands or missions.

*2. Couple* (Zajor): For seven days, practices and rituals for pacification, prosperity, enchantment, and magnetization are excellent. Wrathful rituals should be avoided.

*3. Demon-King* (Dügyal): Favorable for wrathful rituals such as offerings to the Protectors and elimination of inimical forces.

*4. Practice* (Drub Nyi): Excellent day. All important activities are favored, including special meditations.

*5. Luck* (Tashi Nyi): It is excellent to perform virtuous actions, to give or receive initiations, to perform consecrations and to invoke the local deities.

*6. Growth* (Pel Nyi): Favorable for study, education, digging ditches, making dams, irrigation, and work on the land.

*7. Accomplishment* (Thob): It is good to perform virtuous acts. Starting at the gyukar *Trumtö* (Thursday), the indications for the next seven days are similar to those for *Couple*.

*8. Harmony* (Thun Nyi): All benefic activities, such as building a house, are favored.

*9. Union* (Jor Nyi): It is good to invoke the local deities, perform virtuous acts, make predictions, and give festivals. Wrathful rituals should not be performed.

*10. Demon* (Dü Nyi): A day that favors all negativity. The country is weakened. In general, all activity is abortive. Malefic rites such as casting spells are favored. Negative for journeys, marriages, funerals, and all important events such as marriage, birth, and death.

*11. Death* (Chijor): No beneficent act, consecration, long-life ritual, etc., will be of any use and may even become dangerous. Such work as house-building should be avoided, as should ceremonies, marriages, and important journeys.

*12. Bad Meeting* (Mitrö Nyi): No chance for positive acts. The preparation and prescription of medicines should be avoided. Marriage will have negative consequences for the mother-in-law, the spouse, and later on, the children. Bad acts are successful.

*13. Disharmony* (Mithun Nyi): This is a day of disagreement. All important activities should be avoided. Marriage will have negative consequences for oneself, one's parents, and the mother-in-law. Funerals held on this day will bring dangers and cause negativities for the younger members of the family. Only bad acts are successful—creating discord, for example.

*14. Destruction* (Jig nyi): Very unfavorable for marriage, contracts, treaties between countries or people. Horse-training should be avoided, as should journeys, and funerals, which will have very bad consequences for a grandson. Favors bad acts and domination.

*15. Burning* (Sejor): All activities connected with fire should be avoided, including fire offerings and sacrifices. All important activities should be avoided. Inauspicious for surgical operations. Nothing significant for ordinary activities.

THE TWENTY-SEVEN COMBINATIONS

These are the twenty-seven *jorwas* or *yogas*, which are undoubtedly connected with the twenty-seven gyukar. The calculation of these combinations is based on the longitude of the sun and moon, to the sum of which is added 93°20'. The result corresponds to a position in one of the twemty-seven gyukar.

The following list shows the twenty-seven combinations, along with their calculation and their interpretation, first in a natal horoscope and then for a particular day.

Here $x$ = solar longitude + lunar longitude + 93°20'.

*1. Elimination* (Sel): $x = 120° - 133°20'$
Conquest of enemies, prosperity, possession of land and cattle.
Natal: Power of attraction.
Particular Day: Good day for clarifying the vows that one follows.

*2. Lover* (Dzawo): $x = 133°20' - 146°40'$
Natal: Loved by all.
Particular Day: Day of universal love.

*3. Lively* (Tseden): $x = 146°40' - 160°$
Natal: Good health and longevity.
Particular Day: Favorable.

*4. Good Fortune* (Kelzang): $x = 160' - 173°20'$
Natal: Good luck and satisfaction.
Particular Day: A day on which everything goes well.

5. *Good* (Zangpo): $x = 173°20' - 186°40'$
Natal: Lascivious character, sexual attraction
Particular Day: A day on which everyone will be pleasant.

6. *Totally Empty* (Rabtong): $x = 186°40' - 200°$
Natal: Criminal tendencies, meeting with many obstacles and accidents.
Particular Day: Depletion of wealth and cattle.

7. *Good Karma* (Le Zang): $x = 200° - 213°20'$
Natal: Good and noble deeds.
Particular Day: Prosperity resulting from good karma.

8. *Possession* (Dzinpa): $x = 213°20' - 226°40'$
Natal: Weakness for women and other people's money.
Particular Day: Accumulation of property, increase in number of sons. Rejoicing.

9. *Nail* (Zer): $x = 226°40' - 240°$
Natal: Bad tempered and argumentative.
Particular Day: A day on which one's aims may be upset by great misfortune.

10. *Grain* (Dre): $x = 240° - 253°20'$
Natal: Bad character.
Particular Day: A day on which illness caused by the Nāgas may arise.

11. *Growth* (Pel): $x = 253°20' - 266°40'$
Natal: Progress day by day, intelligence.
Particular Day: A positive day in all respects, increased prosperity.

12. *Certainty* (Nge): $x = 266°40' - 280°$
Natal: Fixity of mind, concentration, and prosperity.
Particular Day: A day on which enemies are always overcome.

*13. Great Wound* (Men): $x = 280° - 293°20'$
Natal: Cruel mind.
Particular Day: People suffering from infectious diseases should
be avoided.

*14. Joy* (Gawa): $x = 293°20' - 306°40'$
Natal: Joyful and intelligent character.
Particular Day: A day of good luck.

*15. Diamond* (Dorje): $x = 306°40' - 320°$
Natal: Prosperous and lascivious.
Particular Day: A day on which wishes are fulfilled.

*16. Accomplishment* (Ngödrub): $x = 320° - 333°20'$
Natal: Will attain certain spiritual accomplishments. Protector
of others.
Particular Day: A day on which all projects are successful.

*17. Fall* (Trung): $x = 333°20' - 346°40'$
Natal: Unstable character, untrustworthy.
Particular Day: Everything will go badly if one travels far.

*18. Hero* (Pawo): $x = 346°40' - 360°$
Natal: Bad character, pugnacious, and lascivious.
Particular Day: A day on which an enemy will be overcome.

*19. Terrace* (Yongjom): $x = 0° - 13°20'$
Natal: Quarrelsome character, prosperous.
Particular Day: A day on which there is a risk of imprisonment.

*20. Peace* (Zhiwa): $x = 13°20' - 26°40'$
Natal: Respected by kings, cool and calm, learned, well-versed
in the commentaries, prosperous.
Particular Day: A day on which results will certainly be
obtained.

*21. Accomplished Being* (Drup): $x = 26°40' - 40°$
Natal: Good nature, interested in religious rituals, successful.
Particular Day: A day on which all plans succeed.

*22. What Is Attained* (Drubja): $x = 40° - 53°20'$
Natal: Good manners.
Particular Day: Excellent day for trade.

*23. Virtue* (Gewa): $x = 53°20' - 66°40'$
Natal: Prosperous, handsome, and brilliant, but poor health.
Particular Day: Favorable day for religious activities and virtuous deeds.

*24. White* (Karpo): $x = 66°40' - 80°$
Natal: Good manners, indecisive mind, thoughtless chatterbox.
Particular Day: A day on which everything goes well whether one travels or remains.

*25. Brahma* (Tsangpa): $x = 80° - 93°20'$
Natal: Trustworthy, sound judgment, high aspirations.
Particular Day: A day on which the dignity of a god is obtained.

*26. Indra* (Wangpo): $x = 93°20' - 106°40'$
Natal: Prosperous, learned, and helpful.
Particular Day: A good day for attending to the needs of a spiritual master.

*27. Hostility* (Shakhön): $x = 106°40' - 120°$
Natal: Deceitful or devious nature, blameworthy, prosperous, and strong.
Particular Day: A day on which there is no love between men and women.

The combination that rules a person's day of birth affects both character and abilities. However, if the natal horoscope is particularly good, the effects of a bad combination may be greatly reduced; and vice versa.

## THE FIERY LUNAR DAYS

Of the 30 days that comprise the lunar month, a number are known as "fiery" when they fall on a particular day of the week. On these days, few activities will have positive results. The use of heat and fire must be avoided, particularly cremations and the hot needles used in medicine. Surgical operations are dangerous. The only favorable activities are fighting and acts of war.

| Day of week | Sunday | Monday | Tuesday | Wednesday | Thursday | Friday | Saturday |
|---|---|---|---|---|---|---|---|
| Lunar date | 12, 27 | 11, 26 | 10, 25 | 3, 18 | 6, 21 | 2, 17 | 7, 22 |

---

# THE HOURS

The Tibetan day is divided into twelve double hours or *Dutsö,* six during daylight (approximately 5:00 A.M. to 5:00 P.M.) and six at night (5:00 P.M. to 5:00 A.M.). Each double hour is designated by a name corresponding to the period of the day and by an animal of the twelve-year cycle. Since there are twelve hours in a day, the same cycle of animals is repeated every day. The *Jungtsi Men Ngak* says:

> Each day has six hours of day and six of night. Daybreak is the hour of the Hare, sunrise is the hour of the Dragon, morning is the hour of the Snake, and noon is the hour of the Horse. The afternoon is the hour of the Sheep, and the evening is the hour of the Monkey.
>
> Sunset is the hour of the Bird, twilight is the hour of the Dog. The beginning of night is the hour of the Pig. Midnight is the hour of the Rat. The end of the night is called the hour of the Cow and dawn is the hour of the Tiger.

The hours are natural periods of the day that mark different phases of the sun's journey across the sky. The length of day and night and the time of sunrise vary throughout the year, and the correspondence between the Tibetan hours and Western hours is therefore only approximate. In order to calculate the Tibetan hour correctly, it is necessary to know the length of the day and night and the time of sunrise. The Tibetan system is thus one of unequal hours.

The names of the animals associated with the hours correspond to the sun's position: the Tiger and the Hare have the natural direction East. They are associated with dawn and daybreak, when the sun appears in the East. The Horse corresponds to the South, the position of the sun at midday; and so on. (There is an interesting parallel between the names of the hours and the behavior of the associated animals: at sunset, birds are very loud, and dogs bark at dawn; at midnight, rats and mice are very active.)

Kartsi astrology associates the double hours with the signs of the zodiac (*khyim*). Table 34 shows the associations.

It does not seem to be necessary to convert to Lhasa time in order to calculate one's birth hour according to Tibetan hours. As we have seen, this system is concerned with local solar time, which is based on the apparent movement of the sun in the course of the day.

TABLE 34

## THE CHARACTERISTICS OF THE TIBETAN HOURS

| Period | Tibetan name | Approximate Solar Time | Animal | Sign | Direction |
|---|---|---|---|---|---|
| Daybreak | Namlang | 05–07 | Hare | ♈ | East |
| Sunrise | Nyishar | 07–09 | Dragon | ♉ | Southeast |
| Morning | Nyidrong | 09–11 | Snake | ♊ | South |
| Noon | Nyiche | 11–13 | Horse | ♋ | South |
| Afternoon | Cheyöl | 13–15 | Sheep | ♌ | Southwest |
| Evening | Nyinyur | 15–17 | Monkey | ♍ | West |
| Sunset | Nyinub | 17–19 | Bird | ♎ | West |
| Dusk | Sasö | 19–21 | Dog | ♏ | Northwest |
| Start of night | Sökhor | 21–23 | Pig | ♐ | North |
| Midnight | Namche | 23–01 | Rat | ♑ | North |
| End of night | Cheyöl | 01–03 | Cow | ♒ | Northeast |
| Dawn | Thörang | 03–05 | Tiger | ♓ | East |

On the other hand, the birth hour does have to be converted to solar time. Winter hours, for example, are at the moment one hour ahead of solar time and summer hours are two hours ahead. An ephemeris or a calendar can be checked to find out which system was in force at the time of birth. It is then necessary to subtract one or two hours in order to obtain local solar time.[1]

## THE HOURLY CYCLE OF ELEMENTS

The hours follow a sexagenary cycle. Each hourly animal is therefore associated with an element. To work out the hourly cycle of elements for a given day, it is necessary only to know the rules of Jungtsi astrology.

1. The element of the first hour of the day (Hare) is the son of the element of the day.
2. The elements follow each other in their order of production and change each double hour.

In our example, 12/25/84 is a Water Dragon day. The son of Water is Wood. The double hours therefore have the following elements and animals:

Wood Hare—Fire Dragon—Earth Snake—Metal Horse— Water Sheep—Wood Monkey—Fire Bird—Earth Dog— Metal Pig—Water Rat—Wood Cow—Fire Tiger.

## INTERPRETATION

Knowing the native's hour of birth and the element-animal combination allows one to refine one's judgment. The animal of the hour of birth is the most important—some writers on Chinese astrology have compared it to the ascendant in Western astrology. The hourly animal is therefore compared with the animal of the year of birth, and their relationship is considered:

1. These considerations, of course, apply specifically to French conditions. However, daylight saving time as applied elsewhere must be taken into account.

- If the two animals are the same, the characteristics indicated by the birth animal are strengthened.
- If they are in harmony, this denotes a second facet of the personality, complementary to the first, which is shown by the animal of the year of birth.
- If they are opposed, this indicates a double personality with internal contradictions.

Although the element is less important, it can also be compared with the element of the day, month, and year of birth. This would give a complete table of the individual's element makeup, which would allow the strength of certain forces to be considered and would reveal possible tensions.

We now have a set of data concerning year, month, day, and hour. It is time to combine these and apply them to the interpretation of a horoscope.

# 10

## CASTING
## AND
## INTERPRETING
## A HOROSCOPE

### The Chart Data

The intention of this chapter is to give the reader a simple method that will allow a horoscope to be quickly drawn up for analysis. Three types of horoscope can be cast in this way: the natal horoscope, a horoscope for yearly predictions, and one for daily predictions. To cast these horoscopes, it is necessary first to calculate the data in Jungtsi astrology and then factor in the elements of Kartsi astrology.

In the name of ease of understanding and learning of our method, we shall use a sample horoscope throughout the following explanation. Our example will be for a male born in Paris, November 15, 1950, at 5:00 P.M. local time.

### *The Chart Components in Jungtsi Astrology*

1. CONVERTING THE BIRTHDATE
   FROM WESTERN TO TIBETAN DATE

Here we shall use table 22 to convert to the Tibetan year, month, and day. Our native was born in November 1950, which falls in the Tibetan Male Metal Tiger year. November 15 falls in the 10th month of that year. This month begins on November 10, and there are no irregularities between November 10 and 15. Our day is therefore the 6th day of the Tibetan month.

The hour of birth can be worked out from table 34, after converting to local solar time. In the present case, 1950, we must subtract one hour:

Local solar time = 5:00 P.M. − 1 h = 4:00 P.M.

This is therefore the "evening hour" or "hour of the Monkey" in the Tibetan system. Our native's particulars are thus:

6th Day, 10th Month, Male Metal Tiger year, hour of the Monkey

## 2. DETERMINING THE ANIMAL-ELEMENT PAIRS

These pairs must be determined for the year, month, day, and hour of birth. We have already worked them out for the year. For the month, we use table 24: 1950 ends in 0, so the 10th month is Water Cow.

The pair for the day of birth is given in table 28: the year ends in 0 and the 1st day of the 10th month is Wood Monkey; the 2nd is thus Fire Bird, the 3rd Earth Dog, the 4th Metal Pig, the 5th Water Rat, and the 6th Wood Cow. The rule for determining the hour element is as follows: the day is Wood, the son-element for Wood is Fire, the element for the first hour (05:00–07:00). Our hour is the sixth and its element is therefore Fire.

Combining all these details:

| Year | Male Tiger—Metal |
| Month | Female Cow—Water |
| Day | Female Cow—Wood |
| Hour | Male Monkey—Fire |

## 3. FINDING THE ELEMENTS
### FOR THE FIVE PERSONAL ENERGIES

These are the elements of Vitality, Health, Power, Luck (Wind Horse), and *La*. Table 9 is used to establish these elements. One can use the elements for the birth year only, but it is also possible, using the same table, to determine the elements for month and day of birth. However, we shall confine ourselves here to the elements for the birth year. For the Metal Tiger year we find:

| | |
|---|---|
| Vitality: | Wood |
| Health: | Wood |
| Power: | Metal |
| Luck: | Metal |
| *La:* | Water |

These elements will be used in annual predictions.

### 4. DETERMINING THE MEWAS

The Mewas for the year of birth are given in table 13. For 1950, the Mewa is Yellow 5. Given this, it is easy to determine the Mewas for Vitality, Power, and Luck.

Since the Natal Mewa or Body Mewa is Yellow 5, the Vitality Mewa will be Black 2 and the Power Mewa will be White 8. The Luck Mewa will be Black 2. These will be used in annual predictions.

The Mewa of the day of birth can be calculated from table 29: the Mewa of the 1st day of the 10th month is Red 7. Since the Mewas follow in numerical order, we arrive at Blue 3 for the 6th day.

### 5. DETERMINING THE PARKHAS

The Parkha for the year of birth is Li because our native is male. The Parkha for the natal day can be worked out from table 30: the 1st day of the 10th month is Da, and the 2nd is therefore Zön.

We have now established all the components of the natal horoscope in Jungtsi astrology. We shall now consider the Kartsi components.

## *The Chart Components in Kartsi Astrology*

The components of Kartsi astrology are exceedingly numerous and call to mind the calculations of classical astrology as used by Western astrologers. We therefore recommend the use of Western ephemerides, taking due account of the precessional shifts. For our present purposes, we shall confine ourselves to a limited number of components, those which are emphasized in modern Tibetan astrology.

## 1. CASTING THE NATAL HOROSCOPE

The natal horoscope shows the planetary positions in their signs (*khyim*) so that their relationships can be further studied.

The first step is to determine the planetary positions in Sayana (Western) longitude in accordance with the classical method.

Let us briefly recall that once local time has been converted to local solar time, which we have already done, it must next be converted to Greenwich Mean Time:

$$GMT = 16h + 9m = 16:09$$

Let us begin with the position of the Sun. At 00:00 GMT, its position is 22° ♏ 03′12″ in Sayana longitude. Its daily movement is the difference between that position and its position at 00:000 GMT the following day:

$$\text{Daily movement: } 23°03′40″ - 22°03′12″ = 1°00′28″$$

The exact position of the sun at 16:09 GMT can be calculated using a table of logarithms: adding the log of time elapsed between 00:00 and 16:09 to the log of the daily solar movement, we obtain the distance covered by the sun in this period:

$$
\begin{array}{ll}
\text{Log } 16:09 & 1720 \\
+\text{Log } 1°00′ & 13802 \\
\hline
 & 15522 \\
\end{array}
$$

Log 15522 corresponds to a movement of 0°40′. The sun's position is therefore:

$$\text{Solar longitude} = 22°03′ + 0°40′ = 22° ♏ 43′$$

Carrying out the same calcuations for the other planets, we have:

Moon:      10° ≈ 49'
Mercury:   00° ♐ 30'
Venus:     23° ♏ 08'
Mars:      07° ♑ 04'
Jupiter:   28° ≈ 24
Saturn:    29° ♍ 32'
Rāhu:      26° ♓ 16'
Ketu:      26° ♍ 16'

We may add to these values the position of the Lagna or Ascendant, which is worked out according to the Western method: GMT is converted into Sidereal Time.

00:00 Sidereal Time  = 03:34
∴ 16:09 Sidereal Time = 03:34 + 16:09 = 19:53.

Using a table of astrological houses, we then determine the Ascendant for the latitude of Paris (approximately 49°) at that time: 23° ♉ 53'.

The second step is to subtract the Ayanaṃsa of these longitudes in order to obtain the Nirayana longitudes of the Indo-Tibetan horoscope:

Ayanaṃsa = (1950 − 285) × 0.014 = 23.31 = 23°81'

We now have the final coordinates:

| Sun | 29° ♎ 25' | Jupiter | 05° ≈ 06' |
|---|---|---|---|
| Moon | 17° ♑ 31' | Saturn | 06° ♍ 14' |
| Mercury | 07° ♐ 12' | Rāhu | 02° ♓ 58' |
| Venus | 29° ♎ 50' | Ketu | 02° ♍ 58 |
| Mars | 13° ♐ 46 | Lagna | 00° ♉ 35' |

These are now placed in a diagram to make interpretation easier. The charts used by the Tibetans do not seem very clear, and I prefer the South Indian style, as shown in the illustration on page 221.

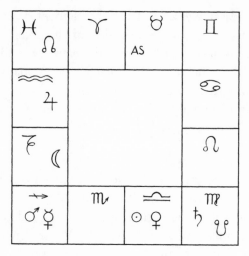

*Horoscope in the South Indian style*

## 2. GYUKAR POSITION OF THE NATAL MOON

The moon's longitude is 17°♑31', which corresponds to the double lunar mansion of Drozhin/Jizhin. The element of this lunar mansion is Earth and its ruling planet is the Moon.

## 3. THE DAILY PLANET AND ITS ELEMENT

An ephemeris or a perpetual calendar may be used to determine the day of the week upon which the birth date falls. November 15, 1950, falls on a Wednesday. The planet is therefore Mercury and its element is Water.

We now have all the important data for the native's horoscope in both systems. It now remains only to decipher, read, compare, and synthesize—in other words, to interpret the chart.

---

## INTERPRETATION

## *Interpreting the Natal Chart in Jungtsi Astrology*

Interpreting a chart in Jungtsi astrology consists first of all in appreciating the qualities of the animal signs and the elements of the horoscope, according to the following rules:

221

1.  A study of the animal and the element of the birth year gives a very general indication of character.
2.  In considering the month, the element is more important than the animal. Similarly, the animal is more important in daily prognostication.
3.  For the hour of birth, the animal is more important than the element.

Let us therefore trace the broad character of our native using the element and animal of the birth year, Metal Tiger. The Tiger indicates a bold and energetic character, very independent: this is a nonconformist and an idealist. The Metal element does not weaken these characteristics but tends to push them to their limits. The native will thus have a tendency to impose his idealist views in a sharp and lively manner—one might say, then, a great deal of style but a lack of adaptability.

Our native was born during the hour of the Monkey, which is the enemy of the Tiger. Both signs are bold and energetic, but the Tiger is a noble and plain-speaking idealist, occasionally a little mad, while the Monkey is rather more calculating: the Monkey is wily and prepared to leave his scruples on one side. There will thus be a conflict between the ideal and the tendency to manipulate.

THE ELEMENTS

In studying an individual's overall balance of elements, it is necessary to determine the proportions of each element in the year, month, day, and hour of birth; and to do so not only for Power but also for Vitality and Body (Physical Health).

|  | Animal | Polarity | Power Element | Vitality Element | Body Element |
|---|---|---|---|---|---|
| Year | Tiger | + | Metal | Wood | Wood |
| Month | Cow | − | Water | Earth | Wood |
| Day | Cow | − | Wood | Earth | Metal |
| Hour | Monkey | + | Fire | Metal | Fire |

Thus we have 4 Woods, 2 Fires, 2 Earths, 3 Metals, and 1 Water. All the elements are present, but in unequal proportions: the ideal is 20 percent of each. Here we have an excess of Wood (33 percent), which shows a tendency toward innovation, but also a tendency to scattering and anger. There is not enough Water (8.33 percent) to temper this excess. The native will be impatient and somewhat unreflective. The Metal element is quite strong (25 percent), which confirms the lack of adaptability. Earth and Fire are in reasonably good proportion (16.6 percent) and are sufficient to ensure the native's stability and capacity for transformation.

POLARITY

As a general rule, a man should have a little more Pho (+) than Mo (−), and the opposite applies to women. Here we have a balance of polarity.

THE MEWAS

The characteristics of the Mewas of the natal year are studied and compared with those of the natal day, particularly with regard to harmony among the elements.

Our native's natal-year Mewa is Yellow 5. This is the central Mewa, the crossroads where everything can topple over. The passionate side of the nature is taken to extremes. One can look for the best, spiritual realization and a good material situation; or the worst, depravity, hard times, and disaster.

The daily Mewa is Blue 3, which favors independence and dynamism. But action should not be confused with precipitate behavior, which will bring obstacles. However, the daily Mewa is Water, which is the friend of the yearly element, Earth. The relationship is positive and indicates that energy should be wisely controlled and placed at the service of success.

THE PARKHAS

The Parkha of the natal day is Zön, the Parkha of Wind, a sign of mobility, even instability and dispersion.

We may now formulate a judgment combining all these elements. Here we have a bold and energetic man, who combines independence and idealism. If he is successful in social life, he may be a leader, but his rigidity may make him a fanatic. If he fails, he will probably become bitter and rebel. Nevertheless, he has the capacity to avoid disaster, and can be crafty. He needs always to center himself, and his dynamism will be of great benefit to him in this regard. If not, the flair of Wood will be cut through by the blade of Metal.

## Interpreting the Natal Chart in Kartsi Astrology

### 1. PLANETS IN SIGNS

In Kartsi astrology, as in Western astrology, the planets can be in their own house, in their exaltation, or in their fall, to which is also added the *Mūlatrikona*. Table 35 shows these.

In our horoscope (see chart on page 221), we see that the Sun is in its Fall in Libra, and that Venus is in its Exaltation, also in Libra. The Sun is therefore weakened and Venus is a strong planet.

### 2. RELATIONS BETWEEN PLANETS

As we have seen, planets in Kartsi astrology can be permanent friends, enemies, or neutral. In addition, there are temporary

TABLE 35

| Planet | Rules | Exaltation | Fall | Mūlatrikona |
|--------|-------|-----------|------|-------------|
| Sun | ♌ | 10° ♈ | 10° ♎ | 0°–20° ♌ |
| Moon | ♋ | 3° ♉ | 3° ♏ | 4°–20° ♉ |
| Mars | ♈, ♏ | 28° ♑ | 28° ♋ | 0°–12° ♈ |
| Mercury | ♊, ♍ | 15° ♍ | 15° ♓ | 16°–20° ♍ |
| Jupiter | ♐, ♓ | 5° ♋ | 5° ♑ | 0°–10° ♐ |
| Venus | ♉, ♎ | 27° ♓ | 27° ♍ | 9°–15° ♎ |
| Saturn | ♑, ♒ | 20° ♎ | 20° ♈ | 0°–20° ♒ |
| Rāhu | ♌ | 20° ♉ | 20° ♏ | — |
| Ketu | ♒ | 20° ♏ | 20° ♉ | — |

friendships and enmities, which depend on the respective positions of the planets in question. It will be recalled that any planet placed in the 2nd, 3rd, 4th, 10th, 11th, or 12th sign from another becomes its temporary friend; while any planet in the same sign or in the 5th, 6th, 7th, 8th, or 9th sign from another becomes its temporary enemy.

We therefore have six possible relationships (see table 36):

| Permanent friend | + | Temporary friend | = | Best friend |
| Permanent friend | + | Temporary enemy | = | Neutral |
| Permanent neutral | + | Temporary friend | = | Friend |
| Permanent neutral | + | Temporary enemy | = | Enemy |
| Permanent enemy | + | Temporary friend | = | Neutral |

(*Continued on next page*)

TABLE 36

| Planet | Best Friend | Friend | Neutral | Enemy | Worst Enemy |
|---|---|---|---|---|---|
| Sun | Sun, Mars | Mercury | Jupiter, Saturn | — | Venus |
| Moon | Sun, Mercury | Mars, Jupiter, Venus | — | Saturn | — |
| Mars | Sun, Moon, Jupiter | Venus, Saturn | — | — | Mercury |
| Mercury | Sun, Venus | Jupiter, Saturn | Moon | Mars | — |
| Jupiter | Moon, Mars | — | Sun, Mercury | Saturn | Venus |
| Venus | Mercury, Saturn | Mars | Moon | Jupiter | Sun |
| Saturn | Mercury, Venus | — | Sun, Mars | Jupiter | Moon |

$$\begin{array}{ccccc} \text{Permanent} & + & \text{Temporary} & = & \text{Worst} \\ \text{enemy} & & \text{enemy} & & \text{enemy} \end{array}$$

Thus for our native's Sun, the Moon is both permanent friend and temporary friend (4th sign from the Sun). It is therefore a best friend. Mars is also permanent and temporary friend (3rd sign) of the Sun, and therefore its best friend. Mercury is a permanent neutral and temporary friend and therefore a friend. Jupiter is permanent friend and temporary enemy, and therefore neutral. Venus is permanent and temporary enemy and therefore the Sun's worst enemy. Saturn is a permanent enemy and temporary friend (12th sign from Sun) and therefore neutral.


3. ASPECTS

In Indo-Tibetan astrology, the aspects differ considerably from their counterparts in Western astrology.

1. Aspects are measured from sign to sign.
2. The conjunction is not an aspect.
3. The aspect to the 7th sign—the opposition—is the most important.
4. Mars, Jupiter, and Saturn have special aspects: Mars aspects the 4th and 8th signs, Jupiter the 5th and 9th, and Saturn the 3rd and 10th.
5. In judging the positive or negative value of the aspect, the relations between planets and their positions in the signs must be considered.

Looking at our example chart, we have several aspects:

Mars aspects Rāhu (4th sign)
Jupiter aspects Venus and the Sun (9th sign)
Saturn aspects Rāhu (7th sign)

A complete interpretation of aspects lies beyond the scope of this book—this matter is studied in excellent Indian works by

B. V. Raman, S. Kannan, Dr. G. S. Kapoor, and others (see bibliography). We shall confine ourselves to a few simple words regarding the sample chart.

Mars, which is in a friend sign (Sagittarius, ruled by Jupiter—the best friend of Mars in this chart) aspects Rāhu (in Pisces, also ruled by Jupiter). Rāhu in Pisces indicates meticulous habits, a methodical and careful mind, and often a failure to grasp the overall picture. The aspects of Mars will tend to counteract these tendencies and force the native to be open, but it also indicates impatience and haste. This aspect will operate above all in the realms governed by Jupiter (education, religion, social life, success, etc.).

Jupiter, the natural benefic in the sign of human communication (Aquarius), aspects Venus, also a benefic and in its domicile, Libra. However, these two planets are in an inimical relationship in this chart, which makes the aspect ambiguous. The native is strongly influenced by Venus, ruler of the Ascendant (Taurus) and the birth sign (Libra). This aspect may signify a struggle to harmonize the values of Venus (love, sensuality, arts, entertainment) with those of Jupiter (law, religion, social success).

The Jupiter aspect to the Sun in its fall tends to strengthen the Sun.

Saturn, the natural malefic but in a friendly sign, is in opposition to Rāhu in Pisces. This indicates trials and sacrifices.

Aside from these broad lines of interpretation, there are many other methods which cannot be discussed here. These, however, are connected with Indian astrology, to which the interested reader is referred.

We come now to a number of elements of lunar astrology that are widely used in Tibetan astrology.

## 4. THE COMBINATION OF NATAL-DAY ELEMENTS

This is concerned with the connection between the element of the daily planet and the element of the natal lunar mansion. The native was born on a Wednesday, day of Mercury, whose element is Water. The lunar mansion is Drozhin/Jizhin, or more precisely, the beginning of Jizhin, whose element is Earth. The combination Water-Earth is known as the "combination of youth" and is very favorable for good luck.

### 5. THE PLANET–NATAL GYUKAR COMBINATION
The Mercury-Jizhin conjunction is Parasol, which is excellent for energy, activity, and overcoming hostility.

### 6. CONJUNCTION
There is no conjunction except between certain planets and certain gyukar. The Mercury-Jizhin conjunction is not a conjunction.

### 7. THE TWENTY-SEVEN COMBINATIONS
Adding the longitudes of the sun and the moon and adding 93°20' to the sum gives the figure corresponding to a combination:

$$x = 209°25' + 287°31' + 93°20' = 590°16' = (590° - 360°)\ 230°16'$$

This gives us the combination Nail (*Zer*), which indicates a bad-tempered and quarrelsome temperament.

### 8. JUDGING THE GYUKAR PLANETS
### ACCORDING TO THE NATAL ANIMAL
This analysis links Jungtsi and Kartsi astrology. The native is a Tiger. Table 21 (page 151) lists the Gyukar planets that are favorable or inauspicious to the Tiger.

| | |
|---|---|
| *La* Planet | Jupiter |
| Vitality Planet | Saturn |
| Destructive Planet | Venus |
| *La* Gyukar | Go 4 |
| Vitality Gyukar | Namdru 26 |
| Power Gyukar | Kak 8 |
| Obstacle Gyukar | Nakpa 13 |
| Demon Gyukar | Wo 11 |
| Destructive Gyukar | Dranye 1 |

The planets of the La and the Vitality indicate the native's positive days. Thus, Thursday (Jupiter) and Saturday (Saturn) are good days for him. The day of the destructive planet is inauspicious: in this case, Friday (Venus). The native was born on a Wednesday, which is a neutral day for him.

The positions of the planets in the Gyukar are:

| | |
|---|---|
| Sun | Saga 15 |
| Moon | Jizhin 21 |
| Mercury | Nub 18 |
| Venus | Saga 15 |
| Mars | Chutö 19 |
| Jupiter | Möndre 22 |
| Saturn | Wo 11 |
| Rāhu | Trumtö 24 |
| Ketu | Wo 11 |
| Lagna | Mindruk 2 |

Here we see that Saturn, the planet of Vitality, is in Gyukar Wo 11, known in the case of the Tiger as "the demon." This means that the native's Vitality will be threatened by illnesses or by demonic spirits of the eight classes. Ketu in the same place indicates probable karmic debts owing to the spirits or again, obstacles deriving from old karma threatening the Vitality.

## Annual Predictions

In Jungtsi astrology, the yearly animals and elements for the coming year can be compared with those of the natal year. This enables one to make certain predictions as to how the native will fare during this period, as well as revealing his or her weak and strong points.

Here we shall consider how the native will fare during 1989–90.

### 1. COMPARISON OF ANIMAL SIGNS

This comparison shows the general tone of the year. The native is a Tiger, while 1989–90 is a Snake year. Table 6 shows that this is a neutral year for the Tiger. The Snake and the Tiger are not harmonious signs: the Tiger native should pause and reflect rather than rush in.

## 2. COMPARISON OF ELEMENTS

The elements are always compared by relating the yearly element to the element of the natal year. Referring to table 9 to determine the elements for the year to be studied, a table can be drawn up to compare these with the natal year and a prognosis can be made in accordance with table 10:

|  | *1989–90* | *1950* | *Prognosis* |
|---|---|---|---|
| Power | Earth | Metal | ${}^{O}_{O}{}^{O}$ |
| Vitality | Fire | Wood | OX |
| Body | Wood | Wood | X |
| Luck | Water | Metal | OX |
| *La* | Wood | Water | OX |

During 1989–90, the native will enjoy excellent "personal power," that is, he will be able to carry through his projects. However, as the animal signs show, he will always have to act with calm and reflection—if he does so, the year can be prosperous. The Vitality and the *La* are neutral. Body energy, on the other hand, is negative, which indicates signs of ill health. He must therefore keep a close eye on his body and avoid overexertion during the year. The Wind or Luck is neutral: no big wins at poker!

## 3. COMPARISON OF THE MEWAS

***Comparison of Yearly Mewa and Natal Mewa.*** The elements of the two Mewas are compared in accordance with the usual relations:

1989–90:   Black 2
1950:       Yellow 5

The element of Black 2 is Water, while that of Yellow 5 if Earth. The relationship is friendly and the prognosis for the year is *very good.*

*Comparison of Other Mewas (Vitality, Power, Wind).* We have already compared the yearly Mewas or Body Mewas. The Mewas of Vitality, Power, and Wind (Luck) remain to be considered. Having worked these out for the year 1989–90, a table can be drawn up to compare them with those of the natal year.

| | 1989–90 | 1950 | Prognosis |
|---|---|---|---|
| Power | Yellow 5 (Earth) | White 8 (Metal) | o°o |
| Vitality | White 8 (Metal) | Black 2 (Water) | o°o |
| Body | Black 2 (Water) | Yellow 5 (Earth) | oo |
| Luck | White 8 (Metal) | Black 2 (Water) | o°o |

Thus for the Mewa comparison we have only positive prognoses for the year 1989–90. The prognosis for the Body Mewa contradicts that of the Body element, which would seem to suggest that the native's health is not really threatened. Similarly, the prognoses for Vitality and Luck are also enhanced.

*Study of the Papme.* This Mewa depends on the native's age, the Natal Mewa, and the male or female characteristics of the natal year. It will be recalled that Tibetans reckon a child as one year old at birth. In 1989, the native is therefore 40. The natal Mewa is Yellow 5 and the year is masculine (Male Metal Tiger). Consulting table 15, we find the Papme White 1. White 1 is Metal, which is in a son-relationship with Earth, the element of the Natal Mewa. This is a neutral relationship—the year will not present any danger for the native.

4. THE PARKHA

In order to determine the Parkha, it is only necessary to know the native's gender and his or her age in 1989. Our native is male,

231

so we count from Li at birth, moving toward Khön, Da, and so on. He is 40 years old, which gives us the Parkha Zön for 1989.

Consulting table 17, the table of geomantic houses, we can determine the favorable and unfavorable directions for this year.

*Favorable Directions*

| | |
|---|---|
| South (Prosperity) | Favors growth of property |
| Southwest (Message of Luck) | Favorable for traveling |
| East (Sky Medicine) | Favorable for health and healing |
| North (Life Support) | Favorable for recouping energy |

*Unfavorable Directions*

| | |
|---|---|
| Southwest (Five Demons) | Threats from demons |
| West (Corporal Punishment) | Risks of bodily injury |
| Northwest (Injury) | Risks of accidents |
| Northeast (Life-Cutting Demons) | Danger to life from demonic influences |

These judgments must, of course, be refined with reference to the other elements of the yearly prognosis. Thus, we have seen that in 1989 there is no real threat to the vitality, health, power, or luck of the native—this may assist in making choices such as choosing a place of rest, and so on. On the other hand, in years of great danger (poor vitality, Papme the same as that of the year of birth, etc.) these readings would call for closer attention.

## Elective Charts

Elective astrology is that branch of astrology that is concerned with determining the auspicious or inauspicious qualities of a given day. This forms a very important part of Tibetan astrology. When a day takes on special significance—when there is a serious decision to be made, a contract to be signed, or a piece of business to be concluded—it is good to know whether the prognosis for that day is favorable. When the circumstances allow a date to be chosen, it is also possible to find the best time for a particular project. Bearing in mind the laws of karma and interdependence, it is easy to understand that the success of an action is dependent not only on the actor but also on the circumstances in which it is performed. The elective chart is thus a method for selecting the moment when interdependent origins are most favorable to success.

This is certainly not a question of carefully analyzing every day in the future—clearly it would become difficult even to lift one's little finger without meeting astrological difficulties. Only important days demand our attention. In Tibet, the peasants would take account of predictions before beginning a job or planting seeds, and merchants would also do so before setting out in caravans.

A number of types of prediction are possible: general predictions concerning the tone of a day for everybody; predictions relating to a particular activity; and predictions that concern the native personally.

1. THE TONE OF THE DAY

In order to determine the more or less auspicious quality of a day, it is necessary to consider above all the ruling planet, the daily gyukar, and their various relations. Let us take as an example May 23, 1988.

*Determine the Tibetan Lunar Date.* The Tibetan lunar date is given in table 22. This is a double day, 7b of the 4th month. We now inspect the general characteristics of the thirty lunar days: the 7th day is said to be good for journeys.

*The Day of the Week and Its Planet.* The almanac or ephemeris shows that this day is a Monday, which is ruled by the Moon, whose element is Water. The daily planet and its energy are the main data for the day.

Monday is unfavorable for violent or energetic acts, for the use of fire, physical exercise, and journeys. It is favorable for reflection, writing, purification, and contact with water.

*The Daily Gyukar.* The entire movement of the moon for the day in question must be considered. The moon travels very fast (about 13° per day) and often passes through two gyukar in the same day. The ephemeris shows the following lunar coordinates:

Position at 00:00 GMT: 24° ♌ 29'
Position at 12:00 GMT: 00° ♍ 23'
At midnight, it reaches 6° ♍ 17'

Since these coordinates are in tropical longitudes, the Ayanaṃsa (which in 1988 is equal to 23°50') must be subtracted. Thus, between 0:00 and 12:00, the moon travels from 00° ♌ 39' to 12° ♌ 27'. Table 20 shows that the moon only travels through one Gyukar on that day, namely no. 9, Chu. The element associated with this constellation is Fire.

*The Daily Element Combination.* The daily element combination is known as the "Little Combination," but it is nevertheless a determining factor in the favorable or unfavorable character of the day. In the order of importance, this combination is the strongest.

In our example, the combination is Water-Fire, a bad combination known as "the combination of death," and unfavorable for any undertaking. One can immediately declare that this is not an auspicious day.

*The Daily Conjunction.* This is also known as the "Great Combination." Although it is not so powerful as the Little Combination, it should not be neglected. In this case, the combination Moon-Chu gives the constellation Crow, which indicates quarrels and destruction.

*The Daily Juncture.* This is a combination that may or may not occur, depending on the planet and Gyukar concerned. In our example, the Moon-Chu association does not give any juncture.

When there is a juncture, it may either confirm or contradict the judgment of the daily conjunction, and the judgment must be modified accordingly.

*The Daily Combination (Yoga).* The daily yoga is concerned with the twenty-seven combinations that involve the positions of the Sun and Moon. It therefore entails calculating the longitudes of the Sun and Moon, the latter of which changes considerably, so that there will be two combinations in the course of a day.

In our example, the Sun's longitude is 62°05' − 23°50' (Ayanaṃsa) = 38°15'. As we saw above, the Moon's longitude extends from 00° ♌ 39', or 120°39', to 12° ♌ 39', or 132°27'.

The value of $x$ (solar longitude + lunar longitude + 93°20') therefore lies between 252°14' and 264°92', thus corresponding to the 11th combination, *Pel* or Growth. This combination in itself is positive, favorable to the increase of prosperity, but the aggregate of the preceding components destroys its force.

It remains only to check whether this is a "fiery" day, which is unfavorable. This is a matter of comparing the lunar date and the day of the week, and in our case, the relation Monday–7th lunar day is not fiery. These are the main components to be considered at a general level. If one wishes to determine the chances of success for a specific activity, certain components of Jungtsi astrology must be added, as well as certain judgments connected with the nature of Gyukar.

## 2. SELECTING A DAY FOR
## A PARTICULAR ACTIVITY

In addition to the factors already discussed, one must take account of the following:

*The Daily Animal.* Since the day is given as a Tibetan date, it is necessary to determine the animal that rules the day by consulting table 28. For example, May 23, 1988 is day 7b of the 4th month in a year ending with 8: the 1st day of the month is Monkey, therefore the 7th is Tiger. This is an unfavorable day for marriage and public ceremonies.

*The Daily Mewa.* The daily Mewa can be calculated from table 29. Looking at our example again, we see that the 1st day of the 4th month is Red 7. Days 7 and 7b are therefore Green 4.

*The Daily Parkha.* The daily Parkha can be calculated from table 30. The Parkha for the 1st day of the 4th month is Tsin. Days 7 and 7b are therefore Kham.

Certain daily factors specify exactly which activities are favorable and unfavorable under their aegis: the position of the day in the lunar month, the day of the week, the constellation through which the Moon is traveling, and the daily animal, Mewa and Parkha. The following list shows the positive and negative factors for certain daily or important activities.

*Marriage.* Marriage is favorable if it takes place during the 1st month (Chu dawa), the 2nd month (Phalguna Dawa), the 4th month (Saga Dawa), or the 5th month (Nrön Dawa). The most auspicious days are Monday, Wednesday, and Thursday. In terms of the lunar month, the 1st, 9th, 10th, 19th, and 24th days are the most auspicious. The days of the Sheep and the Monkey are favorable for marriage, as are those ruled by Mewa White 6 and White 8. The positive lunar constellations are 3 (Narma), 4 (Go), 9 (Chu), 11 (Wo), 12 (Mezhi), 14 (Sari), 16 (Lhatsam), 18 (Nub), 20 (Chume), 25 (Trume), and 26 (Namdru). Marriage should be avoided on Tuesdays and Sundays, while Saturdays are moderately good. The 6th, 8th, 15th (full moon), and 30th (new moon) days of the lunar month should also be avoided. The days of the Tiger, Snake, Horse, and Dog are inauspicious, as are days ruled by the Mewas Black 2 and Blue 3 and Parkha Li.

*Journeys.* The days of the week are divided as follows:

Sunday: Favorable for traveling toward the North, unfavorable for traveling toward the West.

Monday: Not favorable for traveling, except toward the South. The East in particular should be avoided.

Tuesday: Also unfavorable, particularly for traveling toward the North. However, traveling to the East is possible.

Wednesday: Favorable for traveling, except toward the North.

Thursday: Favorable for traveling toward the West, unfavorable for traveling toward the South.

Friday:         Favorable for traveling, except toward the West.

Saturday:       Not favorable for traveling, particularly toward the East. Travel to the South, however, is possible.

The 7th, 10th, 22nd, 24th, and 25th days of the lunar month are favorable for travel. The 6th, 14th, 15th, 21st, 29th, and 30th should be avoided. Days of the Cow, Tiger (East and West), Snake (South), and Monkey (North and East) are favorable. Days of the Rat and Snake (North, West, and East) are unfavorable. Mewa White 6 is favorable. Parkha Da is good for travel to the East.

The lunar constellations 0 (Takar), 4 (Go), 6 (Nabso), 7 (Gyal), 12 (Mezhi), 16 (Lhatsam), 18 (Nub), 21b (Jizhin) are favorable for travel. Constellations 5 (Lag), 8 (Kak), 17 (Nön), 22 (Möndre), and 13 (Nakpa) are unfavorable.

*Starting a Building.* Monday, Wednesday, Thursday, Friday, and Saturday are favorable, as are the 1st, 3rd, 9th, 10th, 11th, 19th, 20th, 23rd, 24th, and 25th days of the lunar month. Days of the Cow, Tiger, and Dragon are also favorable. Days ruled by the Parkhas Kin and Tsin are excellent for laying foundations. Days on which the moon is in constellation 0 (Takar), 3 (Narma), 4 (Go), 11 (Wo), 12 (Mezhi), 13 (Nakpa), 14 (Sari), 16 (Lhatsam), 18 (Nub), 19 (Chutö), or 20 (Chume) are favorable.

Tuesdays, the 26th day of the lunar month, and days ruled by the Parkhas Khön and Khen should be avoided. The most favorable times of the year are when the sun is in Aries, Taurus, Cancer, Leo, Libra, Scorpio, Capricorn, or Aquarius.

The following lunar months must be avoided: 6th (Chutö Dawa), 7th (Drozhin Dawa), 8th (Trume Dawa), 9th (Takar Dawa), and 12th (Gyal Dawa).

*Moving into a New House.* Monday, Tuesday, Thursday, Friday, and Saturday are favorable; and even more so during the following lunar months: 1st (Chu Dawa), 2nd (Wo Dawa), 4th (Saga Dawa), or 5th (Nrön Dawa). Days during which the moon travels through constellations 3 (Narma), 20 (Chume), and 25 (Trume) are auspicious.

Sundays should be avoided, as should days on which the moon is in constellations 0 (Takar), 6 (Nabso), 7 (Gyal), 12 (Mezhi), 14 (Sari), and 21b (Jizhin).

*Giving a Name.* This refers, for example, to naming a child or a place. Favorable days are Tuesday, Wednesday, Thursday, and Friday. Days on which the moon is in the constellations 0 (Takar), 3 (Narma), 4 (Go), 7 (Gyal), 11 (Wo), 12 (Mezhi), 16 (Lhatsam), 20 (Chume), 21b (Jizhin), 22 (Möndre), 25 (Trume) or 26 (Namdru) are also auspicious. Tuesday and Saturday should be avoided.

*Funerals.* The best days are Wednesday, Friday, and the days of the Hare and the Monkey. Monday, Tuesday, Thursday, and Sunday should be avoided, as should the days of the Dragon, Snake, and Horse and days when the Parkha is Li or Khön or when the moon is in constellation 13 (Nakpa).

It is considered very important in Tibetan astrology to select the right day for a funeral, not only in the interests of the deceased but also for the family. A bad choice can lead to disagreements in the family or the descendants of the deceased.

*Taking on a Responsibility.* The auspicious days are Sunday, Monday, Tuesday, and Thursday, and days of the Dragon and the Horse. Saturday and the day of the Monkey should be avoided.

*Starting a Fight.* This can mean beginning hostilities, provoking a battle, setting off for war, or struggling against something. The most favorable days are Sunday, Tuesday, and the day of the Cow. Constellations 5 (Lak), 10 (Dre), 17 (Nrön), and 18 (Nub) are also favorable.

Combat should be avoided on Wednesday, Thursday, and Saturday, days of the Tiger, Hare, Dragon, Sheep, and Dog. Days when the Mewa is White 6 or Red 7 or when the Parkha is Khön,

Kham, or Da are inauspicious. The portents are not good when the Moon is in constellation 16 (Lhatsam): massacres are to be feared.

*Trade.* Monday, Wednesday, Thursday, and Friday are favorable, as are days of the Rat and Hare. The day of the Bird is good for selling and the day of the Dog is good for buying. Constellations 7 (Gyal), 14 (Sari), 20 (Chume), and 26 (Namdru) are good for trade.

Saturday should be avoided for transferring or selling (buying only); and Sunday and Tuesday are also bad for selling. Days of the Snake and Cow are negative; however, the Day of the Horse is good for dealing in horses. Goods should not be given or taken out on days when the Mewa is Red 9, but purchasing is good on those days. Days when the Parkha is Kin or Da should also be avoided.

**Work on the Land.** Agricultural work related to the land is favored on Monday, Wednesday, Thursday, and Friday. Saturday is auspicious for planting seeds but not for ploughing. The day of the Sheep is favorable, as are days when the Parkha is Tsin. For ploughing, a day should be chosen when the Moon is in constellation 3 (Narma), 4 (Go), 7 (Gyal), 9 (Chu), 11 (Wo), 12 (Mezhi), 13 (Nakpa), 20 (Chume), 21b (Jizhin), 23 (Möndru), 25 (Trume), or 26 (Namdru).

Sunday, Tuesday, and days of the Snake, Dragon, Hare, and Pig should be avoided, and the day of the Dog is not good for planting. Other unfavorable days are those with Yellow 5, days of the full and new moon (15th and 30th), and the 23rd, 24th, and 29th days of the lunar month.

*Planting Trees.* This is best done on Mondays, Wednesdays, Fridays, or Saturdays. The day of the Monkey and the Parkha Tsin are excellent. Sunday and Tuesday should be avoided.

*Felling Trees.* This is best done on days when the Parkha is Khön or Da. It should be carefully avoided on days of the Snake or days ruled by the Mewa Blue 3 or Parkha Tsin—on these days, felling trees will expose one to the wrath of the Nyen spirits and the Nāgas, who send diseases to those who injure them.

*Irrigation and Work Connected with Water.* Favorable days are Monday, Wednesday, Saturday, and days of the Cow. Days when the Mewa is White 1 or White 8 are also positive.

Sunday, Tuesday, days of the Dragon, Snake, or Hare, and days when the Mewa is Blue 3 or the Parkha is Kham should be avoided.

*Medical Treatment.* Sunday, Monday, and particularly Thursday are excellent for preparing remedies. Friday is good for surgical operations. The day of the Bird is auspicious for making medicines and for medical treatment of all sorts. Days when the Mewa is Blue 3 or Green 4 are also favorable. The auspicious constellations for administering remedies are 0 (Takar), 3 (Narma), 4 (Go), 6 (Nabso), 11 (Wo), 12 (Mezhi), 13 (Nakpa), 14 (Sari), 15 (Lhatsam), 20 (Chume), 21b (Jizhin), 22 (Möndre), 23 (Möndru), and 26 (Namdru).

Saturday and Tuesday are not favorable for administering remedies, and Wednesday is not good for preparing medicines. The day of the Tiger is not good for medical treatment and the day of the Dragon is harmful for operations. The day of the Snake is negative for everything connected with medicine and treatment. The 4th day of the lunar month and days when the constellation is 18 (Nub) are unfavorable.

In the case of operations, it is also necessary to check the circulation of the *La* (the vital soul) in the body throughout the course of the month. For example, on the 13th of the month, the *La* is in the teeth, and on those days dental treatment should be avoided.

*Cutting the Hair.* The day of the Pig is good. In the lunar month, the following days are excellent: 8th (for longevity), 9th and 10th (magnetism), 11th (intelligence), 26th and 27th (good luck). The following constellations are favorable: 0 (Takar), 4

(Go), 6 (Nabso), 7 (Gyal), 12 (Mezhi), 13 (Nakpa), 14 (Sari), 17 (Nön), 21b (Jizhin), 22 (Möndre), 23 (Möndru), and 26 (Namdru).

The following days of the lunar month should be avoided as prejudicial to Vitality: days of the Horse, Dog, or Tiger, the 4th, 6th, 14th, 15th (New Moon), 16th, 17th and 30th (Full Moon).

*Important Steps and Petitions.* These should preferably be made on Wednesdays, Thursdays, or days of the Rat, Monkey, or Bird. Days of the Horse, Sheep, and Dog should be avoided. These are the astrological recommendations for certain activities. There are also a number of special recommendations for particular ritual or religious activities:

*The practice of astrology* is favored on Monday, Wednesday, Thursday, and Friday. Saturday is good for calculation but not for divination, and the same holds for the day of the Rat.

*Purification* is best on Monday and days when the Mewa is White 1, White 6, or White 8. Tuesday and the day of the Tiger should be avoided. The day of the Full Moon (15th) is excellent for purification.

*Offering ceremonies (Gānacakra pūjā).* The day of the Horse and days ruled by White 1 are excellent, as are the 10th and 25th days of the lunar month. The day of the Tiger should be avoided.

*Prosperity rituals* are favored on Monday, the day of the Tiger, and days when the Mewa is White 6 of Red 9. The day of the Hare should be avoided.

*Rituals for dispelling negativity* or *Dogpa* are favored on Tuesday, Friday, the day of the Dragon, days when the Mewa is Black 2, or when the Parkha is Khön, Kham, Kin, or Zön. The days of the Hare, Bird, Snake, Cow, Rat, Pig, and Monday should be avoided.

*Rituals for the local deities* are beneficial on Friday, the day of the Snake, and days ruled by Blue 3, Red 7, Kham, Kin, or Tsin.

*Fire rituals* are favored on Sunday, Tuesday, days of the Tiger and Bird, and days when the Parkha is Li. It is not good to perform them on Mondays or Wednesdays.

*Rituals to produce rain* are favored on Days of the Monkey,

Bird, Pig, and Rat. They should not be performed on days of the Dragon, Horse, Sheep, or Cow.

## 3. SELECTION OF A DAY FOR THE NATIVE

The selection of a day for the native consists of an evaluation of the day's qualities as they relate to the native: the positive or negative characteristics of the day are determined by comparing certain factors of that day with the natal chart. We shall use again the example of a person born on 11/15/1950. We shall take the date May 23, 1988, and see whether it is favorable for the native.

*Comparing Animal Signs.* Comparing the animal signs is a matter of comparing the animal that rules the day with that which rules the natal day. In this connection, table 6 can be consulted. Thus, our native is a Tiger and the day in question is also Tiger. The relationship is neutral.

*Comparing Elements.* Comparing elements consists of comparing the ruling element for the day with that of the natal year: their relationship is analyzed and the favorable or unfavorable quality of the day is determined. Thus, May 23 is Earth (table 28), and our native's ruling element is Metal. The Metal-Earth relationship is a mother-relationship. Thus the day is very favorable in terms of elements.

The elements of Vitality, Body, Luck, or *La* can also be studied in the same way. For example, let us determine whether the day in question is a lucky one for the native. The Wind element of Earth Tiger is Metal, while that of Metal Tiger is also Metal. The Metal-Metal relationship is a bad one (table 10), so this is not a favorable day for luck.

*Comparing Mewas.* In comparing Mewas, the daily Mewa is compared with the Mewa of the natal year from the element point of view. In our example, the daily Mewa is Green 4, whose element is Wood; while the Mewa for the natal year, Yellow 5, is linked with Earth. The Wood-Earth relationship is an enemy relationship, and therefore very bad.

The Mewas for Vitality, Power, and Luck can be studied in the same way. Thus, the daily Power Mewa is Black 1, while the natal Power Mewa is White 8; and the Water-Metal relationship must therefore be considered: this is a son-relationship, which is neutral.

In order to form an overall judgment of the tone of the day for the native, it is enough to consider the relationship between the ruling element of the day and the ruling natal element, and then the relationship between the Mewas of the natal year and the day in question. If both judgments are positive, the day will be good. If they are contradictory, as is the case here, the day will be a mediocre one. If both are bad, the day will be inauspicious.

*The Days and Constellations with Reference to the Natal Animal.* For any given animal, there are auspicious and inauspicious days throughout the lunar month (table 27). May 23, 1988 is the 7th day of the lunar month, which is neutral for the Tiger. If, on the other hand, the native had been a Bird, this would be a powerful day.

The days of the week can also have a particular quality according to the natal animal (table 26). Thus for the Tiger, Tuesday is the day of the La and thus positive, and Saturday is the day of Vitality, also positive. Friday, however, is the day of Obstacles and is negative. May 23 is a Monday and therefore does not enter into consideration in this case.

There are also Gyukar with special meanings for each animal (table 21). For the Tiger, the Gyukar in question are 4 (Go), the star of the La; 26 (Namdru), the star of Vitality; 8 (Kak), the star of Power; 13 (Nakpa), the star of Obstacles; 11 (Wo), the demon star; and 1 (Dranye), the destructive star. Our day, May 23, 1988, has Gyukar 9 (Chu), which is not significant.

*Comparing Gyukar.* The procedure for comparing Gyukar is as follows. Count from the natal constellation to the constellation for the day being considered, divide the number obtained by 9, and use the remainder, except for the numbers from 1 to 9, which are used as they are for the purposes of interpretation.

1   Danger to the body
2   Wealth and prosperity
3   Danger, loss, and accident
4   Prosperity
5   Obstacles
6   Actions are successful, gains
7   Danger of death
8   Favorable day or Excellent
9
0

In our example, the natal constellation is 21b (Jizhin) and the constellation for the day is 9 (Chu). Counting from Jizhin to Chu gives 16; and $^{16}/_9$ gives a remainder of 7, which indicates danger of death. Nothing important or risky should therefore be undertaken on that day.

# APPENDIX I

# *TIBETAN COSMOLOGY*

## PLANETARY SPIRITS AND LOCAL DEITIES

A great many demons, local deities, and elemental spirits are found in Tibetan astrology, many of which were present well before the establishment of Buddhism. Some of them, such as the nāgas, are mentioned in Indian Brahmanism, but they derive chiefly from the pre-Buddhist religious matrix. Thanks to its great flexibility, Tantric Buddhism has been able to assimilate these beings into its worldview.

Similar spirits and deities are also present in Western folklore and magic: here they are known as "nature spirits," "elementals," and "planetary demons," and a great number of popular deities such as dwarves, elves, gnomes, goblins, trolls, naiads, nymphs, satyrs, and so on are found.

In Tibetan astrology, these deities symbolize the natural forces of places, tree, mountains, and elements; and the forces connected with the earth are equally connected with the planets and the constellations. They are therefore subject to the yearly, monthly, and daily cycles of manifestation and movement. Since humans are in constant contact with the natural environment, they must be vigilant and take care not to disturb these forces if they wish to maintain a harmonious relationship with nature. When disturbed, these deities are said to be capable of causing bad harvests or provoking disease in humans and their cattle. Thus the Tibetans are concerned to respect a "magical ecology."

These deities are encountered in most rituals. The Tibetans are concerned to live on good terms with the local deities. They avoid disturbing them and expect their concern to be reciprocated. They are often asked for protection, and it is not unusual for a local deity to become the protector of a village, a region, a monastery, or a spiritual lineage.

When Padmasambhava crossed the Himalayas on his way to Tibet, he subdued many hostile demons and local deities; indeed, not only did he subdue them, he forced them to take vows to protect the tantric teachings and practices. The following episode is recounted in a short biography of Padmasambhava, a treasure text discovered in the nineteenth century by the tertön Chogyur Lingpa (1829–1879):

> At Phuru, I subjugated Dorje Legpa, king of the tenacious evil spirits; at Yasru and Yönru, I subdued specters and cannibal spirits. At Osam, I tamed Thaglha, the Lord of epidemics and plagues. All of these I bound by solemn oath to the Dharma.

Padmasambhava also dominated hostile planetary forces.

> At Mount Ti Se (Kailash), I bound the stellar forces of the lunar mansions (Gyukar) and on the Targo I placed the dark forces of the planets under the control of the Dharma.

When a lama is preparing to bestow an initiation or when a yogi begins a retreat in a wild and lonely place, their first concern is the local deities. They ask those deities to lend them the place and they offer them a torma or ritual cake.

The traveler going over a pass will note a pile of stones or Lha Tho or sometimes even a "citadel," a square construction known as a Ten Khar. These structures mark the sites of mountain-deity cults. Colored cloth is arranged on these mounds, as well as wind-horse flags and above all weapons and even suits of armor, for these deities are wrathful and warlike. On the banks of rivers and near springs one sometimes finds pieces of colored cloth tied to a branch as offerings to the nāgas.

All these gods of natural forces appear as personal beings like those who populate the phenomenal world. They are no more or less real than other beings. Among the six classes of being, some are known as *Lha*, "gods," but this is to be understood as referring to a category of being midway between the gods of the sense realm, the āsuras, animals, and spirits.

The Buddhist teachings show the causes of the existence of these beings. If at death the consciousness leaves the body through the nostrils, this is a sign of rebirth among the nature spirits. Birth among the spirits may follow a life in the hell realms. The karmic circumstances surrounding the moment of death—assassination, violent death, hatred or passionate attachment, the breaking of monastic vows—may also bring about such a rebirth.

There are numerous categories of such beings and it would be very difficult to compile a clear and coherent list. Here I shall confine myself to citing the principles entailed, the eight classes of gods and demons.

The *Lu* are water deities. These are of pre-Buddhist origin and were assimilated at an early date to the Indian nāgas. They live below the ground, in springs, lakes, and rivers. They are in this sense local deities. However, by reason of their identification with the nāgas, they are believed to have an underground kingdom at the base of Mount Meru, the axial mountain. Patala is a kingdom filled with wealth, with rich and sumptuous palaces, for the nāgas are the guardians of underground treasures. Their king is Nanda Takṣaka (*Jogpo* in Tibetan), and they are divided into five castes like those of the Hindus: the kingly caste, the nobles, the Brahmins, the Vaiśya, and the Śūdra. Their bodies are half-human, half-snake. In Buddhism, they are considered to be under the authority of Virupakṣa, the guardian king of the West. Nāgas occur frequently in the history of Buddhism: when the Buddha attained enlightenment under the Bodhi tree at Bodhgayā, the king of the nāgas and his subjects protected him from the weather by forming an umbrella over his head; and when the Buddha taught the Prajñāpāramitā, the teaching on emptiness, on Vulture's Peak, the volumes of his teaching are said to have been entrusted to the protection of the nāgas. According to legend, the great master Nāgārjuna visited the nāga realm and brought the teachings back to reveal them to humankind. The nāgas are often entrusted with termas, treasure texts attributed to Padmasambhava. In the Tibetan era, the hero Gesar of Ling was born of a nāga mother.

As local deities, the nāgas may be vindictive when their natural environment is disturbed. The pollution of water, the building of dams and dikes, irrigation works, and the diversion of the course of rivers are all acts that may bring about sickness if they are not performed at the astrologically correct time. The nāgas are then capable of wreaking vengeance by sending such diseases as leprosy to the responsible humans.

The *Nyen* are generally malicious spirits who live in the atmosphere or at the surface of the earth, in fields and woods. Many of them live in trees, and it is therefore important not to cut timber on certain days indicated by the astrological almanacs. The Nyen are the cause of numerous ailments and certain types of cancer are also attributed to them. They are described as having a cowlike form and being yellow or green.

The *Sadak* are the "Lords of the Earth." They are generally neuter. The Sadak become irritated when their home, the earth, is "injured" by earthworks, the digging of wells, or the construction of a building. Certain days are therefore indicated as unfavorable for such activities; and before one builds a house or temple, offerings are made to them and their permission is sought to use the site.

The Sadak are an important group and are frequently met with in astrology. The *Vaidurya Karpo* gives complete lists of them. In the almanacs, the locations of some of them are indicated, for the Sadak are subject to the annual, seasonal, and even daily cycles. While a Sadak is in residence in a particular direction, it will sometimes be necessary to postpone work in that direction or even to cancel a journey.

The Sadak have a king, The se, whose body is red. He wears a robe of the same color and holds a large copper Garuḍa (a mythical bird). He is the chief of the Sadak of the cycle of twelve years. Each year, he occupies the direction of the ruling animal: in the Year of the Rat, he is in the North, in the Year of the Cow he is in the Northeast, and so on. He is accompanied by his principal consort, The Khyim, who is dark brown and holds a jar and a mirror. His second consort, Hang ne, is white and holds a large golden jar. The king's retinue comprises numerous deities: his son Te so, his minister Lonpo Trangkun, his astrolger Sewa La Khyen, his servant Hal Khyi, the guardian of his treasures Se Chi, his bodyguard Se Shar, his squire Ta Tri, his charger Rang Ta, and so on.

Each of these moves throughout the year. By way of illustration, we reproduce a diagram showing the movement of the Sadak in the Year of the Rat. These diagrams show the directions

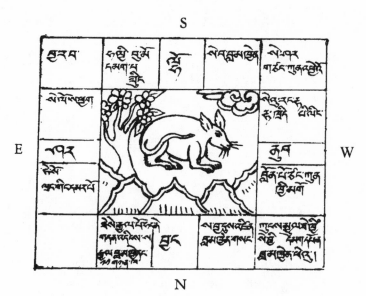

*Movement of the Sadak in the Year of the Rat*

occupied by different Sadak and are accompanied by commentaries that explain the appropriate activities. The almanac says:

> The horse Rang Ta of the god The se and his squire Ta Tri dwell in the West. One should avoid (in this direction) the purchase or sale of stables or horses, journeys on horseback, taking a corpse for burial in a horse-drawn cart and, in short, all equestrian activities and all funerary rites without exception.

The twelve-year cycle is not the only one associated with the Sadak: the same applies to the Mewas and the Parkhas. The nine Mewas are thus the residents of a group of nine Sadak:

> White 1 is inhabited by Sa yi Lhamo, the white "Earth Goddess."
>
> Black 2 is the place of Dud kyi Gyal po, the black "Demon King."
>
> Blue 3 is occupied by Sa den Duk je, the blue-black "Poisoning Sen Demon."
>
> Green 4 is the residence of Lugyal Waru, the green nāga with the goiter.
>
> Yellow 5 is inhabited by Sadak Gyalpo, the yellow-gold "King of the Sadak."
>
> White 6 is the residence of Gyalpo, the white spirit king.
>
> Red 7 is occupied by Tsen mar Chen po, the "Great Red Tsen."
>
> White 8 is the place of Lhachen Wangchuk, the white-colored "Great and Mighty God."
>
> Red 9 is the residence of Mamo Dzamunti, the dark red "Dzamunti Sorceress."

All these deities symbolize elemental earth-energies as they enter into relationship with the astrological configuration of the moment.

The *Tsen,* the red spirits that haunt rocks, are all male, the spirits of erring monks of earlier times. When they are subdued by a great practitioner, the Tsen often become the guardian of

*A number of the Sadak figures shown in the* Vaid-urya dkar po
*by Sangye Gyatso, regent of the Fifth Dalai Lama.*

temples, shrines, and monasteries. Red offerings are made to them.

The *Gyalpo* or "Spirit Kings" are said to be the spirits of evil kings or high lamas who had broken their vows. They are white in color and often wear armor. They are often local deities of great importance, such as mountain gods.

The *Dud* (Skt. *Māra*) are openly malevolent spirits who had been fiercely opposed to the Dharma in their previous lives. They create obstacles for practitioners and live on human flesh. They are black in color.

The *Mamo* constitute a very numerous class of fierce female deities. Although they predate Buddhism, they have been assimilated to the Matrika, a type of sorcerer of the charnel grounds. These black goddesses personify natural forces that become destructive when disturbed. They carry bags full of disease germs and comprise the retinue of the Great Dharma Protectresses.

The *Za* (Skt. *Graha*) are malevolent planetary spirits who cause diseases such as epilepsy. Some of them are seasonal: the Black Dog in Spring, the Dragon-tailed Monster in summer, the Knight on the Black Horse in autumn, and the Phoenix in Winter. Their movements have to be kept in mind and protective diagrams have to be made.

The *Nöchin*, assimilated in Buddhism to the Yakṣas, are the guardian-deities of the natural riches of the earth. Their chief is Vaiśrāvaṇa, the guardian-king of the North, who is also a wealth god. They are also associated with medicine: twelve Yakṣa generals took a vow before the Medicine Buddha to protect all those who read his sūtra or pronounced his mantra.

The *Lha* are white deities who are well-disposed toward humans.

Eight classes of spirit were foreshadowed, but ten types have been described. In fact, there is some variation and overlapping in the lists of the eight classes. We may note also the Shinje, "Lords of Death," who are often included in the lists of eight and who form the entourage of Yama, the personification of death.

Most of these spirits are capable of causing illness or "stealing one's vitality." There are karmic reasons for this: a person who disturbed the spirits in a past life, in this one may suffer an illness brought about by the spirits. The circumstances that make such an attack possible are always linked to a loss of vitality or an imbalance of elements in the victim. It is even said that when they are unable to touch a person whose vitality is intact, certain spirits will attack the weakest member of that person's family—this is the explanation given by Tibetan doctors for certain family diseases and many conditions that do not respond to any sort of treatment. In such cases, it is necessary to perform specific practices that make good the harm done to the spirits in the past.

There are many other types of "demon," "creators of obstacles," and so on. According to the sources, the number of demon species varies between 360 and 84,000!

A distinction is made between external demons, who cause obstacles external to the practitioner; internal demons, who cause internal sicknesses and disturbances; and secret demons, who are none other than disturbing thoughts. As a general rule, the latter symbolize our neuroses, our unconscious fears, and our spiritual obstacles. The story is told of the poet and yogi Milarepa that one day he found himself confronting a group of demons who had taken up residence in his cave in order to disturb him. He applied all means possible to defeat them, but to no avail. Finally, he abandoned the fight, relaxed his mind, and realized that they were nothing but the play of his perturbed mind. As soon as he realized their void nature, the manifestations disappeared.

## PROTECTIVE DIAGRAMS AND TALISMANS

For those who are unable to realize that demons are no more than a manifestation of the mind, there are many protective rituals and articles. Most of the latter are designs on paper, intended to be carried on the person or installed in the house.

The seals of Sipaho, designed to neutralize the influence of malefic planets, generally feature the cosmic turtle at their center, with the twelve animals of the twelve-year cycle on its belly, along with the eight Parkhas and the magic square of the Mewas. Circular protective diagrams are arranged around it, with their corresponding mantras. On each side there are geometric seals, reminiscent of Chinese Taoist seals, which are intended to repel evil influences in the twelve-year cycle, as well as those caused by the Lu, Nyen, and Sadak spirits. Mañjuśrī, the protector of astrology, sits at the top, along with the Kālacakra emblem, the "Ten Powers," an important apotropaic talisman made up of the six intertwined syllables of the Kālacakra mantra (OM HA KṢA MA LA VA RA YAM SVĀHĀ) in Lentsa letters.

The design is accompanied by a prayer of invocation to the astrological deities, who are the same as the local deities.

Eight Great Planets, respect your vows!
God of the element Wood, dwelling in the East,
God of the element Fire, dwelling in the South,
God of the element Metal, dwelling in the West,
God of the element Water, dwelling in the North,
God of the element Earth, dwelling in the four intermediate
    directions, all of you, maintain your great oath!
And you also, the five deities of the cosmic turtle!
Pay attention!
Take no notice of us, who are making offerings!
Do not go astray!
All you deities of the five elements, keep to your vows!
You twenty-eight constellations, Mindruk, Dranye, and the
    others, keep your vows!
May all the malevolent Sadaks keep their oath in this great
    assembly today!
Sagyal, King of the Earth, do not be angry today!
Do not break the Parkhas or the Mewas!
Do not destroy the year or trouble the months, do not steal
    the days or change the hours!
Do not invert the rising and setting of the stars!
Do not cause all the Düd demons to descend!
Do not bewitch the Earth!

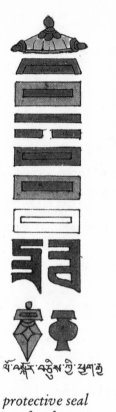

ཡོ་འཁོར་འཆུས་ཀྱི་ཕྱག་རྒྱ

*protective seal
for the
twelve-year cycle*

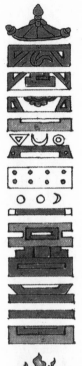

ས་བདག་རྗེ་བློན་གྱི་ཕྱག་རྒྱ

*protective seal
for the
lords and ministers
of the Sadak*

ཀླུ་གཉན་ས་བདག་གི་
ཕྱག་རྒྱ

*protective seal
against
Lu, Nyen, and Sadak*

སྲིད་པ་ཧོའི་ཕྱག་རྒྱ

*Seal of
Sipaho*

*Some protective talismans*

Do not act from jealousy or malice!
Do not have any hatred!

TAD YATHĀ OṂ HALA HALA SVĀHĀ HILI HILI
SVĀHĀ HULU HULU SVĀHĀ ATIMUKTI PAṆAYE
SVĀHĀ OṂ AKANINI KANA ĀBHĪLA-MAṆḌALA-
MANTRALE SVĀHĀ YE DHARMĀ HETU-PRABHAVĀ
HETUṂ TEṢĀM TATHĀGATO HYAVADAT
TEṢAṂ CA YO NIRODHA EVAṂ VĀDĪ MAHĀ
ŚRAMAṆAḤ OṂ SUPRATIṢṬHA VAJRAYE SVĀHĀ

The mantras with which the text concludes are of three sorts:
the first group consists of mantras invoking the planetary forces.
The second is the "Mantra of Interdependent Origination,"
which can be translated as follows: "Of all that which has a
causal origin, the Tathāgata has explained the cause; and of all
those things the Great Ascetic has also explained the cessation."
The third is a mantra of authentication of the seal.

On the back, there are also two prayers:

> King of the nāgas, Nanda Takṣaka, nāga of the royal caste, the
> nobel caste, the people, the Brahmins and the Śūdras, all the
> Nyen and all the Sadak, be cured!
>
> We, the yogis, despite the irreverent acts that we have com-
> mitted, whether peacefully or violently, such as turning the
> earth, removing stones, cutting trees where the Nyen dwell, or
> removing their rock fortresses, we ask you, do not act out of
> jealousy or hatred!
>
> And you also, the four great classes of Nyen, the sixteen
> classes of small Nyen, the lords of the soil belonging to the
> clans of the country, the full complement of Sadak, nāgas, and
> Nyen, be pacified, happy, and healed!
>
> Give us your friendly aid and be vigilant!

TATHĀGATA SARVA-ŚĀNTIṂ KURUYE SVĀHĀ
(Tathāgata, make everything pacified.)

> You who govern the year, the months, the days, and the
> hours, the King of the year, the ministers of the months, the

soldiers of the day, and the armies of the hours, lords and ministers of the Sadak, the Yoginī, the Lord of Death, Düd Tsenma, Kikang, Mamakhyi the Celestial Dog, Tsin Pung, Piling, Tsegyi, Hal Khyi, the Sadak of the twelve-year cycle, the Mewas, the Parkhas, the planets, and the lunar constellations, evil spirits of the hours, all of you, pay attention to this seal of Sipaho!

Do not act out of malevolence or jealousy, be pacified and happy!

OM AKANINI KANI ĀBHĪLA-MAṆḌALE
MANTRALE SVĀHĀ YE DHARMĀ HETU-PRAHBAVĀ
HETUṂ TEṢĀM TATHĀGATO HYAVADAT
TEṢAṂ CA YO NIRODHA EVAṂ VĀDĪ MAHĀ
ŚRAMAṆAḤ SVĀHĀ!

The practice of these prayers is accompanied by offerings, which may take the form of tormas, colored threads, medicines, and juniper smoke. These rituals are used to ward off bad astrological configurations, and also against drought or the danger of poor harvests.

## THE UNIVERSE

Tibetan cosmology is that of the Abhidharma and the Kālacakra, in which the universe is considered at the same time in spatial terms and in terms of the realms of existence. It includes all the levels of saṃsāric existence, hells, and the most exalted divine kingdoms. A "great universe" consists of one hundred times ten million small universes such as our own—this illustrates the vast scale of Buddhist cosmology. We shall describe here the structure of our small universe.

### The Small Universe

The small universe consists of a group of mountains, oceans, and continents, inhabited by sentient beings of the six realms. In the center is the great axial mountain, Mount Meru, which is structured as a conic section: the Eastern face is made of white crystal, the Southern face of blue lapis-lazuli, the Western face of rubies, and the Northern of emeralds or gold. Its base is located deep below the level of the ocean and its summit reaches into the skies. A fabulous tree grows from its base to its summit.

At its base, in ocean caves and rock caves, there live the āsuras or jealous gods, whose kingdom consists of four great cities, each ruled by a king. One of these kings is Rāhu, Lord of the Eclipse. The āsuras live at the level of the roots of the Wish-fulfilling Tree, and although their lives are pleasant, they can never enjoy the fruits of the tree, whose branches are in the realms of the gods. Consumed by jealousy and ambition, they wage ceaseless war against the god in order to obtain their pleasures. They are always vanquished, but they continue to fight.

The first four levels of Mount Meru are inhabited by the nāgas, the guardians of treasures, and various classes of demigod occupying the second to fourth levels: Suparnas, Danavas, Rakṣasas and Yakṣas. The fifth level is inhabited by the guardian kings of the four directions, who protect the divine realms and the universe against the demons. Dhritiraśtra, the lutenist, guards the East and rules the people of the Gandharvas, the celestial musicians. Virudhaka, king of the Kumbhandas, with a saber in his right hand, keeps watch over the South. Virūpakṣa, who is shown holding a stūpa, is the guardian of the West and King of the Nāgas. Vaiśrāvana, the guardian of the North, holds a banner of victory and a mongoose—he is the King of the Yakṣas and keeps watch over the riches of the universe.

The kingdom of the Four Great Kings is the gateway to the divine realms. The devas or gods are divided into three large groups according to their degree of spiritual advancement: the gods of the realm of desire (kāmaloka), who are still part of the sensual realm; the gods of the realm of pure form (rūpaloka), who are beyond desire but still possess a material body; and the gods of the formless realm (arūpaloka), absorbed in the most elevated meditation, beyond all concepts.

The gods of desire or kāmadevas occupy five different realms:

1. The Heavens of the Thirty-three, located at the summit of Mount Meru, which is also the site of the palace of Indra, king of the thirty-three gods.
2. The heavens of Yama, the first realm below the summit.
3. The Tuṣita heavens or "Heavens of Beatitude," the divine realm in which buddhas dwell before incarnating on earth.
4. The Nimāṇarati heavens, inhabited by gods "who create their own pleasures."
5. The Paranirmita heavens, inhabited by the gods "who arrange the creation of others." This is the summit of the desire realm.

The gods of pure form, the Rūpavacaras, have luminous bodies of great beauty. Their heavens are celestial material realms composed of the essence of the five elements. Their chief is Brahmā. They are divided into 17 or 18 kingdoms and their hierarchy reflects the four levels of meditative absorption, the four dhyānas. The highest of these heavens is Akaniṣṭa or "the unequaled."

The formless gods are "pure spirits," consciousness absorbed in the highest meditation, and they are divided into four realms depending on their meditative attainment. This is the highest level that can be attained in saṃsāra.

All the devas are very long-lived, their life span being proportional to their level of attainment. The gods of the Heaven of the Thirty-three live for 1,000 years, and each day in this realm is equal to 100 years in the human realm. The Tuṣita gods live for 4,000 years of like duration. The Parinirmita gods live for 160,000 years, and each day is equivalent to 16,000 human years. The life span in the form realms ranges from 16,000 kalpas to one quarter of a great kalpa. In the formless realms, consciousness is absorbed in meditation for between 20,000 and 80,000 great kalpas. Although these periods of time are almost inconceivable, none of the gods is immortal. At the end of their lives, they are condemned to rebirth in another realm, like all other beings, because they are subject to the law of karma.

Around the foot of Mount Meru there are walls formed by seven four-sided golden mountains, each half the height of the one behind it. Between these walls are located the seven square Sitas, lakes whose pure water is endowed with eight perfect qualities: lightness, luminosity, clarity, purity, freshness, sweetness, and perfect taste and scent.

The whole is surrounded by a great ocean of salt water, which supports the continents.

In each of the cardinal directions, there is an island continent surrounded by two smaller continents. There are thus twelve continents in total. At the East is Videha (*Lu Pakpo*), surrounded by Dehu (*Lu*) and Videha (*Lu pak*). This continent is white and shaped like a half-moon. The people who live there are twice as tall as us and their faces resemble half-moons. They are peaceful vegetarians and live in towns and villages. Their life span is between 250 and 500 years. Although their lives are pleasant, it is not greatly advisable to be reborn in their realm since they do not have the true Dharma. The chief characteristic of Videha is its mountain of diamonds, lapis-lazuli, saphires, emeralds, pearls, gold, silver, and crystal.

In the South is Jumbudvīpa (*Dzambuling*), our own continent, surrounded by Camara (*Nga yap*) and Upacamara (*Ngayap zhen*). Our world is a fortunate one, where buddhas are born and the Dharma flourishes. It is blue and trapezoidal in shape. Its inhabitants have a life span of a century. Its main feature is the thicket of trees that accomplish all desires and whose fruits fall as rain.

In the West is the continent of Godaniya (*Nub pa tangcho ling*), surrounded by Shatha (*Yoden*) and Uttaramantrini (*Lamchok dro*). Godaniya is ruby red and circular in shape. Its inhabitants have round faces and they are four times as tall as us. They live for five centuries and follow a pastoral life, living on the dairy produce of their beasts. Its main feature is the herd of wish-fulfilling heifers, each of whose udders give all that is desired.

To the North lies Uttarakuru (*Draminyen Ling*), surrounded

by Kurava (*Draminyen*) and Karuava (*Draminyen gyi Da*). The northern continent is green and square. Its inhabitants are giants, with square faces "like those of horses." They live in great abundance for more than a thousand years, without effort or worry, for the land is very rich. They live on cereals that grow spontaneously, and they do not for a moment feel the need to wear clothes or build shelters, towns, or villages. But Draminyen means "with an unpleasant voice"; and indeed, a week before they die, the inhabitants of Draminyen hear the grating voice of death, which announces to them the way in which they will die and what sort of bad rebirth awaits them. Their suffering then exceeds what we undergo in a whole lifetime. The main attribute of this continent is the cereal that grows without effort, an inexhaustible and delicious food.

Although they are all inhabited by humans, these continents remain invisible to the eyes of the inhabitants of other worlds, except for clairvoyants. Jambudvīpa is the only one in which buddhas appear in perceptible form and it is said to be the best place in which to be born.

Beyond the continents, the great external ocean reaches as far as the iron mountains that surround the universe, Cakravala. The entire universe rests on a base of gold.

In the depths of the continent of Jambudvīpa are the hells. There are eight levels of hot hells on top of each other. From top to bottom, these are the Reviving Hell, the Hell of Black Lines, Mass Destruction, Lamentation, Great Lamentation, Heat, Extreme Heat, and the Avīci Hell or Vajra Hell, whose tortures are unimaginable.

The *Longhchen Nyingtik* describes the hot hells as follows:

> If I am born in the hell realms, on an earth of red-hot iron, my head and body will be separated with weapons and my body will be ripped apart with saws and crushed by hammers of burning metal. I will call out for help as I am suffocating, imprisoned in an iron house without doors. I will be transfixed on burning, razor-sharp stakes and I will boil in liquid bronze. I will burn in a fire of intense heat.

There are also eight cold hells, tiered in the same way and located next to the hot hells, under the iron mountains of Cakravala. These are called Pustules, Bursting Pustules, Groaning, Great Groaning, Trembling, Blue Lotus, Lotus, and Great Lotus.

> In the great snow-covered mountains, in narrow crevasses and glaciers, I will be swept by the torment of snow. Battered by a glacial wind, my tender flesh will be covered with blisters and bursting ulcerations. My lamentations and moanings will be endless. Enduring the sensation of intolerable pain, like a sick man close to death whose strength is exhausted, I will cry out from behind clenched teeth, my skin will crack, my flesh coming out of wounds where the skin is deeply cleft. Such are the eight cold hells.

Finally, there are four peripheral hells located around Avīci:

> In a field of razors, my feet will be chopped and my body will be torn apart in a forest of swords. I will be sucked into the mire of the swamp of rotting corpses and I will suffer in an expanse of burning ashes. These are the peripheral hells surrounding the unimaginable hell.

The diffused hells have no specific location: "Imprisoned in doors, pillars, hearths, and ropes, I will be endlessly used and exploited. Such are the diffused hells."

The karmic causes of birth in the hell realms are principally anger, hatred, murder, and suicide. Although extremely long, residence in these worlds of suffering is in no case eternal.

The *pretas* or hungry ghosts, constantly tortured by hunger, thirst, exhaustion, and hallucinations, live in underground cities or in the realm of Yama, or death, while others are scattered throughout the universe.

Animals live in all the continents of the universe.

Such is the Buddhist view of the world.

## Time

The universes are not eternal—they have a beginning and an end. In order to express the duration of these periods, the Buddhists use the concept of *kalpa*. The Mahākalpa is the unit of time that measures the life of a universe, from its formation to its destruction. A Mahākalpa comprises four medium kalpas, representing the four phases of the evolution of a great universe: formation, endurance, destruction, and void. Each medium kalpa is divided into twenty lesser kalpas.

### THE PERIOD OF THE FORMATION OF THE UNIVERSE

The cause of the creation of the universe is none other than the karma of the beings whose consciousness survives the destruction of the previous Mahākalpa. By the strength of this karma, there appears little by little in the voice a calm wind, whose power gradually increases to form the maṇḍala of air. Clouds form and develop, giving rise to the element liquid, the maṇḍala of water. The great mass of water supported by the wind becomes the primordial ocean. This ocean, which resembles milk, is then whipped by the wind—this is compared with the churning of milk to make cream. The golden base of the universe then separates out, and a thick yellow foam forms on its surface, which then solidifies and gives birth to Earth, in the same way as butter separates from cream. The earth becomes a mountain around which the clouds condense, and the resulting rainfall gives rise to the saltwater oceans.

Jewels then crystalize and form Mount Meru, the axial mountain, and the seven mountains that surround it. Finally there appear the continents and the iron mountain that encircles the universe. One hundred times ten million universes are born simultaneously in this way, thus forming a great universe.

The gods of the form realm then leave Mount Meru and colonize the empty continents—this is the golden age, when people are like gods, free of illness and taking nourishment only from meditation. Their bodies emit their own light, and so there is neither day nor night; and their life span is so long that it is incalculable. However, as a result of karmic defilement, one of these divine beings one day tastes the creamy substance that covers the earth, and soon the others follow suit. Little by little, as a result of taking this material nourishment, their bodies become more gross and their powers decrease. When this delicious food is exhausted, they all begin to live on the fruits of the earth. As their luminosity diminishes and their longevity declines, desires and passions appear. The earth has to be cultivated and the concept of property arises; and along with it jealousy and conflict appear. As a result of desire, sexual organs form. Children are born from the contact between men and women, and the world is soon peopled by numerous humans. Shadows now envelop the world, and then the sun, moon, and stars appear in the sky as a result of past karma. Because of the many conflicts that arise among humans, they choose a king, Mangkur, who decrees laws.

From this time, humans become subject to birth, disease, old age, and death. Some of them go into solitude to practice meditation, and these become the first Mahārisis. Others, as a result of the accumulation of bad karma, are reborn after death in lower realms, and thus the hells and the realms of the *pretas* come into existence. The cruel cycle of samsāra begins again.

This period of formation lasts for twenty lesser kalpas, in the course of which life span is reduced to 84,000 years.

THE PERIOD OF ENDURANCE

The period of endurance also lasts for 20 lesser kalpas, during the first of which life span diminishes by one year every two centuries until it reaches 10 years.

During the following 18 kalpas, periods of growth alternate with periods of decay. In the first half of a kalpa, life span increases from 10 years to 84,000 years at the rate of one year per century, and in the second half it is again reduced to 10 years. During periods of growth, the universe is ruled by a king, the Cakravartin, but he disappears during periods of decay; and that is the time when Buddhas appear in the world.

We are at the moment going through a period of decay in a "fortunate kalpa," during which 1,002 buddhas will appear. Śākyamuni, the historical Buddha, is only the fourth of these. The next will be Maitreya, the Buddha of Love.

When life expectancy drops to 30 years, a terrible famine breaks out; and when it reaches 20, there are seven months of epidemic. When it reaches 10, a rain of weapons falls for seven days. The few people who survive, under the inspiration of the buddhas, practice virtue once more and life expectancy begins to increase again. In the twentieth minor kalpa, life expectancy increases by one year per every 200 years and reaches 84,000 years.

## PERIOD OF DESTRUCTION

Beings' karma matures during this period. Destruction begins with the hells and then proceeds from the lower to the higher realms. Certain beings are reborn in the divine realms, but this does not delay their destruction. Of the three spheres of existence, the sphere of desire is the first to be destroyed: seven suns rise and dry out the world before reducing it to an immense brazier and reducing it to ashes. It is thus the Fire element that destroys the *kāmaloka* or world of desire. All but the highest of the gods of the *rūpaloka* or sphere of pure form are then destroyed by the elements of Water and Air. The highest gods, those of the fourth dhyāna, as well as the gods of the *arūpaloka* or formless realm, are never destroyed, due to their great purity.

## PERIOD OF VOID

No universe exists and none is created for the 20 kalpas that constitute the Great Kalpa. At the end of this period, a new Mahākalpa begins and a new universe appears.

In concluding this brief survey of cosmic time, we may note that a minor kalpa is divided into a number of subperiods, such as the Four Yugas: the Satya Yuga or age of gold; the Tretā Yuga or age of silver; the Dvāpara Yuga or age of bronze, and the Kāli

Yuga or age of iron. In the course of these periods, which are of decreasing length, there is a progressive degeneration in the conditions of life, brought about by negative karma. We are at present in the Kāli Yuga, the dark age which the Tibetans call "the dregs of time," a period during which everything is accelerated and intensified as a result of the pressure of karma. Karma ripens more rapidly and energy is greater; and most beings are quickly engulfed in suffering. It is nevertheless possible to clear away the fog and attain realization more quickly.

## THE COSMIC MAN

As we have seen, the Tantras view the human being as a microcosm containing all the energies of the cosmos. The gross body is considered to be like the universe: the spinal column is like Mount Meru, the axial mountain; the four limbs are like the four continents; and the eyes are like the Sun (right eye) and the Moon (left eye).

At the subtle level, the body contains certain channels, the *nāḍīs* (*tsa*) and energy centers, the *cakras* (*khorlo*). A subtle air known as the *prāṇa* (*lung*), circulates in the *nāḍīs*, acting as the vehicle for various energies. These in their turn are located in the cakras in the form of drops, the *bindu* (*thikle*). All of these are connected with the cosmic symbolism of the elements of the planets.

In Tibetan yoga, there are said to be three main channels. The first is the central channel or Tsa Uma, which stretches from a point below the navel to the crown of the head. Connected with the element of space, its function is to ensure that the vital energy descends into the body and to connect the different cakras. This is also known as "Drachen," the planet Rāhula. The right channel or Roma Tsa, is red and is associated with the Fire element and masculine energies. It reaches from the base of the right nostril to the root of the sexual organ, passing up through the cranium and then down through the vertical axis. This is also known as Nyima, the Sun. The left channel, Kyangma Tsa, is associated with the water element and feminine energies. Its location is similar to that of the right channel except that it is on the left side of the body. It is also known as Dawa, the Moon.

The five cakras are arranged along the central channel. The "hundred-thousand petaled" Dab Tong cakra at the crown of the head includes the two head cakras of the Indian system, Sahasrara and Ajña, which are located between the eyebrows. These are also known to the Kālacakra system. This cakra is connected with the element of Space. In the system of the five Buddha families, it is linked with Vairocana and the all-pervading wisdom of the Buddha family. The throat cakra, connected with the element of Air and the energy of speech, corresponds to the Buddha Amitābha of the Padma family and discriminating wisdom. The heart cakra is associated with the element of Fire, the Buddha Akṣobhya of the Vajra family, and the mirrorlike wisdom. The navel cakra is connected with the Water element, the Buddha Ratnasambhava of the Ratna family, and the wisdom of equality. The cakra of the secret place comprises the two cakras Svadhistana and Mūladhara of the Indian tradition. It is connected with the Earth element and the karma family, the Buddha Amoghasiddhi and the all-accomplishing wisdom.

The arrangement of the energies in the cakras corresponds with the symbolism of stūpas or *chorten*, reliquary mounds representing the mind of the buddhas. The object of yoga is to purify our elements and internal energies, which normally operate at a gross level as negative emotions and the aggregates of the ego. Once this transmutation is complete, we are able to realize our awakened state, the Buddha nature.

In certain Tantric practices of Tsongkhapa and Padmavajra, the twelve petals of the heart cakra are identified with the internal zodiac. Prāṇa circulates inside this cakra in accord with the day and night movements of the signs of the zodiac in the sky.

The cosmic turtle, symbolizing the universe, is sometimes understood also as representing the energy structure of the human body. Thus the axis running from its head to its tail is both Mount Meru and the central channel. Three vajras emerge from

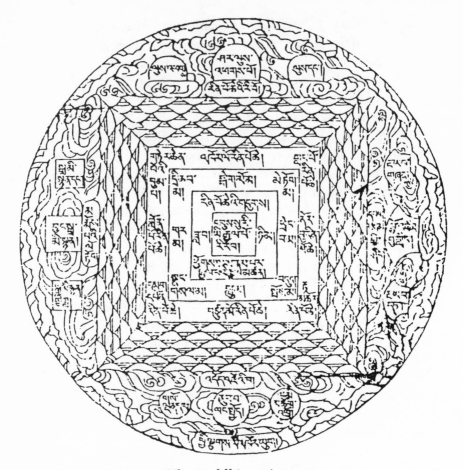

*The Buddhist universe*

its head: one, at the crown and in the body axis, denotes the blue central channel; the second, at the right and red in color, represents the right channel; and the third, white, represents the left channel or Kyangma. Another vajra emerges from the tail. Snakes entwined around this vajra and those of the lateral head vajras symbolize the subtle energies of the body.

# CALENDAR
# OF SPECIAL DAYS
# AND RELIGIOUS
# FESTIVALS

In the Tibetan lunar calendar, there are a number of special days on which festivals are celebrated and rituals are performed. We note here the most important annual and monthly days.

## GREAT ANNUAL CEREMONIES

*Losar* (*lo gsar*) is the Tibetan new year and the occasion for a great number of celebrations and ceremonies. These begin on the 29th day of the 12th month, the day of Gütor, when all the negativities of the preceding year are exorcised. In the monasteries, the monks and lamas perform rituals and offering *pūjās* to the *Dharmapālas*, the protective deities of Buddhism, in order to persuade them to remove obstacles and demons. They also offer prayers to Dharmapālas, asking them to protect the new year and bring about favorable circumstances.

The last day of the year, the 30th day of the 12th month, is devoted to purification. The Tibetans clean their houses from top to bottom and wash their hair. In the monasteries, the *Tashi* or good luck ceremony is performed to the accompaniment of somber music played on long trumpets.

On New Year's Day, people dress in clean or new clothes. New prayer flags are hung on the roofs of houses and monasteries, and the *Losar* ceremonies begin, lasting for the best part of the first month. They consist of group practices in which both monks and laypeople take part—prayer rituals (*Mönlam*), and rituals for the purification of houses, sacred lama dances (*Cham*), fasting, group prayers, and so on.

The official New Year is *Gyalpo Losar*, or "Royal New Year," which is celebrated on the 1st day of the 1st month (new moon in February or early March) in all the large urban centers. There is also a "Farmer's New Year" (*Sonam losar*), celebrated chiefly in the country and in the border areas of Tibetan culture (Dolpo, Nepal, etc.). This New Year occurs toward the winter solstice, the 1st day of the 12th month. In Ladakh, following a custom introduced during the 17th century by King Jamyang Namgyal, New Year is even celebrated on the first day of the 11th month, two months before the official Losar. Again the Kālacakra New Year falls on the 1st day of the 3rd month, in April–May.

The principal religious anniversaries and special days are:

*1st month, 14th day:* Anniversary of Milarepa, the great yogipoet and founder of the Kagyü school.

*1st month, 15th day: Chonga Chöpa.* This day celebrates the miracle of Śrasvati. On this day, in order to increase the devotion and merits of his disciples, the Buddha Śākyamuni performed many different miracles. Merits are multiplied by ten million.

*1st month, 21st day:* Anniversary of Jamyang Khyentse Wangpo, one of the greatest masters of the nineteenth century.

*3rd month, 15th day:* Day when the Buddha taught the Kālacakra.

*3rd month, 25th day:* Anniversary of the fifth Dalai Lama.

The 4th month is important in the sphere of religious practice. It is said that the merits of practice are multiplied by one million during this month.

*4th month, 7th or 8th day:* Anniversary of the birth of the Buddha.

*4th month, 15th day:* Enlightenment and *parinirvāṇa* of the Buddha. This is a day for intensive practice and the reading of the sūtras. Pūjās are performed in celebration. Merits are multiplied by 10 million.

*4th month, 23rd day:* Anniversary of Virapa, founder of the Sakya school. This anniversary is celebrated for 7 days in Sakyapa monasteries.

*5th month, 15th day:* Dzamling Chi Sang, day of local deities. Smoke rituals are performed and offerings are made to the local deities and protectors. According to Theravāda tradition, this is also the day upon which the Buddha first gave teachings.

*6th month, 4th day:* Chökor Düchen, the day upon which the Buddha gave the First Turning teachings (the Four Noble Truths) at Sārnath. This is a day of practice, upon which merits are multiplied by ten million.

*6th month, 10th day:* Birth of Guru Rinpoche.

*7th month, 15th day:* Anniversary of the discovery of the four Medical Tantras (*gyü zhi*) by Trapa Ngönshe. Celebrations of the Medicine Buddha.

*9th month, 3rd day:* Annniversary of Jigme Lingpa, one of the great Nyingma masters.

*9th month, 4th day:* Anniversary of Karma Pakṣi, second Karmapa.

*9th month, 22nd day:* Lhabap Düchen, the descent of the Buddha from heaven. On this day, texts are read and offering ceremonies are performed. Merits are multiplied by 10 million.

*10th month, 25th day:* Anniversary of Tsongkapa, founder of the Geluk school.

*11th month, 3rd day:* Anniversary of Düsum Khyenpa, first Karmapa.

*11th month, 6th or 7th day:* Ngenpa Gu Dzom, the day on which nine ill omens coincide. It is advised not to undertake any important activity on this inauspicious day.

*11th month, 26th day:* Anniversary of Jamgön Kongtrul the Great, an eminent master of the tenth century.

*12th month, 18th day:* Anniversary of Longchenpa, the greatest master of the Nyingma school.

*12th month, 29th day:* Gütor (see above).

On the anniversaries of great masters, offering ceremonies are performed in the monasteries belonging to the corresponding schools.

The most important of the special days are the four *Düchen,* or "Great Times": the birth of the Buddha, his enlightenment and parinirvāṇa, his first teachings, and his descent from the Tuṣita heaven.

Each of the great monasteries, morever, used to have its own special day and ceremonies, when sacred dances and other rituals were performed. This was the case, for example, with the monastery of Kubum, where, on the 15th day of the 1st month great numbers of butter sculptures were displayed. The exquisite beauty of these sculptures astonished travelers such as Pierre Huc in the nineteenth century.

## Important Days of the Month

Each month has a number of days dedicated to particular practices.

The 8th is the day of Tārā, protectress deity of Tibet. Pūjās are performed to Tārā.

The 10th is Guru Rinpoche day. Guru Rinpoche or Padmasambhava is the Buddha who established Tantric Buddhism in Tibet. At the esoteric level, he is the essence of all buddhas and masters. He is the Buddha of our troubled age, dispelling all negativities, and as such he occupies an important place in the hearts and in the practice of the Tibetans, particularly those of the Nyingma school. Each Guru Rinpoche day commemorates an episode from his life. His Holiness Dudjom Rinpoche, late Supreme Head of the Nyingma School, describes these as follows.

*1st month:* Guru Rinpoche renounces his kingdom and practices yoga and meditation in the great creation ground of Sitavana, the "cool grove," where he attains liberation. He gathers around himself the goddesses of the cemeteries, the mātrikas and ḍākinīs, and is known as Śāntarakṣita, "the protector of peace."

*2nd month:* Guru Rinpoche receives monastic ordination (*rabjung*) from Ananda, a disciple of the Buddha. Displaying an unparalleled comprehension and complete mastery both of the sūtras and of the tantras, he is known as Śākya Senge, "Lion of the Śākyas."

*3rd month:* The King of Zahor tries to burn Guru Rinpoche. However, the guru transforms the flames into a lake (the lake Tso Pema or Rewalsar), establishes the Dharma in the land of Zahor and takes the king's daughter, Mandarāva, as his spiritual consort. He is known as Guru Pema Jungne, "the Lotus-Born Teacher."

*4th month:* The deluded ministers and people of Orgyen (Oḍḍiyāna) attempt to burn Guru Rinpoche and his consort Mandarāva alive. The guru transforms the flames into a lake, from which he emerges with his consort seated on a lotus. The king, his ministers, and the people are filled with devotion. He is known as Pema Dorje Tsel, "the Guru with Vajra and Lotus."

*5th month:* The Tirthikas, extreme philosophers, try to damage the Dharma in South India; but through his great power, Guru Rinpoche defeats them all along with their gods and protectors. Raising the banner of victory of the Dharma, he is known as Guru Sangge Dradog, "the Lion's Roar Guru."

*6th month:* At sunrise, Guru Rinpoche is mysteriously born from a dazzling light in Lake Dhanakośa. Turning the wheel of the Dharma for the ḍākinīs, he is known as Guru Tsokye Dorje, "Vajra Lake-Born Guru."

*7th month:* The non-Buddhists of Tamradvipa throw the Guru into the river Ganges. He rises from the waters, reverses the flow of the river, and performs a Vajra dance in the sky. Inspired by devotion, the non-Buddhists begin to follow the Dharma. He is known as Guru Khading Tsel, "the Guru Who Flies Like a Garuḍa."

*8th month:* The non-Buddhists attempt to poison the Guru, but he transforms the poison into amrita (nectar). He becomes luminous and inspires faith in the non-Buddhists. He is known

273

as Guru Nyima Özer, "the Sun-Ray Guru."

*9th month:* Guru Rinpoche takes the wrathful form of Vajra-kumāra at Yang Le Shö, in Nepal. He subdues the local deities and negative forces. He practices the sādhana of Yangdak Heruka and at the same time attains the level of Vidyādhara (holder of knowledge) in the realization of Mahāmudrā. He is known as Guru Dorje Tötrengtsel, "the Guru with the Vajra Garland of Skulls."

*10th month:* Arriving in Central Tibet, the Guru subdues all negative and hostile forces. He founds the great monastery of Samye and lights the lamp of the Dharma, teaching sūtra and tantra. He leads his twenty-five disciples and King Trisong Detsen to liberation and is known as Guru Padmasambhava, "the Lotus-Born Guru."

*11th month:* In Bhutan, the Guru takes wrathful form and places the local deities and protectors under his own control. He converts them into guardians of the termas (hidden teachings) and initiates them into the secret oral teachings, which are only revealed to tertöns (discoverers of termas). He is known as Guru Dorje Drolo, "the Vajra-Wrathful Guru."

*12th month:* King Indrabhūti invites Guru Rinpoche to Orgyen, where he is proclaimed heir to the throne and marries the princess Bhaśadhāra. He is known as Guru Pema Gyalpo, "Lotus-Prince Guru."

These are the twelve deeds of Guru Rinpoche, commemorated in the course of the twelve months of the year. Each one reflects the profound symbolism of the tantras and cannot be interpreted according to ordinary thought patterns.

In the three schools of the New Tradition (Kagyü, Sakya, and Geluk), the 10th day of the month is sacred to Heruka, the wrathful form of the buddhas. Thus on the 10th day, male energy is at its peak.

*15th day:* Day of the Buddha, devoted to meditation and the recitation of sūtras.

*19th day:* Performance of pūjās to the protectors and the Medicine Buddha.

*25th day:* Day of the ḍākinīs, "those who fly in space." The ḍākinīs symbolize the female energy of enlightenment and are the inspiration of the great yogis. On this day, female energy is at its peak.

*29th day:* Day of the Dharmapālas, protectors of the Dharma.

*30th day:* Buddha day, devoted to recitation of the sūtras.

# THE
# WRITTEN SOURCES
# AND THEIR AUTHORS

Most of the great Tibetan scholars have left one or more works on astrology, whence there is a great deal of literature on the subject.

Certain Sanskrit astrological works have been translated into Tibetan. Many of these deal with *dKa rtsis* astrology according to the Kālacakra system, which was introduced into Tibet in the year 1024. The most important of these is the Kālacakra root tantra, the *Dus 'khor rtsa rgyud,* written by Sucandra, king of Shambhala, in accordance with the teachings of the Buddha Śākyamuni himself. We may also note the very important abridged *Kālacakra Tantra,* the *Dus 'khor bsdus rgyud* or *Laghutantra,* composed by Mañjuśrīkīrti, eighth king of Shambhala after Sucandra, who received the title *Kūlika,* "lineage holder." This tantra comprises five chapters with a total of 1,047 stanzas. This text, in its Tibetan translation, is widely consulted.

The Kūlika King Puṇḍarīka, son of Mañjuśrīkīrti, was the author of the great Kālacakra commentary, the *Vimalaprabhā* (Tib. *'Grel chen dri med 'od*). Among other Indian works translated into Tibetan, we may note the *bDe ldan Svarodayai rGyud* or *dbYang 'char gyi rGyud*, which is the source text for a partic-ular system of astrology; the *dbYang 'char;* the *Mig bcu gnyis pa'i mdo;* the *sTag rnga'i rtogs brjod;* and the *Nyi ma'i snying po'i mdo*. All of these have been the subject of many commentaries in Tibetan.

All the authors of astrological texts were also eminent spiri-tual masters, famous in Tibet's religious history.

**The Third Karmapa, Rang byung rDo rje** (1284–1339) was a great Mahāmudrā and rDzogs chen master. He evolved a sys-tem of astrology known as *mTshur phu,* and wrote the *rTsis kun btus pa* and the *Zab mo sngang don*.

**Bu ston Rin chen grub** (1290–1364), the great Sa skya mas-ter, was a Kālacakra scholar. In 1326, he composed the *rTsis gz-hung mkhas pa dga byed*.

**mKhas grub dGe legs dPal bzang** (1385–1438), one of the two main disciples of Tsong kha pa, founder of the dGe lugs pa school, was the author of a number of commentaries on the Kālacakra, and an astrological work, the *Tika che de nyid snang ba*.

**Phug pa lHun grub rGya tsho** was the great astrologer who created the so-called *Phug* system. In 1447, he wrote a treatise entitled *Pad dkar zhal lung mau bu*.

**mKhas grub nor bzang rgya mtsho,** an astrological scholar, wrote the *Dri med 'od rgyan* in 1483.

**Lo chen Dharmaśrī** (1654–1718), brother of the great *gter ton* O rgyan gter bdag gling pa, was a rNying ma pa master and astrological scholar. To him we owe the *'Byung rtsis man ngag zla ba'i 'odzer,* which deals with the astrology of the elements in accordance with Chinese tradition and which was widely used in preparing the present work. He was also the author of the *rTsis kyi man ngag nin yed snang ba* and its commentary *Nyin byed snang ba'i rnam grel gser gyi shing rta,* both of which deal with *dKa rtsis* astrology.

**sDe srid Sangs rgyas rGya mtsho** (1653–1705), regent of the Fifth Dalai Lama, composed the celebrated *Vaidūrya dkar po ma bu,* one of the main works of Tibetan astrology.

Sum pa Ye shes dPal 'byor (1704–1788), a great dGe lugs pa scholar, composed the *dGe ldan rtsis gsar ma bu,* as well as a number of medical treatises.

Thu'u kvan Chos kyi Yyi ma (b. 1737), celebrated for his perfect understanding of the different systems of tenets, composed an astrological treatise, the *mKhas pa'i nying nor.*

Closer to our own times, in 1827 Phyag mdzod gSung rab composed the *Rig ldan snying thig,* which deals with the fundamentals of Kālacakra astrology and the calculations used therein.

Brag dgon bsTan pa Rab rgyas also composed a treatise on Kālacakra astrology in 1867, the *Rigs ldan mchod pa'i 'od snang.*

Finally, the great rNying ma pa scholar 'Ju Mi pham 'Jam dbyags rNam rgyal (1846–1912) wrote a number of commentaries on the Kālacakra and on astronomical and astrological calculations.

# TIBETAN
# TRANSLITERATIONS

This section lists Tibetan terms used in the text except those found in Appendix 2.

| PHONETIC | WYLIE TRANSCRIPTION |
|---|---|
| Amdo | *a mdo* |
| Balchen Geko | *dbal chen ge khod* |
| Bön (po) | *bon (po)* |
| Butön | *bu ston* |
| Chag Shen gyi Thekpa | *phya gshen gyi theg pa* |
| Chak | *lcags* |
| Cham | *'cham* |
| Chama | *bya ma* |
| Che | *dpyad* |
| Chenrezi | *spyan ras gzigs* |
| Chi | *khyi* |
| Chimo | *phyi mo* |
| Chökor düchen | *chos 'khor dus chen* |
| Chonga chö pa | *bco lnga mchod pa* |
| Chu | *chu* |
| Chu (constellation) | *mchu* |

| | |
|---|---|
| Chu tsö | *chu tsod* |
| Chülhamo | *chu'i lha mo* |
| Chume | *chu smad* |
| Chutö | *chu stod* |
| Da | *dva* |
| Da shol | *zla shol* |
| Dakye | *zla skyes* |
| Dalwe lha den ma | *dal ba'i lha ldan ma* |
| Dam sri | *dam sri* |
| Dawa | *zla ba* |
| Del | *rdel* |
| Dengchen lhamo | *gdengs can lha mo* |
| Dö | *mdos* |
| Dokham | *mdo khams* |
| Dön | *gdon* |
| Dorje Drolö | *rdo rje gro lod* |
| Dorje Tötrengtsel | *rdo rje* |
| Dra lha | *dgra lha* |
| Drakshul chen | *drag shul chen* |
| Drakpo Khorlo Chang | *drag po khor lo 'chang* |
| Dranye | *bra nye* |
| Dre | *gre* |
| Dri | *'bri* |
| Drigum | *dri gum* |
| Driza | *dri za* |
| Dro | *'bro* |
| Drokme | *grogs smad* |
| Drokpa | *'brog pa* |
| Droktö | *grogs stod* |
| Drozhin | *'gro bzhin* |
| Druk | *'brug* |
| Drukpa Kunley | *'brug pa kun legs* |
| Drup | *grub* |
| Dubu | *gdu bu* |
| Dudjom Rinpoche | *'bud 'joms rin po che* |
| Dü chö | *bdud spyod* |
| Dü kyi khor lo | *dus kyi khor lo* |
| Dükhor Dügyü | *dus 'khor bsdus rgyud* |
| Dükhor Tsagyü | *dus 'khor rtsa rgyud* |

| | |
|---|---|
| Düsyum Khyenpa | *dus gsum mkhyen pa* |
| Dzam ling chi sang | *dzam gling kyi gsangs* |
| Dzawö lha | *mdza bo'i lha* |
| Dzo | *mdzo* |
| Dzogchen | *rdzogs chen* |
| Dzogrim | *rdzogs rim* |
| Dzong pön | *rdzong dpon* |
| Gar | *mgar* |
| Gekmo | *sgag mo* |
| Gekö | *ge khod* |
| Geluk | *dge lugs* |
| Gerpa | *sger pa* |
| Go | *mgo* |
| Golok | *'go log, mgo log* |
| Gyal | *rgyal* |
| Gyanak | *rgya nag* |
| Gyü zhi | *rgyud bzhi* |
| Gyukang | *rgyu rkang* |
| Gyukar | *rgyu skar* |
| Gyur Bön | *gyur bon* |
| Ja | *bya* |
| Ja nagpa | *bya nag pa* |
| Jamgön Kongtrul | *'jam mgon knog sprul* |
| Jamyang Khyentse Wangpo | *'jam dbyangs mkhyen brtse'i dbang po* |
| Ji | *byi* |
| Jigme Lingpa | *'jig med gling pa* |
| Jigten kyong | *'jig rten skyong* |
| Jinme Lhamo | *sbyin ma'i lha mo* |
| Jizhin | *byi bzhin* |
| Jonang | *jo nang* |
| Jordenma | *'byor ldan ma* |
| Jungtsi | *'byung rtsi* |
| Jungtsi Men Ngak Dawe Öser | *'byung rtsis man ngag zla ba'i 'od zer,* |
| Jungwa | *'byung ba* |
| Juthik | *ju thig* |
| Kagyü | *bka' brgyud* |
| Kak | *skag* |

| | |
|---|---|
| Kama | *bka' ma* |
| Kartsi | *skar rtsi* |
| Kham | *khams* |
| Kham (trigram) | *kham* |
| Khenpo | *mkhan po* |
| Khön | *khon* |
| Khyung | *khyung* |
| Kongjo | *kong jo* |
| Kongpo | *rkong po* |
| Kubum | *sku 'bum* |
| Kün dzop | *kun rdzob* |
| Kün zhi | *kun gzhi* |
| Kye mewa | *skye me ba* |
| Kyegü Dakpo | *skye dgu'i bdag po* |
| Kyerim | *skyed rim* |
| La | *bla* |
| La gyu | *bla gyu* |
| La ri | *bla ri* |
| La shing | *bla shing* |
| Laguk | *bla 'gugs* |
| Lak | *lag* |
| Lakpa | *lag pa* |
| Lane | *bla gnas* |
| Lang | *glang* |
| Langdarma | *glang dar ma* |
| Lha | *lha* |
| Lha ri | *lha ri* |
| Lha sang | *lha bsangs* |
| Lha Wangden | *lha dbang ldan* |
| Lhabab düchen | *lha babs dus chen* |
| Lhakpa | *lhag pa* |
| Lhalhathori | *lha lha tho ri* |
| Lhatsam | *lha mtshams* |
| Li | *li* |
| Ligmikya | *lig mi rgya* |
| Ling gu | *gling dgu* |
| Lo | *klo* |
| Lo tho | *lo tho* |
| Longchenpa | *klong chen pa* |

| | |
|---|---|
| Losar | *lo gsar* |
| Lotsawa | *lo tsa' ba* |
| Lu | *klu* |
| Lü | *lus* |
| Luk | *lug* |
| Lung ta | *rlung rta* |
| Lunggi lhamo | *rlung gi lha mo* |
| Lunggi Wangchuk | *rlung gi dbang phyug* |
| Madrukpa | *ma drug pa* |
| Magakpa | *ma 'gag pa* |
| Makpön dra | *dmag dpon dgra'* |
| Mamo | *mamo* |
| Me | *me* |
| Men Tsi Khang | *sman rtsis khang* |
| Metreng | *sme phreng* |
| Metsa | *me tsa* |
| Mewa | *sme ba* |
| Mewa gu | *sme ba dgu* |
| Mezhi | *me bzhi* |
| Mi ser | *mi ser* |
| Mik mizang | *mig mi bzang* |
| Mikmar | *mig dmar* |
| Milarepa | *mi la ras pa* |
| Mindruk | *smin drug* |
| Miyi Senge | *mi yi seng ge* |
| Mo pa | *mo pa* |
| Mön | *mon* |
| Möndre | *mon gre* |
| Möndru | *mon gru* |
| Mönlam | *smon lam* |
| Mu | *dmu* |
| Nabso | *nabs so* |
| Nak tsi | *nag rtsi* |
| Nakmo | *nag mo* |
| Nakpa | *nag pa* |
| Nam tö se | *rnam thos sras* |
| Namdru | *nam gru* |
| Namkha | *nam mkha'* |
| Namkhemik | *nam mkhai'i mig* |

| | |
|---|---|
| Namri Songtsen | *gnam ri srong btsan* |
| Namtak | *nam thag* |
| Namthong gong | *nam mthong dgong* |
| Namthong Og | *nam mthong 'og* |
| Narma | *snar ma* |
| Natsok | *sna tshogs* |
| Nema | *gnas ma* |
| Ngakpa | *sngags* |
| Ngari | *mnga' ris* |
| Ngak nyen pa | *ngag snyan pa* |
| Ngenpa Gu Dzom | *ngan pa dgu 'dzom* |
| Nö | *gnod* |
| Nön | *snron* |
| Nor lha | *nor lha* |
| Nub | *snubs* |
| Nyang de | *myang 'das* |
| Nyatri Tsenpo | *gnya' khri btsan po* |
| Nyen | *nyan* |
| Nyikye | *nyi skyes* |
| Nyima | *nyi ma* |
| Nyima Özer | *nyi ma 'od zer* |
| Nyime Bu | *nyima'i bu* |
| Nyime lhadenmo | *nri ma'i lha ldan mo* |
| Nyingma | *rnying ma* |
| Olmo Lungring | *'ol mo lung ring* |
| Orgyen Lingpa | *o rgyan gling pa* |
| Padma yang thig | *padma yang thig* |
| Pak kyepo | *'phags skyes po* |
| Palang kang | *ba glang rkang* |
| Parkha | *spar kha* |
| Parkha gye | *par kha brgyad* |
| Pasang | *pa sangs* |
| Pema Gyalpo | *padma rgyal po* |
| Pema Jungne | *padma 'byung gnas* |
| Penpa | *spen pa* |
| Phak | *phag* |
| Phul | *phul* |
| Phurbu | *phur bu* |
| Pö Yü | *bod yul* |

| | |
|---|---|
| Puk lha | *phugs lha* |
| Ra | *rva* |
| Rabjung | *rab byung* |
| Ralpachen | *ral pa can* |
| Rikje | *rig byed* |
| Rilhamo | *ri'i lha mo* |
| Rinchen Zangpo | *rin chen bzang po* |
| Rinpoche | *rin po che* |
| Sa | *sa* |
| Saga | *sa ga* |
| Sakya | *sa skya* |
| Samadrok | *sa ma 'brog* |
| Samye | *bsam yas* |
| Sari | *sa ri* |
| Senalek | *sad na legs* |
| Senge | *seng ge* |
| Shambhale Lam yik | *sham bha la'i lam yig* |
| Shang-Shung | *zhang zhung* |
| Shen | *gshen* |
| Shenrab Miwo | *gshen rab mi bo* |
| Shepa Gyeje | *shes pa skyed byed* |
| Shing | *shing* |
| Shinje Dakpo | *gzhin rje bdag po* |
| Sipe Khorlo | *srid pa'i khor lo* |
| Sok | *srog* |
| Sok lha | *srog lha* |
| Sok lu | *srog bslu* |
| Sokpa | *srog pa* |
| Sonampa | *so nam pa* |
| Songtsen Gampo | *srong btsan sgam po* |
| Sowe lhamo | *gso ba'i lha mo* |
| Sri | *sri, brsi* |
| Ta | *rta* |
| Ta Denma | *rta ldan ma* |
| Tachen | *rta chen* |
| Tachung | *rta cung* |
| Tak | *stag* |
| Takzig | *stag gzig* |
| Tashi | *bkra shis* |

| | |
|---|---|
| Tau | *rta'u* |
| Tendrel | *rten brel* |
| Terma | *gter ma* |
| Tertön | *gter ton* |
| Thobden | *thob ldan* |
| Ti Se | *ti se/ti rtse* |
| To | *gto* |
| Torma | *gtor ma* |
| Trapa Ngönshe | *grwa pa sngon shes* |
| Trawo | *bkra bo* |
| Tre | *spre* |
| Trisong Detsen | *khri srong lde'u btsan* |
| Trokje | *'phrog byed* |
| Trül | *sbrul* |
| Trülching | *sbrul 'ching* |
| Trume | *khrums smad* |
| Trumtö | *khrums stod* |
| Tsami | *rtsa mi* |
| Tsampa | *tsam pa* |
| Tsang | *gtsang* |
| Tsatsa | *tsha tsha* |
| Tsawa | *tsa ba* |
| Tse | *tse* |
| Tsen | *btsan* |
| Tsi | *rtsis* |
| Tsi rik | *rtsi rig* |
| Tsinjema | *tsin 'byed ma* |
| Tsipa | *rtsis pa* |
| Tso Pema | *mtsho padma* |
| Tsokye | *mtsho skyes* |
| Tsokye Dorje | *mtsho skyes rdo rje* |
| Tsongkapa | *tshong kha pa* |
| Tulku | *sprul sku* |
| U | *dbus* |
| Wang thang | *dbang thang* |
| Wangpo denma | *dbang ldan ma* |
| Wo | *dbo* |
| Yak | *g.yag* |
| Yang | *g.yang* |

| | |
|---|---|
| Yarlung | *yar klungs* |
| Yö | *yos* |
| Yül lha | *yul lha* |
| Yülkhor srung | *yul 'khor srung* |
| Zadak | *gza' bdag* |
| Zhang lha | *zhang lha* |
| Zhingpa | *zhing pa* |
| Ziji | *zi brjid* |
| Zin | *zin* |
| Zön | *zon* |

# Bibliography

GENERAL WORKS ON TIBET, ITS CIVILIZATION,
AND ITS RELIGIONS

CHANDRAKIRTI. *L'Entrée au milieu*. Anduze: Ed. Dharma, 1985.

DALAI LAMA, H.H. the Fourteenth. *La Lumière du Dharma*. Paris: Ed. Seghers, 1973.

———. *L'Enseignement du Dalai-lama*. Paris: Albin Michel, 1976.

———, and J. HOPKINS. *The Kalacakra Tantra*. London: Wisdom Publications, 1985.

DAVID-NÉEL, A. *The Superhuman Life of Gesar of Ling*. North Stratford, N.H.: Ayer, 1978.

FREMANTLE, F., and C. TRUNGPA, trans. *The Tibetan Book of the Dead*. Boston & London: Shambhala Publications, 1987.

GENDEN DRUB, and GLEN H. MULLIN, trans. *Bridging the Sutras and Tantras*. Ithaca, N.Y.: Snow Lion Publications, 1982.

GESHE, KELSANG GYATSO. *Claire lumière de felicité*. Ed. Dharma, 1984.

GESHE, RABTEN. *Echoes of Voidness*. London: Wisdom Publications, 1983.

GRUNWEDEL, A. *La Voie vers Shambhala*. Arche Milano, 1983.

HOPKINS, J. *Meditation on Emptiness*. London: Wisdom Publications, 1983.

JEST, C. *Dolpo, Communautés de langue tibétaine du Népal*. C.N.R.S., 1975.

————. *Tarap, Une Vallée dans l'Himalaya*. Paris: Le Seuil, 1974.

KARMAY, S. G. "Introduction générale à l'histoire et aux doctrines du Bon." *Nouvelle Revue Tibetaine*, nos. 11, 12, and 13 (1985–1986).

KHENSUR, LEKDEN. *Méditation d'un supérieur de collège tantrique*. Ed. Dharma, 1979.

LATI RINPOCHE and J. HOPKINS. *La Mort, l'état intermédiaire et la renaissance dans le bouddhisme tibétain*. Ed. Dharma, 1980.

DE NEBESKY-WOJKOWITZ, R. *Oracles and Demons of Tibet*. Gravenhage, La Haye, 1956.

NORBU, NAMKHAI. *The Necklace of Gzi: a Cultural History of Tibet*. Dharamsala: I.O.H.H.D.L., 1981.

SNELLGROVE, D. L. *Buddhist Himalaya*. Oxford, 1957.

————. *Nine Ways of Bön*. Boulder: Prajñā Press, 1980.

STEIN, ROLF A. *Tibetan Civilization*. Paris: Le Sycomore–Asiathèque, 1981.

TOUSSAINT, G. C. *Le dict de Padma*. Paris: Ed. Ernest Leroux, 1933.

TRUNGPA, C. *Cutting Through Spiritual Materialism*. Boston & London: Shambhala Publications, 1987.

————. *The Myth of Freedom and the Way of Meditation*. Boston & London: Shambhala Publications, 1988.

TUCCI, G., and W. HEISSIG. *The Religions of Tibet and Mongolia*. Paris: Payot, 1973.

WADDELL, L. A. *The Buddhism of Tibet or Lamaism*. Cambridge, 1958.

## WORKS ON TIBETAN ASTROLOGY

HENNING, E. "Fundamentals of the Tibetan Calendar." *Tibetan News Review* 2.

LAFITTE, JEAN-JACQUES. "Le Calendrier tibétaine." *Nouvelle Revue Tibétaine*, no. 12 (October 1985).

MOSTAERT, A. *Manual of Mongolian Astrology and Divination.* Cambridge: Harvard University Press, 1969.

NORBU, NAMKHAI. *Le Calendrier tibétaine: L'interprétation astrologique.* Paris: Communauté Dzogchen, 1984.

———. *Une Introduction à l'astrologie tibétaine.* Paris: Communauté Dzogchen, 1984.

RIGPA FELLOWSHIP. *Tibetan Calendar*: 1980/81, 1981/82, 1982/83, 1983/84, 1984/85, 1985/86, 1986/87, 1987/88, 1988/89, London.

SCHLISINGWEIT. *Le bouddhisme au Tibet: Calendriers et tables astrologiques.* Annales du Musée Guimet, vol. 3, 1898.

SCHUH, D. *Untersuchungen zur Geschichte der tibetischen Kalenderrechnung.* Weisbaden, 1973.

VAJRANATHA and LYNNE KLAPECKI. *Tibetan Astrological Calendar and Almanac 1977–79.* Kathmandu: Kalacakra Publications, 1978.

## TIBETAN SOURCES

LOCHEN DHARMA SHRI. *'Byung-rtsis Man-ngag Zla-ba'i 'Od-ze*, "A Verse Treatise on the Principles of Tibetan Astrology." *Sman-rtsis Shesrig Spendzod* 82 (March 1976).

———. *Rtsis-kyi Man-ngag Nyin-byed Snang-ba'i Rnam-'grel Gser-gyi Shing-rta.* Ed. Bod-ljongs Mi-dmangs Dpe-skrun Khang, 1983.

*BLA-MA BSOD-NAMS' BRUG-RGYAS LO-THO.* Tibetan Almanacs, 1978, 1984 and 1986–88.

*BOD-KYI RTSIS-RIG GI GO-DON DANG LAG-LEN.* Ed. Mi-rigs Dpe-skrun Khang, 1987.

## WORKS ON INDIAN ASTROLOGY

DETHIER, J. *Astrology of India.* Ed. Dangles, 1985.

GILLET, P. E. A. *Hindu Astrology Manual.* Paris: Ed. Cahiers Astrologiques, 1953.

JAIN, MANIK CHAND. *Rahu and Ketu in Predictive Astrology.* New Delhi: Sagar Publications.

KANNAN, S. *Fundamentals of Hindu Astrology*. New Delhi: Sagar Publications, 1981.

KAPOOR, GAURI SHANKAR. *Learn Astrology the Easy Way*. New Delhi: Ranjan Publications.

RAMAN, B. V. *Astrology for Beginners*. Bangalore: I.B.H.P., 1983.

———. *Elementary Manual of Hindu Astrology*. Paris: Ed. Traditionnelles, 1982.

———. *Hindu Predictive Astrology*. Bangalore: I.B.H.P., 1986.

———. *How to Judge a Horoscope*, vols. 1 and 2. Bangalore: I.B.H.P., 1984.

WORKS ON CHINESE ASTROLOGY

GRANET, M. *La Pensée chinoise*. Paris: Albin Michel, 1968.

DE KERMADEC, J. M. *Les Huit signes de votre destin*. Paris: Asiathèque, 1981.

DE SAUSSURE, L. "Le Cycle des douze animaux." *Journal Asiatique*, January/March 1920.

SCHLEGEL, G. *Uranographie Chinoise*. So-Wen Ed., 1977.

SHERILL, W. A., and W. K. CHU. *An Anthology of I Ching*. London: Routledge & Kegan, 1976.

———. *The Astrology of I Ching*. London: Routledge & Kegan, 1973.

WILHELM, RICHARD. *I Ching, The Book of Changes*. Trans. Cary F. Baynes. Princeton, N.J.: Princeton University Press, 1967.